A BRITISH ARMY NURSE IN THE KOREAN WAR

shadows of the Far Forgotten

Far Away Links to Home

A BRITISH ARMY NURSE IN THE KOREAN WAR

Shadows of the Far Forgotten

E. J. McNAIR

TEMPUS

For Clive, beloved husband

First published 2007

Tempus Publishing
Cirencester Road, Chalford
Stroud, Gloucestershire, GL6 8PE
www.tempus-publishing.com

Tempus Publishing is an imprint of NPI Media Group

British Library Cataloguing in Publication Data.
A catalogue record for this book is available from the British Library.

ISBN 978 0 7524 4317 1

Typesetting and origination by NPI Media Group
Printed and bound in Great Britain

CONTENTS

ACKNOWLEDGEMENTS

With grateful thanks I must acknowledge that permission has been granted to use quotations from the following sources:

Extracts used as chapter headings taken from the Chronology are reproduced from *The Korean War* by Max Hastings (Copyright Max Hastings 1987) by permission of PFD (www.pfd.co.uk) on behalf of Sir Max Hastings.

The Bidding Prayer delivered by the Very Reverend Dr Wesley Carr at the Service of Thanksgiving to Commemorate the Fiftieth Anniversary of the end of hostilities in the Korean War, held at the Abbey on 9 July 2003, by kind permission of the Very Reverend Dr Wesley Carr KCVO and the Dean and Chapter of Westminster Abbey.

Mr Frank Ellison OBE BEM JP, General Secretary of the British Korean Veterans Association, for his helpful advice in my quoting part of the *Select Chronology from British Forces in the Korean War* published by the BKVA, and casualty figures extracted from General Sir Anthony Farrar-Hockley's official history of the Korean War, published by HMSO.

Unless otherwise stated, all photographs – apart from the Myung Jin Orphanage – were provided by the author. For reproduction of the cover portrait (painted in 1957) permission has been sought.

The black and white drawings and sketch maps are by Clive McNair.

I also wish to acknowledge, with special thanks, the author Eric Taylor for his kindness in reading through the manuscript (via the postal network!) and his invaluable help and encouragement.

Dorothy Mercer and Janet Ritchie likewise deserve my heartfelt thanks for their constructive criticism, having read earlier versions of the script.

With sincere thanks to Betty Lawrence OAM, from West Beach, South Australia, for swiftly sending much needed photographs and information regarding her service in Kure and Seoul.

Particular thanks go to my niece Anthea and her husband John Hillman who, due to my computer illiteracy, at a moment's notice, miraculously produced the Rich Text Format disc for the publisher.

Clive, above all, merits my deep gratitude for his long suffering patience in sorting out both my grammatical errors and spelling mistakes, plus his unending support throughout the many years of writing and most especially for his delightful black and white drawings, and for compiling the index.

My lasting thanks too, to Amy Rigg, Publisher, and Sophie Atkins, Editorial Assistant, of Tempus Publishing Ltd, for their helpful encouragement and faith in this book.

The final acknowledgement is in loving memory of my mother who faithfully kept my letters, and of my father, another gallant soldier of the First World War.

AUTHOR'S NOTE

A British Army Nurse in the Korean War: Shadows of the Far Forgotten was written to keep alive the memory of the many thousands who were caught up in this much Forgotten War. It is based on the 160 or so letters written to my parents from Japan and Korea whilst I was on Active Service there.

To protect their anonymity and confidentiality, names of patients and some people portrayed in this book have been changed; likewise some ward emergencies are an amalgam of my nursing experience at that time.

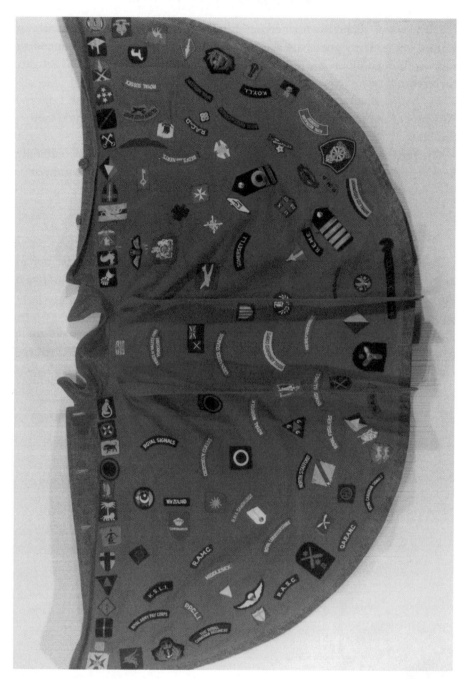

The author's QA cloak with its collection of illicit badges.

SHADOWS OF THE FAR FORGOTTEN

Westminster Abbey, Wednesday 9 July 2003 at noon

Outside the temperature is soaring, inside the atmosphere is close. A fanfare sounds, the packed congregation rises to a resounding National Anthem, as the Dean conducts Her Majesty and their Royal Highnesses to their places in the South Lantern.

Then begins the Service of Thanksgiving to Commemorate the Fiftieth Anniversary of the End of Hostilities in the Korean War.

Sitting several rows behind the royal party, with my husband Clive, I feel a surge of pride as I listen intently to the Dean of Westminster, Dr Wesley Carr, reading the Bidding:

> Customarily on such occasions we meet to thank God for the end of the war. Korea is different; we thank God for the armistice and the end of hostilities fifty years ago. The nuclear threat hung over all. New names entered our vocabulary – Seoul, Pusan, P'yongyang and especially P'anmunjom. But to the soldiers such places as Old Baldy, Capital, Pork Chop, and Heartbreak Hotel meant more; for these were the hills over which they fought. After three years of sweeping attacks and retreats, a truce was declared. But that war has never formally ended, although it is now so long ago that men lost their lives serving there.
>
> It is, however, with gratitude that we meet, recalling that this war was fought by the United Nations and that by the end more than twenty nations had taken part.

For those who fight, however, the experience is the same as that of any battle and the death of loved ones is the same as in any war. So we shall remember all those who suffer as a result of war, especially members of the British Korean Veterans Association.

But first let us keep a moment's silence and remember God into whose presence we come.

Thus was summarised the conflict in which, for twenty months or more of my service as a young nursing officer in the Queen Alexandra's Royal Army Nursing Corps, I had played a minor role. It was with pride, too, for the privilege of nursing those brave young men and gratitude to be at this service of commemoration, having been one of a small number of British women serving in Korea fifty years ago.

Memories flooded back: of the intense humidity, debilitating heat, penetrating dust, deluging rains and the freezing winds of winter. But above all else, I remembered the endless patience, cheerful courage and stoical sense of humour of the frost-bitten, the fractured, the amputees, the badly burned, the multiple gunshot wounds, the yellow-rimmed eyes of the jaundiced and the unseeing eyes of the blind. Indeed, the shadows of all those young men, war weary, exhausted and far from home.

CHAPTER ONE

ALDERSHOT

I<small>N</small> K<small>OREA</small>, <small>THE</small> UN C<small>OMMAND PROPOSES VOLUNTARY</small>
<small>REPATRIATION OF</small> P<small>RISONERS OF</small> W<small>AR</small>.

Matron's Office, the Cambridge Military Hospital, Aldershot,
Thursday 3 January 1952

As I entered, Lieutenant Colonel Somerville looked up from a pile of papers and
smiled, 'Ah Hall, good morning, I have just received a telephone call from the War
Office. At rather short notice, I'm afraid, you have been posted to Japan and you
are to report to the QARANC Depot & TE on 14 January. From there you will
be sent on fourteen days' leave, returning to Hindhead on the 28th to be available
for embarkation 29th.'

Handing me a slip of paper she said, 'This is a copy of your posting order;
check it with me please.' And in a firm voice she read out:

Authority: 112/MED/5292/206/AMD4(S) dated 3rd January 1952. Report to
Depot & TE. 14.1.52 Draft DPANU available 29.1.52.

She added, 'And keep it safe.'

With a frisson of excitement, but simultaneously feeling dazed, I started to
thank her. Interrupting me, Matron continued: 'You are in charge of 6, the acute
surgical orthopaedic ward, aren't you? I will arrange for the handover in ten days'

time, and will let you know as soon as possible who will take over from you. That is all for the time being, thank you, Hall.' And with a kindly nod, I was dismissed.

With excitement growing, I positively floated back down the long, lofty, corridor, past the busy operating theatres on my right, then turned left into my ward.

'Is that more comfortable for you, and what about your plaster cast, shall I raise it up a bit, Private Smith?' I enquired, organising some extra pillows.

'Please Sister, but what are you grinning about, something special must have happened. Has your boyfriend popped the question?'

'Heavens no, but I've just had my overseas posting.'

'Where to, Sister? I bet it's the Isle of Wight.'

'Japan.'

'Wow! You are a lucky one, 'cos I missed out on that when I copped it in Korea; I was shipped straight home from Pusan, with no chance of recovering in the arms of one of them lovely geisha girls!'

'How's that? And can you wriggle your toes for me? Great, the circulation's fine. What about doing a bit of occupational therapy now, whilst you listen to your earphones, shall I give you the loom?' Settling him down with the tartan scarf he was weaving on the tiny Red Cross loom, he grinned broadly, and I dashed on to my next patient.

In my office later that evening, when writing the day report, I paused for a moment, to think of my Japanese adventure ahead, and of some of the wounded repatriated from Korea whom I had nursed since arriving here at this 500-bed, busy hospital in December 1950. That was after surviving one month's rugged, basic training when I joined the QARANC as a twenty-three-year-old trained nurse the previous November.

In particular, there was a quietly spoken, uncomplaining young officer on the eye ward for whom I was responsible when Night Superintendent. This lad, who was probably no older than me, I was shocked to discover, had suffered such dreadful blast injuries that the retinas of both eyes were dislodged. His sight was failing and, tragically, nothing could be done to prevent his ensuing blindness.

For some inexplicable reason, it seemed that fate had linked me to this war, despite the fact that three months ago my original overseas posting had been to the Middle East. This, because of a suddenly inflamed appendix on my part, was cancelled at the last moment.

It was after lunch a couple of days later that Pat Fitzgerald, one of my QA colleagues, caught up with me over coffee in the ante-room.

'Jilly, I've only just heard that you have also been posted to the FARELF. Matron's told me that we shall be going together'.

'Gosh that's good, as it will be much nicer to travel so far with someone I know. Are you pleased about Japan?'

'Yep, it should be fun, but I'm on duty now and have to dash, 'bye.'

Pat, a pretty, petite, Irish brunette, had joined the Corps some time after me, and had only been living in the Mess at Gun Hill House for a few months. Working in such a large hospital on different wards and shifts seldom gave us the opportunity to meet.

The following few days were a mad rush, preparing my ward for the dreaded handover. This meant that every single item on the inventory had to be checked and in place. Everything from a tin mug to a hospital bed was my responsibility, and woe betide my pay packet if anything was missing.

Dividing up my precious off-duty time was something of a problem: writing to friends and relatives, explaining to Miles that I was shortly going overseas, and being called to have extra inoculations, including cholera and yellow fever.

Simultaneously, I hurriedly searched for some new clothes, which not only had to skilfully increase my wardrobe but, more importantly, had to be suitable for the climatic vagaries of a three-year Far East posting. Although clothes rationing had ended in 1949, there were still some post-war shortages, as well as the problem of trying to buy anything summery in the middle of winter. However, Whites, the Aldershot department store, came up trumps when, after searching diligently in the stock room, they eventually found a cool cotton, daisy-white patterned, pale lemon evening dress, a simple cotton frock and a couple of pairs of silk stockings.

My uniform presented no difficulties as it was plentiful, with two scarlet tippets – the famous short capes, with matching cuffs, designed by Queen Alexandra herself – four grey dresses, plus brass buttons, four white monogrammed veils and, to protect our indoor uniform on cold days, the long grey cloak, with its scarlet lining, and Aristoc stockings of a particular shade. The new Norman Hartnell's smart, grey No.1 uniform suit for special occasions, with matching grey shirts and heavy grey Crombie great coat, topped with an expensive grey felt and shiny black peaked cap. One cream riding mackintosh for wet days, black leather gloves and shoes, one khaki battledress skirt and pair of slacks, two matching shirts, thick lisle stockings and a khaki cap, plus the addition of the much maligned Quartermaster's tropical kit with which we would be issued at the Depot. Hopefully all this, plus everything else, would cram into my black tin trunk.

Amidst these preparations, Miles and an Army colleague, with Elizabeth Mills, my QA friend and I, managed to grab a day in London, with prized tickets for the current West End box office hit *South Pacific*. Listening to Mary Martin singing 'I'm going to wash that man right out of my hair', made me wonder just how I could do it. Kind as Miles was, all I wanted was to sail to Japan in a couple of weeks' time.

As so often happens in life, what seemed insoluble then, resolved unexpectedly some time later.

Packing up was the next big hurdle, as I endeavoured to keep my luggage down to one standard size Army issue tin trunk, my recent purchase of a large Globetrotter suitcase and an overnight bag.

Handing over Ward Six was smooth; the hardest part was saying goodbye to my 'Boys'. As I shook his hand, Private Smith pressed the Black Watch Scarf he had just finished weaving into mine, with a cheery 'Good Luck, Sister – you might need this, as it can be mighty cold out there.'

Monday 14 January was crisp and sunny as, clad in khaki, we clambered into the back of the small truck, our combined luggage scattered between us. Once settled, Pat leant across, whispering in her inimitable way, 'Now you'll not be missing your boyfriend and be too miserable, will you, Jilly? So that we'll not be able to enjoy the boat trip out. I heard on the grapevine yesterday, that there are another two QAs going with us, whom no doubt we shall be meeting, as soon as we arrive at the Depot today.'

'Don't be silly, of course I shan't, in fact Miles and I have agreed to depend on the pigeon post whilst I'm away. Anyway, he has a promotion course coming up soon and so, like me, will be far too busy coping in a different environment to become involved at this stage.'

'That's a relief!' and smiling, Pat pulled a paperback from her pocket, whilst I, with a twinge of sadness, watched the imposing edifice of the Cambridge Military Hospital, with its familiar clock tower, slowly slip away as we drove off to an uncertain destination.

Returning from Sussex to Hindhead on the 29th, after spending an enjoyable but hectic embarkation leave with my parents, at the Depot I met up with Pat who had also just arrived, soon to be followed by the other two QAs who were on our draft. Georgina Johnstone, another slim and attractive brunette, was the eldest of we four, and Helen Strachan was a wee Scot with a lovely soft accent and dark hair.

Reporting to the Draftings Officer, we were informed that the sailing date had been postponed and we were to go on temporary duty, for immediate recall once the date was confirmed. The following morning, Georgina and I were to report for duty at Tidworth Military Hospital.

During our two weeks there, whilst suffering the mid-winter cold of Salisbury Plain, an event of great sadness occurred. This was the sudden death of HM King

George VI, on 6 February 1952. At the hospital everyone felt quite stunned and, almost immediately, we ourselves were issued with black mourning bands to be worn for the next three months on the left sleeve of our outdoor uniform as a mark of respect.

Having just reported for duty at 0730hrs on our final day at Tidworth, I had an unexpected telephone call from Georgina, asking me to hurry down to her ward straightaway. With permission, I shot down the dingy old corridors, to find her waiting at the ward door.

'Jilly I didn't want to worry you with this on the 'phone, but apparently late last night, after he left you, Miles had a fall from his motorbike, and was admitted here. But don't worry, he's fine, just had a bit of a bump on the head. Come and see him.'

Sitting up in bed but looking rather pale, Miles assured me that he really was feeling okay, explaining that his bike had skidded on rutted ice, soon after he had left me in the Mess. No one else was involved, and that the MO would be discharging him back to his unit that morning.

This was confirmed when I rang the ward an hour or so later.

Back at the Depot again forty-eight hours later, that evening at dinner we met Major Priscilla Stewart QARANC – an extremely neat and somewhat reserved lady, with an air of authority, and destined to become our deputy matron – who would be in charge of the four of us whilst en route to Japan.

Some time later the following afternoon we were all packed, ready to leave by rail for embarkation the next day. Pat, popping her head round my door, asked, 'How about coming out for a last drink with us tonight, Jilly? Helen, Georgina and I feel like celebrating, because at long last we are on our way to the exotic East!'

Feeling the need for some quiet reflection, I replied – 'That's really sweet of you, Pat. Sorry, but no thanks. You see, I've just realised that tonight is positively the last chance I've got to write some letters and to tie up a few loose ends.'

CHAPTER TWO

SLOW BOAT TO KURE VIA PUSAN

In Korea, disorder in POW camps as
screening of prisoners began.

Friday, 15 February 1952

After a tedious six-hour journey from Liphook full of delays and missed rail con-
nections, we finally arrived at the dockside in Southampton where the air smelt
fresh and invigoratingly salty. Since it was late, the cranes were silent, the wharf
almost deserted but out of the gloom the gleaming portholes and bright lights
illuminating Her Majesty's Troopship, *Empire Trooper*, shone an exciting welcome.
Standing on the quayside, we gazed upward at the yellow funnel of the small,
compact and white-hulled ship, with its familiar blue painted band. Small, in fact
not looking much larger than a cross-Channel steamer, because berthed right
next to her lay the majestic bulk of the *Queen Mary*.

However, there was little welcome from the irate RTO (Regimental Transport
Officer), as he strode down the gangway towards us demanding 'Are you the long-
awaited party of QAs? You are extremely late. What happened, did you get lost or
something?' Followed by a curt, 'Leave your heavy baggage there, and follow me.'

The gangway appeared poorly lit and rather slippery, but that did not prevent
the upsurge of excitement I experienced as I climbed on up to board the ship.

Blinking in the bright lights of the main foyer, with its oak panelled walls
and impressive double staircase, an Indian steward was instructed to show Major

Stewart to her quarters and another to direct us to our cabin. We followed him down the oak stairs and along a long narrow corridor, until he came to a door on the left and throwing it open with a flourish said, 'Your cabin, Memsahibs', and disappeared.

Piling into the cramped space we took stock of our new surroundings, instantly discovering that four QAs standing were two too many!

Hastily Pat and I subsided on to a lower bunk, whilst Georgina exclaimed, 'Heavens above, there's not much room is there?' as she surveyed the scantily furnished cabin, with upper and lower berths on opposite sides, one camp stool, a very small sink with an even smaller mirror above it. Beside the right-hand bunks there were two tiny wardrobes, and next to the ones on the left there was a closed door.

Opening this gingerly, I said, 'Hey look at this – we have our very own bathroom – that will make life a darn sight easier, although hang on – I've just noticed that other door facing it; so maybe we have to share.'

'And look we do have a porthole, my mother always said how important it is to have an outside cabin, and it will be great to see the sea.'

'Especially when it's rough,' Helen chipped in.

'Ugh! Don't even think about it,' moaned Georgina.

There was a tap on the door and in came a steward with our suitcases. 'We had better shove these out of the way under the lower bunks; who's going to sleep where?' organised Pat.

'Message for you from Major Memsahib, dinner is in twenty minutes, gong will go. No changee tonight – first night on board.'

Passing the Purser's Office, on our way up to the Dining Saloon, I was handed a yellow-enveloped telegram. I ripped it open to read a Bon Voyage message from my loving parents. Just for a second, I felt a deep pang of homesickness, immediately dispelled by Pat's urging me to 'Buck up, Jilly or we shall miss the best seats!'

However, on arrival in the busy, grand saloon, we were allocated to share a table with Major Stewart, an RAF officer and an Army captain, all of whom were senior ranks and rather daunting to us junior lieutenants.

Arranged in the middle of the spacious table, amongst the snowy white linen and sparkling cutlery, there was a large vase of fresh daffodils and tulips and two attractive menu cards. Surrounded by such comfort, but sitting there in our crumpled battledress and hastily applied lipstick, I felt untidy and bedraggled until, glancing around, I realised that the majority of the passengers looked just as dishevelled as we did.

After enduring so many post-war years of food rationing, the freshly baked bread rolls – which we later discovered miraculously appeared at every meal – and the unexpected courses that followed, were amazingly rich and by the end of the meal we all felt comfortably satisfied.

❖

Acclimatising to the different sounds and stuffy ventilation, our first night on board was a somewhat sleepless one, ultimately grabbing a few hours just before dawn, only to be disturbed by our Goanese steward with a cup of cold tea at 0630hrs. As breakfast was not for another couple of hours we almost threw him out.

Sleeping on a lower bunk, and being quite tall, it was quite a work of art to crawl out each time without cracking my head and it was then we decided that it was only possible for two of us to be up and dress at a time, whilst the other two must wait patiently on their bunks.

My first ever saltwater bath was refreshingly hot, despite the lack of soapy lather but with the added attraction of scraps of floating seaweed. These I rinsed off with the bowl of fresh water, thoughtfully supplied by our faithful bath steward, a handsome gentleman with long greasy dark curls, scuttling around in bare feet, whilst carrying pitchers of 'running' water to various cabins.

After breakfast the time passed quickly, sorting out our kit, stowing our personal belongings in the space available and squashing our No.1 dress and posher clothes into half a small wardrobe apiece, the rest remaining in suitcases under the bunks.

Reporting to the Major-Ma'am, who gave us details of the current posting addresses and dates for our families, I enclosed the following in a rushed note home for my parents:

LT E J Hall QARANC.
HMT EMPIRE TROOPER. C/O GPO.
Post before 19th FEB: for Port Said

"	"	26th	"	"	Aden
"	"	5th March	"		Colombo
"	"	11th	"	"	Singapore
"	"	14th	"	"	Hong Kong
"	"	19th	"	"	Japan

By 1100hrs we four were up on deck, watching the cranes busily swinging more stores and last-minute luggage aboard.

'My God look at that!' cried Pat, pointing to an uncrated tin trunk swaying perilously in mid-air.

'I'm just hoping that ours are safely in the hold. Ma'am said we shall need permission to get to them later, when we have to change our kit over.' The trunk finally made it across, and we were distracted by uniformed Customs and Embarkation people coming up the gangway.

By now the ship was a hive of noisy activity, with a full passenger list of about 900 troops and a number of families, with an approximate total of

1,200 passengers embarked for service in the varied destinations of the Middle and Far East. Strangely, we had just deduced that we were the only five QAs on board and, apart from the two RAF nursing sisters looking after the tiny ship's hospital, most probably the only single women.

Ma'am, suddenly appearing out of nowhere, kindly thrust a buff envelope in my hand. 'This has just arrived for you, Hall.' Thanking her and at the same time recognising Miles's handwriting, I shoved it in my pocket, to read when unaccompanied.

The different decks were buzzing when, just before noon, the gangway was hoisted away. Promptly at 1200hrs, the ship's siren blew and the engines throbbed to life, as the troopship slowly and cautiously manoeuvred sideways away from her berth.

'Gosh! We are really on our way this time, Jilly, can you believe it?'

'Hardly, but isn't it thrilling. You know, Pat, I'm already quite attached to this little ship; it's incredible to realise too, that she is now our home, for the next six weeks.'

'Rather like travelling into the unknown, making me wonder what exactly lies ahead for us. Not just for the next six weeks but for the next three years,' Georgina added soberly.

'Let's stay put until lunchtime,' said Helen. We continued to lean over the ship's rail, at the same time waving indiscriminately, to the small crowd of unknown onlookers gathered on the quayside as they receded into the distance.

Despite feeling chilled on this typically raw February morning, we watched with fascination the misty grey landscape, as we slowly sailed down the Solent, past the imposing façade of the Royal Victoria Hospital at Netley and on past the Needles, as the ship progressed towards the open sea. Albeit it was with some relief when, at 1300hrs, the pretty dulcimer chimes of the ship's British India Steam Navigation Co. luncheon gong sounded, inviting us down to another delicious, and hot, meal!

One hour later the ship's siren blasted off, this time urging us to assemble for our first lifeboat drill. After donning the bosomy life-jackets, tying the tough cords firmly around our waists, and getting covered in kapok, we were inspected by our superiors, sensibly, to make certain these were positioned correctly and also to ensure that we were standing precisely to attention, with our khaki caps sitting squarely and black leather gloves buttoned up.

'What a way to go, King Neptune would be much impressed!' I whispered to Pat, giggling beside me.

Murmuring, she replied, 'Have a shifty at the two Naval Officers to your left, see they are still struggling to do theirs up!'

For the rest of the afternoon, whilst the other two took a nap, Helen and I remained on the now-deserted deck, absorbing the muted, swishing of the ship and feeling her gently roll as she pushed on through the waves, while at the same time admiring the intermingling of the absolute greyness of sea and sky, relieved intermittently by small flocks of chalky white gulls, noisily following in our wake.

Dashing back to the cabin after a quick cup of tea, we spent the next hour or so busily polishing the brass buttons on our No.1 dress and cleaning the loathsome black beetle-squashers until they shone, before finally taking it in turns to change for dinner. Then, smartly dressed in our relatively new grey Hartnell with matching shirt, uncomfortably stiff collar and tie, we guessed that that evening we might cause something of a sensation when walking into the saloon, because few people, as yet, were familiar with the new QARANC uniform.

Heralded by a noisy crackle, the tannoy came over loud and clear with the unexpected and timbered voice of the ship's captain, informing us that because of the situation in Suez we cannot take on water until we reach Aden, and that from now all fresh water will be strictly rationed.

'Anyway, at least we can still have our seawater baths, so it could be worse,' said Helen.

Major Stewart, whom for practical reasons we later nicknamed 'Lucy', had invited us to join her in the Lounge Bar for drinks before dinner. Meeting Ma'am in such comfortable surroundings was more relaxing and, in her rather stiff formal way, she tried to put us at ease. Over a glass of sherry, she informed us it was exactly twenty years ago that she had joined the QAs, which to us then seemed something like a life sentence...

During another superb meal, we learned some interesting history about our ship, discovering she was originally the German *Cap Norte* and had been captured by the Allies during the war.

Another, perhaps more important, discovery for us was to hear that the ship's shop, located on B deck, would be opening at midday tomorrow. Rumour had it that there were actually nylon stockings on board, as well as a plentiful supply of chocolate!

Walking into the Lounge after dinner, Georgina, Helen, Pat and I found a quiet corner of comfortable armchairs and before we could decide how to spend the rest of the evening, we looked up in some surprise to see four young and somewhat shy-looking subalterns encircling us.

The tallest smiled, asking quite sweetly if we would like to join them for a game of canasta, but first of all perhaps they should introduce themselves.

'This is Angus Mackie, he and I are bound for Hong Kong. Fergus Lindsay, another Scot, David Beaumont from the 'Penny' regiment, and I am James Macfarlane, also from the Argyle and Sutherland Higlanders, unlike Fergus who belongs to the Kings Own Scottish Borderers.'

After introducing ourselves and shaking hands, the boys pulled up some more chairs, quickly rearranging us into a comfortable octet.

James was the tallest and fair haired; Angus, with a shock of auburn hair, a little shorter. Fergus, who was dark, with a small burgeoning moustache, was almost the same height as David, whom I noticed was hazel-eyed, with a good-natured smile.

Attempting to play the comparatively new card game canasta provided something of a challenge because, as yet, none of us had had the opportunity to learn. This was soon remedied by our patient tutors, thus setting a pattern so that even before we arrived at Port Said we were more than adept.

Much later, before turning in, escaping from the heat of the lounge I crossed the high threshold of the bulkhead door, out into the coolness of the deck and on up to the bows of the ship. Almost alone, there it was blissfully quiet, with the exception of a handful of troops on the deck below, singing softly to the strains of a mouth organ.

The sky was misty, with tiny clusters of stars peeping out, as the ship glided gracefully on, throughout the darkness of the night.

Despite nearing the infamous Bay of Biscay, the sea was surprisingly calm and the weather pleasantly warmer with just a gentle breeze that Sunday morning, as Georgina, Helen and I sat like the three proverbial old maids, perched on a large lifeboat box, up forward.

'Crumbs, I had a narrow escape in our bathroom this morning – dashed in late as usual for a quick bath – when to my embarrassment there was a stray gentleman disrobed in there – Gosh did I do a bunk!' Helen told us breathlessly, rolling her large brown eyes.

'Oh blast! I am sorry, I should have warned you, because last night a similar thing happened to me, only this chap was in uniform – tallish, elderly, with a crown and three pips up – that's a Brigadier's rank isn't it? Anyway he was charming and explained that the two of them have the cabin opposite and so share the bathroom with us,' Georgina spelled out apologetically, adding drily, 'Poor chaps won't get much of a chance with the four of us continually using it!'

'Did you hear the radio programme earlier?' I enquired. 'Not that there was anything of note, but apparently we have BBC bulletins broadcast twice a day at 0800hrs and at 1800hrs: rather comforting to keep up with news from home.'

'Which reminds me, what about a little exercise before we have to assemble in the lounge at midday, to attend the Memorial Service for the late King George being relayed from St Paul's Cathedral. Shall we join the many pounding around the deck, intent on doing their daily dozen?' interrupted Pat, who had suddenly appeared.

Having by now familiarised ourselves with the comfortable public rooms on board, from the attractive lounge with its authentic looking fireplace, the spacious, impressive dining saloon to the smaller smoking room with its convenient bar and a modest but well-stocked little library room tucked away, all that remained for us to explore now was the ship's shop due to open after lunch.

This, we found, was a tiny affair located in a gloomy corner on B deck but none the less magical to us, having been subjected to years of post-war shortages through rationing, with little other than the unattractive utility items still on sale.

Joining the small queue which had formed outside the miniature hatched shop window, Pat and I gazed at the selection of chocolate bars arranged on the back shelves and above them, with sheer amazement, at the display of small boxes of Yardley, Coty, Elizabeth Arden and even Chanel No.5, somewhat mixed up with pads of writing paper, tins of fifty cigarettes and, to the right-hand side, a small case of costume jewellery, plus much more stuffed into this precious little Aladdin's cave.

'Look at the prices,' I whispered to Pat, 'everything appears to be much, much cheaper than at home, don't you think? See those ciggies are only 2s 4d a tin, for fifty.'

'Yes, but that's because now we are at sea, there's no luxury tax on anything, didn't you realise that?

'But I can't see any nylons, can you? Perhaps they are under the counter. Look, Jilly, there, do you see that notice, yippee, this is a hairdresser's shop as well!'

'I don't believe it! But yes, you are right, that is really marvellous, but how on earth can it fit into this tiny space?'

'We'll soon find out.'

The kind lady serving confirmed that she was indeed the hairdresser, explaining to us that was why the shop opening hours were somewhat limited, as she had to look after both. Out of one of the many cupboards below she found us a treasured pair of nylon stockings each, and we both left, well satisfied with our purchases.

Back in the cabin, having shown off my loot of chocolate and told Georgina that limited nylons were available, she in turn reminded me that we only had the standard overseas allowance of £5 each to cover our personal expenditure for the whole six weeks of this voyage. Hopefully, with extras like laundry bills, drinks such as tomato juice at 4d a glass and with some shore leave ahead, this would be sufficient.

Less than forty-eight hours after leaving Southampton, regardless of the confines of our cabin, we four had settled down into a pleasant routine, mainly regulated by mealtimes. Starting with breakfast at 0830hrs, lunch was at 1300hrs and dinner at 1900hrs, and associated with this was the obligatory three-times daily change of dress:

Battledress for breakfast until 1100hrs.

Mufti from then on, until…

No.1 dress for dinner.

Quite a feat; nonetheless, but for the occasional fraying of tempers, and by coping with a sense of humour and certain amount of generosity, we managed extremely well.

Finally, the carefree and happy atmosphere pervading throughout the ship, combined with the unexpected freedom after years of disciplined training, with the added advantage of unlimited fresh air and superb food, all contributed to a sense of well-being and relaxation. Notwithstanding that, travelling on a troopship we were still subject to the bounds of military law, even though this particular ship was run by the RAF!

Gradually a daily pattern was emerging involving some sort of activity each morning, from washing one's smalls in the laundry room below decks to a game of deck quoits or a swift trot around the deck. Lunch usually took a pleasant three quarters of an hour, resulting in a traditional siesta when, to our surprise, we all flaked out on our bunks, crawling down later to grab a cup of unpleasant tasting tea and a bun from the saloon. Then it was a mad session of badge and button polishing and desperately trying to extinguish the smell of Brasso by liberally sprinkling ourselves with scent.

After dinner, unless we had to do our duty with Ma'am at some social gathering, we usually spent the evening with our new friends the subalterns, either playing canasta, pontoon for matchsticks or watching the weekly film show organised by the Entertainment Committee. One evening, however, as we strolled on deck, Angus Mackie pulled a mouth organ from out of his pocket to softly play *The Dashing White Sergeant*. Helen started dancing, the rest of us followed and there began the many nights of our impromtu Scottish country dancing.

Passing Cape Finistere at 0600hrs on Monday, apart from a heavy swell causing the ship to roll, the sea was calm and it was fascinating to glimpse the Spanish coast with its hills shrouded in mist. Twenty-four hours later we sailed on past Cape St Vincent and the Portuguese shoreline, with bright green fields sloping down to the chalky cliffs below. Disappointingly, we missed Gibraltar, passing through the Straits in the early hours of Wednesday into an unusually grey, dismal and rough Mediterranean, with a bitter head wind blowing.

Two days later it was all change, as we followed the North African coast with its magnificent backdrop of the Atlas Mountains, partially obscured by cloud but with their snow-capped summits just visible. The sun shone warmly, shimmering down on the roofs of distant houses. The sky was a deep sapphire, with the sea constantly changing from dark indigo to a sparkling turquoise.

This was utterly refreshing for the four of us, having recently experienced some unexpected mood swings during the past day or so; apparently a commonplace occurrence at sea, or so we had been told, by those more widely travelled. Added to this, the previous evening Lucy had put her foot down, insisting that we should all join her small party. This consisted of playing poker dice with her boring and very ex-Poona companions, when we all would have been a lot happier practising our Scottish sets with the others and with whom we seemed to have made quite a hit.

Finding myself to be a Sassenach untutored in Scottish dancing, Helen kindly suggested a crash course by teaching me the basic steps. This we did, practising in the only available space, which was the next-door bathroom!

Exactly ten days after leaving Southampton, the *Empire Trooper* docked at Port Said at about 0400hrs on Tuesday 26 February. Prior to our arrival, due to the tense situation in Egypt, the O/C Troops had ordered that under no circumstances was anyone permitted to leave the ship whilst in port. Armed guards would protect and patrol all entrances and exits and no local traders in bum boats were to be allowed anywhere near the troopship.

'That's dashed any hopes we might have had to go on a shopping binge at Simon Artz,' remarked Pat gloomily.

'Or even to stretch our legs,' concluded Georgina, as we hung over the rail trying to assimilate something of the atmosphere on the dingy quayside below.

'It just looks tatty to me, apart from that impressive building over there,' said Helen, pointing across the water to the dome of the Suez Canal Offices.

At midday, tugs came alongside to turn and tow us out to join the thirteen other ships forming a long convoy at the commencement of the Suez Canal. Earlier, to our joy, the first mail from home had been delivered and I had had letters from my parents, as well as a rather worrisome one from Miles explaining that, although he had fully recovered from his motor bike accident, unfortunately the sight in his right eye had been affected by the bump on his head and he was waiting to see another eye specialist, for a second opinion.

The journey down the canal was incredibly fascinating; its noticeably restricted width allowed a superb view of the adjacent scenery as we slowly sailed ahead at just seven knots. It was a wonderfully warm day, with hot sunshine and a cool breeze, as the decks filled with curious onlookers during our passage through.

En route, to the right, we passed El Tina and El Cap and several other small canal signal stations, plus the occasional little town, sparsely populated and in desolate surroundings. At intervals along the canal we saw military outposts, including Ismailia, with groups of khaki-clad troops cheerily waving to us from the steep banks, and frequently shouting, 'Get your knees brown', or 'Come for a swim!' where a number of them were wallowing in the water.

On the opposite side, after leaving El Qantara, the further down we travelled the more barren the landscape became, with large stretches of desert and little habitation, apart from odd clumps of tiny straw-covered mud-brick dwellings, built next to a few dusty-looking palm trees for shade.

Focusing David's binoculars, through the distant haze I could see the railway line with a couple of wrecked trains lying abandoned beside the tracks. A few minutes later, to my astonishment, smoke appeared on the horizon from a steam train puffing along.

Swivelling the glasses towards the desert, I inadvertently came across another type of train, but this was a caravan of camels swaying majestically across the sand-dunes accompanied by Biblical figures, some walking and some riding.

About halfway through, the convoy pulled into a cutting, stopping there for three hours to allow the north-bound convoy of fourteen ships to pass on their homeward journey. One of the many unforgettable sights that day was that of a tall, bright red ship's funnel seemingly riding high out of the nothingness of desert.

Sailing onward again, that evening we were entertained by the ship's band. Taking advantage of the lively music we hastily organised an informal dance on the deck, joined by an ever increasing circle of young friends, including Anne, the pretty teenage daughter of one of the families on board.

Suddenly, in the middle of a slow waltz, the ship lurched quite violently, sending us slithering across the teakwood planks to grab on to the rail.

The band continued to play but as most of the excitement was on deck the dancing came to an abrupt halt and we hung over the side in the darkness to try to see what had happened.

From the grapevine we soon gathered that the ship had accidently got stuck on a sandbank, at the same time hitting a buoy. For the next hour there was a much activity, as the ship's crew worked tirelessly to free her, which fortuitously they did. As for the rest of us, after watching the drama successfully unfold, we concluded the evening traditionally, by dancing a conga around the ship!

By the following Thursday we were well into the Red Sea, having sailed through the Gulf of Suez with its spectacular panorama of high, rugged, barren mountains, with a glimpse of Mount Sinai as an unexpected bonus. The temperature was increasing by the hour, getting hotter and hotter, and at the same time it was hard to believe most everyone at home was probably feeling miserably cold, with coal rationing still in force.

The previous day, the O/C Troops had given the order to change from battle-dress to khaki drill and personally gave permission to the QAs to wear mufti from 1100hrs onwards; it was such a relief to be able to wear a cotton dress, instead of a stiff collar and shirt each evening. We were also given the privilege of our own tiny sun deck, which had been especially rigged up with an awning. Pat and I had already taken advantage of sunbathing there, and were now rather an unbecoming shade of lobster pink.

So far during the voyage we had lost three hours but by the time of arrival in Japan, we would be eight hours ahead of GMT. This, combined with the unaccustomed heat, was beginning to have a tiring effect.

'Aren't they so beautiful! Quickly look, there, dancing along beside the ship,' Helen exclaimed as, enchanted, we watched a school of porpoise, leaping gracefully across the bows, their silvery bodies glistening in the sunlight.

'What's more I bet they will go on following us for ages. Incidentally did you know that there is a brown owl with three young, nesting on the ship? But to change the subject, Jilly, I've just heard from Lucy that the hospital we are posted to in Japan is in Kure, on the island of Honshu and not far from Hiroshima. Apparently it is the busy base hospital for the sick and wounded from Korea and it sounds as though we shall have some acute nursing ahead.'

'That's great, but do you think that we might just get over to Korea?'

'No, not from what Ma'am was saying, but you never know, and I hope so.'

As we progressed the temperature rose, the sea became quite rough with a stiff head wind and for several hours the ship pitched badly. This was when I almost disgraced myself, while pressing my uniform down below in the intense heat of the laundry room, suddenly I felt very, very sick! Crawling back to the cabin I found that the other three were feeling much the same. We took some Kwells and flaked out on our bunks until lunchtime, where we did our level best to avoid eating. However, there, at Lucy's insistence, we had to swallow a bowl of fatty oxtail soup which, to my surprise and relief, instead of immediately throwing up, I kept down and unexpectedly felt much better.

Later that day, Georgina and I had to go down to the hold of the ship to locate our trunks.

On our way, we passed through the troops' quarters which seemed to be unbearably hot and poorly ventilated and we felt really sorry for them, but at least they had more deck space than us, which was something of an asset.

That night we had our first formal dance on board, where it was almost too hot to dance, and even more difficult to keep any powder on one's nose! Amusingly, we four were outnumbered by the opposite sex and were much in demand, and at one time, as I tried to cool off on deck, I discovered that I had an escort of two kilted Highlanders, with another two bringing up the rear! Despite the intense heat and perspiring in places that one had never dreamt of, we finished the evening with an explosive eightsome reel.

Approaching Aden in the late afternoon of Sunday 4 March the ship sailed along at a leisurely pace, waiting for the pilot to board whilst we all waited on deck to hear if this time we would be lucky enough to be granted any shore leave.

Watching the advancing landscape as the ship closed in towards the shore was an amazing experience, as it progressively unfurled into a Walt Disney scene. Silhouetted in a purple haze were high jagged desolate peaks and rocky prominences, with a sparse foreground of one or two green trees and clumps of small white houses, neatly placed like cardboard cut outs. This, combined with the magnificence of the setting sun and glittering cerulean sea, created a dramatic technicolour backdrop to a constantly changing scene.

Originally David had invited me to have dinner ashore with him, but because of what seemed to be interminable delays, we decided to eat on board to save what precious time we might have. Dressed in khaki drill ready for the excursion, I boldly excused myself to Lucy and before she could say No! dashed over to David's table to join him and his companions, James, Angus, Fergus and Charlie who was a Gunner.

Just as the coffee was served, it was announced over the tannoy that the ferries were ready to leave. Clutching our leave passes, we rose with one accord making a mad dash to the side of the ship, to scramble down the accommodation ladder onto the waiting tender below.

By then it was very dark and especially exciting to chug across the black water to see the bright lights of Aden beckoning us for our first step ashore into the mysterious East. Determined to make the most of the miserly one and a half hours' shore leave, the six of us decided to stick together and set off in the heat and humidity of the evening, walking along the harbour road to the Crescent Hotel for a cool Swedish beer.

Soon refreshed, we then trooped off to look at a nearby bazaar, but most of the stuff was tawdry, and with an allowance of only ten East African Shillings each, we could not afford to waste any of it.

Frankly, although we had been forewarned, Aden appeared drab and somewhat disappointing, and nothing like the exotic East I had imagined. Wondering what on earth to do for our remaining precious hour ashore, Charlie had the bright idea of going up to the Club, so that if nothing else we could see a bit of the local scenery. Finding a cab, which just happened to be a large open Ford, we all piled in and, not surprisingly, had some difficulty in making the driver understand the whereabouts of our destination.

When eventually he did, down went his foot and we shot up the main street at about sixty miles per hour, hanging on tightly, whilst Abdul did his utmost to avoid flattening any pedestrians who ventured too near! We arrived at the Club in one piece, only to discover that being a Sunday it was closed. So Abdul, as we had named him, returned us at speed to the bright lights, dropping us at the Crescent Hotel.

Feeling somewhat peckish, we ordered some sandwiches and beer. The beer was deliciously cool as ever. The sandwiches when they finally turned up, were huge hunks of warm bread, spread lavishly with warm greasy butter and filled with very warm and very greasy goat's meat. One bite was sufficient!

Although time was rapidly running out, we still wanted to buy some souvenirs and rushed hopefully from the hotel into the adjacent bazaar. There we were pursued by moustachioed vendors trying to flog everything from pseudo 'Indian' brassware – with 'Made in Birmingham' plastered over it. And to my own embarrassment, I was plagued by several enthusiastic vendors of 'Silk pyjamas lady, you buy my silk pyjamas, look very good on you lady!'

The moment came when we had either to buy or not to buy. Simultaneously I spied a lonely little prancing glass horse, begging James to haggle for it, on my behalf. This he accomplished with skill; even so it still cost twelve rupees (18*s*) and was far too expensive. Very generously, the boys insisted that they gave it to me as a memento and on the spot christened it Abdul. We just made it back to the ferry by 2000hrs and concluded the evening by joining the other three in a game of canasta.

To my dismay, the following afternoon Lucy ordered me to report for night duty that evening in the ship's hospital, explaining that the two Princess Mary's Royal Air Force nursing sisters in charge – with whom she was very friendly – were far too busy to look after a sick baby who had recently been admitted. The rest of us suspected that it was really because she had seen me riding through Aden on the back seat of the open Ford, surrounded by five subalterns.

The baby was very sick during the night, and it was unbearably hot and humid in the ward and by the time I finished duty that morning my clothes were positively sticking to me. Fortunately the baby started to recover and I did two more nights on duty before being relieved by Georgina, who had kindly offered to take over from me.

We recently heard on the News that an earthquake, accompanied by a severe tidal wave, had struck Japan, but still had no idea exactly where, leaving the four of us thinking that our new posting would most probably prove to be quite an unusual one.

Having completed three weeks on board, we were now halfway through this incredible voyage of sailing around almost half the world when, at that time, few of us had opportunity to travel so far.

The temperature continued to rise as we entered the Indian Ocean. There it was stiflingly hot, both by day and by night, and we were exhorted to drink plenty of water. Unfortunately, the water which had recently been taken on at Aden was heavily chlorinated and tasted more like warm Soda Bic.

By this time we were also five hours ahead of GMT, so what with the heat, lost time and lack of sleep, understandably we four were sometimes a bit on the scratchy side.

It was a relief to arrive in Colombo and Pat and I felt really excited at the thought of being off in Ceylon with a whole six and a half hours' shore leave in which to catch a glimpse of it.

Leaving the ship promptly at 1000hrs, with Peter, David and Fergus, we hailed a taxi driving slowly through the spacious tree-lined city streets, at the same time observing how little motor traffic there was, instead, what a large number of rickshaws there were. Because it was so baking hot, we drove straight out to the swimming club where we spent one and a half glorious hours wallowing like porpoises in the clear cool water of the huge pool.

After a leisurely lunch at the Grand Oriental Hotel it was time to shop. Sadly, as we wandered through the hundreds of smaller shops and market stalls, we were besieged by lots of little children, with huge dark almond-shaped eyes, begging for buckshees. However, everyone else seemed to be flogging nothing but elephants of all shapes sizes and colours, carved from costly ivory to painted coconut wood.

Eventually I found a small tea merchant's shop, where I arranged for a 2lb-box of best Ceylonese Orange Pekoe tea to be sent to my parents who, like the rest of the country, were still in the grip of food rationing. The tea, which was rather expensive, I was told, would take five weeks to ship home.

After much bargaining, my other purchase was an attractive blue sari made of the finest cotton and decorated with a delicate flower motif. Returning to the ship that afternoon, I found a wonderful cache of eight letters waiting for me.

Bursting into the cabin, whilst I was quietly digesting Miles's latest news, Pat flopped excitedly on to the nearest bunk. 'Jilly, there's to be a fancy dress dance on Thursday night. What on earth are we going to wear, stuck right out at sea?'

'Gosh that's a surprise and I suppose originality will be the order of the day. There's no hope of buying anything on board.'

Three nights later, an hilarious assortment of dress paraded at dinner, from an absent-minded professor minus trousers! to a somewhat tubby middle-aged gentleman sitting at the table next to us, dressed in only a nappy, a pink bonnet perched on top of his bald head, and sucking a baby's bottle full of – what? – milk…

Pat as Gorgeous Gussie, the 1951 darling of Wimbledon, caused something of a stir, swinging in with her racquet and showing off her trim little figure in the shortest of tennis whites, complemented by a pair of very frilly knickers.

Helen wore her traditional Scottish attire and Georgina had made a splendid Ascot hat. Lucy, was just being Lucy, in a plain evening gown.

Thankfully, having just bought the sari, I made good use of it and with Anne's unstinting help, by folding it correctly and staining my face, neck, and arms a dark brown, I dressed up as an Indian lady. Despite my fair hair and blue eyes, I was both flattered and relieved when passing one of the Bearers he spontaneously complimented me with 'It is a good dress'. It was a riotous evening, letting off steam – quite literally – dancing until midnight through the heat and humidity of the Indian Ocean, and much later to marvel at the infinite number of giant stars, glittering like huge diamonds in a black velvet sky.

Less than twelve hours later, when passing through the Malacca Straits with Malaya lying to our left and the mountains of Sumatra to the right, quite suddenly the weather changed to a heavy drizzle and the sea became a shade of steely slate. During that evening and on several others the sky was punctuated by frequent flashes of lightning – electric storms – which apparently are a common occurrence in this area.

One of the ongoing amusements on board was the daily mileage sweep, cheap at 3*d* a go and, amazingly, I won this for a second day running, with a prize money of 13*s* 6*d*!

The little library was such a Godsend, and during opening hours was invariably crammed with avid readers.

In spite of the cramped space and general stuffiness of our cabin, the four of us continued to manage well, even with the self-inflicted difficulty of dressing up each evening.

Docking in Singapore in the early hours of Sunday 18 March, we were very sorry to bid farewell to several of our young friends, especially Anne who, with a considerable number of other passengers, disembarked there. Later that morning, after watching them disappear down the gangway, from the deck I was able to appreciate the stunning beauty of the vast natural harbour, where everything surrounding it appeared to be shaded in a leafy green. Dotted with little green islands, its lovely background of green hills sloped down to red sandy beaches, abutting onto a deeper green sea.

However, apart from its natural charm, there was little else that day which impressed me during my short foray into Singapore. This was partly my own fault; through being somewhat shy, I accidentally missed my friends at the quayside and, not wanting to miss the chance of going ashore, ventured off alone.

It was an extremely hot and humid afternoon as I wandered through the busy main street filled with a polyglot of mainly Chinese, Malays, Indians, plus a few other nationalities. Everywhere there was an abundance of colourful Chinese sign boards hanging above the shop windows. Disappointingly, most of these displayed a monotonous variety of cheap Westernised goods and chewing gum: my sole purchase was an inexpensive Austrian cigarette lighter, which I later discovered behaved like a flame thrower!

Before arriving in Singapore we had been told that there at 1500hrs every afternoon it rained heavily, and as the sky grew darker I checked my watch as the downpour erupted, hastily flagging down a bicycle rickshaw for cover. Sitting in the quaint mode of transport, in my crumpled khaki drill, I felt somewhat conspicuous, slightly apprehensive, and a just a little lonely, deciding that what was needed was a decent cup of tea.

Afternoon tea at the Raffles Hotel was an uplifting experience, with its spacious, comfortable lounge, attentive staff, delicious tasting tea and slice of rich fruit cake. From there, my kind Chinese rickshaw driver gave me a swift tour around the city, driving slowly past the beautiful Anglican cathedral of St Andrew, built from the finest white stone and superbly situated on a broad, grassy green sward.

Returning safely to the ship, I was greeted some time later by the others, demanding to know where I had been all day and emphasising that, because of the present tense situation in Singapore, I should not have gone ashore alone!

Sailing on through the South China Sea towards Hong Kong, the heat was less oppressive and each evening there seemed to be a brilliant sunset, with a dazzling array of colours. But even more enchanting to watch were the myriads of tiny, gossamer-winged flying fish that sometimes appeared at that particular time of day; their gleaming, glistening, bodies were phosphorescent in the sunshine, as they darted to and fro above the water, until suddenly plopping down into a wave.

Another fascination was the passing of ships at night and observing the friendly exchange of signals with lamps, especially if it happened to be a large passenger ship, which was always a blaze of lights.

There was extra excitement that previous afternoon, with organised horse racing on deck. Some of the passengers had been invited to name certain horses. This had been carried out in true spirit, with one cardboard nag aptly christened by the two Brigadiers, 'Locked, by Sisters, out of Bathroom'. Needless to say, it lost heavily!

Twenty-four hours before arriving in Hong Kong we experienced the roughest of seas so far, with the ship pitching badly for a considerable time. It was a relief to reach calmer waters and to dock later that Friday. It was lucky, too, as this was our last evening to spend with our young friends the subalterns, most of whom were disembarking, along with the majority of passengers, apart from David, Charlie and Fergus who were destined for Korea, via Japan. We all made the most of it, playing canasta, Scottish dancing and finishing up, in true Army tradition, with a crazy conga.

Waving them off the next morning was quite sad because, despite the disparity in ages – at twenty-four and having a younger brother of my own, I had felt much like an elder sister – we had all enjoyed their lively company and at the same time become real wizards at canasta.

The remainder of us were granted seven hours' shore leave and because Lucy heard the other three making plans, she astounded us all by kindly inviting me, to go ashore with her and two of her friends. Being somewhat reticent by nature, and acknowledging the difference in seniority, I was not altogether sure, but after my last debacle in Singapore decided quickly that I had better accept, and thanked her very much. Quite unexpectedly, through her thoughtfulness, I spent a most interesting day, with the extra bonus of permission to wear mufti.

Leaving the ship at 1100hrs, with Lucy and her two companions Major Dick Smith and Captain Donald Johnson, to cross over to the mainland by small boat, I was fascinated by the stunning scenery, of high rugged hills surrounding the lovely harbour and the number of impressive buildings on the shore. In Kowloon we made straight for the enormous Peninsular Hotel to have morning coffee because, as Lucy explained, it was far too expensive to have lunch there, but the coffee was the best yet!

Major S suggested the United Services Club, which he said was both pleasant and reasonably priced, adding that anywhere else lunch could cost up to £10 each – which, at that time, was exactly half my month's salary.

The taxi ride there was enjoyable, as the Club was situated some distance away, where it overlooked a range of craggy hills. This was blessed with a beautiful garden which was full of flowers, some typically English and many other exotic species such as hibiscus, with even some banana trees growing there.

After lunch we returned to the shopping centre in Kowloon, with its spotlessly clean, broad chestnut tree-lined streets, huge modern stone buildings and captivating shops. The latter, after the austerity and shortages at home, I found almost overwhelming, stuffed full of rich brocades, exquisite embroidery, crocodile handbags with matching shoes. Spoilt for choice, I plumped for a pretty, pale blue, pure silk, hand-embroidered blouse, unbelievably cheap, at just £1.

The ferry ride over to Hong Kong was very pleasant, with a cool exhilarating freshness briefly enveloping us as we sped across the water to the lovely island. There, we continued with an exciting ride in a taxi which slowly bumped its way up along the uneven edge of the precarious, sheer, alpine road, to the summit of the Peak.

At 1,300ft the view was staggering, and to the right we saw the colossal harbour, bustling with ships from naval frigates to the larger *Empress of Australia* berthed next to our own *Empire Trooper*. The sea was a sparkling blue, as numbers of tiny sampans and the slightly larger Chinese junks deftly wove their way to and fro through the mass of craft at anchor.

The panorama from our left was breathtakingly beautiful, with clear views over an extensive green fertile valley of tropical and sub-tropical trees, inclining down to an azure sea with several odd little islands, where the only craft were Chinese Junks.

'Do you realise that just over there is Red China?' Major Smith asked, as I returned his binoculars.

'No, I'd no idea that we were so close to the Communists.'

After scrambling around the rocky slopes, Lucy sensibly suggested tea and we went over to the small café. Sitting outside, enjoying the coolness of the Peak, we noticed the large mansions built for the lucky few on its hillside. Instead of returning by taxi, we chose the funicular railway. This was an amazing feat of engineering which, during its ten-minute descent, ground slowly down a sick-making and almost perpendicular slope, and at times passing incredibly close to numbers of very small houses, which leant somewhat drunkenly beside it. We were so taken by this incredible ride that by common assent, we boldly made a second round trip!

With fifteen Hong Kong dollars left burning a hole in my pocket, we walked around the shops where I blew it on a couple of tiny glass animals to add to my growing collection.

Crossing back from Kowloon to the ship in the early evening, the water was bathed in the brilliance of a spectacular sunset, until without warning, the huge flaming ball of the sun sank suddenly and swiftly, behind a hill.

By Monday 26 March, twenty-four hours after sailing from Hong Kong, not only had the weather changed dramatically, but also our intended destination.

Once we were well out to sea, the O/C Troops announced over the tannoy that the ship had been diverted to Korea and we should be docking in Pusan to disembark troops and stores in just over forty-eight hours. After the news had broken and the ship changed course to sail between the Chinese mainland and Formosa into the East China Sea, everyone seemed a bit blasé, and went around saying 'Pusan next stop' rather as though it was Victoria Station. Pat, eternally hopeful, went as far as speculating that if we were ever lucky enough to get ashore, we might even get danger money!

The previous night we experienced something of a severe storm when the poor old *Trooper* just pitched, creaked and lurched all night, with a heavy spray splashing loudly on the scuttle. Lying on my bunk was like sleeping on a seesaw.

Thankfully the next day, we changed back into battledress as it was incredibly cold, with a bitter wind blowing over a rough and dull grey sea. A similarly sombre grey atmosphere emanated on board the now-quiet and half-empty ship. Surprisingly, with only eight women remaining and so with more space available, Georgina was given her own cabin; something that would suit her, having had to put up with us three younger ones for so long. And at last I had an upper bunk.

Disappointingly rumour had it that our three-year Kure posting might now only be for eighteen months, although we imagined that that depended on the situation in Korea. While the privilege of living in lovely limbo for the past five weeks was well behind us, the true proximity of the war loomed ahead.

From a practical sense we re-packed our belongings, plus the additional loot we had collected, each of us feeling a certain sadness at the loss of freedom we knew we should experience once disembarked from this dear old, happy, little ship.

Thursday 27 March

All around us there was a cheerless shade of grey, converging with the leaden horizon of sea and sky, as huddled in our heavy greatcoats, we four watched the ship ease into her berth in Pusan harbour. Ahead the old port buildings and sheds looked grey and beyond them the bleak background of barren hills and stunted trees was partially obscured by a haziness of grey. From time to time flurries of sleet swirled around us; it was bitterly cold and gloomy, matching well the mood of sombreness which for several hours had permeated through the ship.

Anchored in the harbour were two hospital ships, the USN *Consolation* and the Danish *Jutlandia*, their large scarlet crosses glowing comfortingly in the pallid light.

Despite the gloom, the freezing wind and the putrid stench of rotten rice drifting over from the shore, we had been rooted to the deck well before docking at 1000hrs.

'Not much happening yet,' observed Pat.

'No, but can't you feel the atmosphere, to me it feels rather sad,' I replied.

'Watch it, here comes Lucy,' warned Helen.

'Blast!' muttered Georgina.

'Morning Ma'am,' we chorused dutifully.

'Good Morning, while things are so quiet, I am determined to put my feet on Korean soil so I am going down now – shan't be long.' And to our utter amazement off she swept.

'It's alright for some!' grumbled Pat, adding, 'Didn't orders state that on no account were any unauthorised persons allowed on shore?'

About twenty minutes later, we heard the familiar sound of clattering boots and peering down, we watched as a steady stream of khaki-clad soldiers marched down the gangways to form up into neat columns on the quayside. Simultaneously we heard the heart-warming sounds of rousing music, when to our surprise and delight we saw marching towards us from around the corner of the sheds the impeccably smart American Negro Military Band. And whilst they played and cheerfully paraded up and down on the cold quayside, our British boys left the security of the ship to march off to what would be for the majority of them, their first experience of war.

'They do look proud,' said Lucy, who had just rejoined us as we watched their fresh English faces grinning responsively to an expert rendition of Jazz Blues.

'But, some of them look so young and I suppose are most probably national servicemen,' I added.

'It must be sobering for them to realise that now they really are on their way, poor boys,' Georgina sighed.

'And I wonder how many of them we shall be nursing soon in Kure?' mused Helen.

At the moment none of us had an inkling, that in less than three weeks, several of those lads would have been admitted with serious wounds and others, tragically, would have been killed.

The band struck up with a lively *If I knew you were coming I'd have baked a cake* and this they continued to play until the last of the troops had filed away out of sight.

'Do you think there is the remotest possibility of any of us serving in Korea, Ma'am?' I enquired.

'No, Hall, none at all. Apparently the conditions are too rough, so that at present all our nursing sisters are based at the British Commonwealth General Hospital in Kure. Don't worry, from what I've already gathered, there's more than enough to do there,' added Lucy, with a wry smile.

Late afternoon, as darkness fell, the *Empire Trooper* slipped away from Pusan. Now a near empty ship, her few remaining passengers were bound for the garrison port of Kure, on the island of Honshu, in Japan.

A BRIEF HISTORY OF THE KOREAN WAR

1910	Korea was annexed by the Japanese Empire.
1945	After the surrender of the Japanese at the end of the Second World War, President Truman ordered the division of Korea at the 38th Parallel, thus to allow the Soviet troops to disarm the Japanese and occupy North Korea, and the American Forces to do likewise in South Korea.
1948	The Republic of Korea (ROK) was declared and by the end of the year all Soviet troops had been withdrawn from the northern republic and American troops from the southern. However, whilst the US supplied just sufficient arms necessary for self defence, the Russians were at the same time pouring in a vast array of weapons into the North and thereby providing a formidable army.
1950	
25 June	North Korean Army invaded the South Korean Republic without warning.
26 June	United Nations Security Council condemned the attack and called upon the North Koreans to withdraw to the 38th Parallel. Twenty-four hours later the Security Council requested all members of the UN to support the ROK and created a Unified Command for Korea. The US immediately committed ground forces and General MacArthur was appointed commander-in-chief of the UN Command.
29 June	British and Australian naval forces arrived in Korean waters and during the following weeks were soon joined by British and Commonwealth troops, and contingents from sixteen other countries in accordance with the UN Resolution. For the first few months the war went badly for the UN Forces and then

	between August and September the decisive battles for the Pusan Perimeter were fought, when the UN troops launched an offensive which finally repelled the North Koreans.
October	After the additional involvement of Chinese Communist Forces, the conflict continued for the next six months or so with both sides alternately advancing and retreating until July 1951, when a stalemate was reached just north of the 38th Parallel.
1951	
10 July	Cease fire talks began at Kaesong, later to be transferred to Panmunjom. Negotiations dragged on and off for another two years until it was accepted that the battle line and not the 38th Parallel should be the demarcation line, which lead to the creation of the DMZee (Demilitarised Zone) and the truce village of Panmumjom.
1953	
27 July	The Armistice was eventually signed at Panmunjom and since then both sides still meet there periodically to exchange opposing views, because as yet it has never been followed by a peace treaty.

By the end of the war Korea was in ruins; Seoul had been flattened and had changed hands several times. Millions of people were homeless, the countryside devastated and industry destroyed. The UN Forces had lost over 37,000 men, a large number of whom had been US Servicemen; thousands had been wounded, and civilian casualties had been horrendous.

The approximate total of Commonwealth casualties killed, wounded and missing was 7,268, which included the British casualties from Royal Navy, Royal Marines, Army and RAF. The total killed was 1,078 and wounded 2,674. Prisoners of War who were repatriated numbered 978, plus those known to have died as POWs numbered seventy-one and presumed to have died as POWs eleven.

Sources: *The Limited War* by Rees and *The British Forces in the Korean War* by General Sir Anthony Farrar-Hockley (the latter being the official history of the British involvement).

CHAPTER THREE

FIRST IMPRESSIONS

In Korea, Armistice negotiations had begun in Kaesong as early as 10 July 1951 but were suspended by the Communists after alleged violation of the neutral zone in Kaesong. On 25 October talks were resumed at Panmunjom, followed by various stalemates, and continued for another eighteen months.

Saturday 29 March 1952

After completing the twenty-four-hour crossing from Pusan, the *Empire Trooper* docked in Kure on Friday night. By 0900hrs on the following morning we QAs were waiting in the saloon, spruced up in khaki battledress, with our hand baggage stacked neatly, in readiness for the arrival of our new Matron.

Five minutes later, the doors swung open and in swept Lt-Col Phylis Widger QARANC, small of stature, awesomely correct, her uniform pressed to perfection. She was accompanied by a large, kindly looking gentleman, our new commanding officer, Colonel Meneces RAMC.

'Welcome, it is good to see you and I hope that you have had an enjoyable voyage', he said, smiling pleasantly at us.

'Which one of you is Hall?' enquired Matron briskly.

'I am, Ma'am,' I responded nervously, wondering what misdemeanour I could have committed already!

'I have a letter for you.'

'Thank you, Ma'am.' Relieved, I took the blue airmail envelope, recognising my mother's handwriting.

Surveying us briefly, Matron then said, 'I'm very glad to meet you all, especially as we are short staffed and I hope that you will enjoy your posting here in Kure. However, I must tell you now, in case you are under the misapprehension that you will be stationed here for the next three years, this is not so. Your posting in Japan is only for the next eighteen months.'

Sucking my teeth with disappointment, at the same time catching Pat's downcast eyes, Ma'am noticed, and looking disapprovingly at the two of us, she continued, 'You may well feel disappointed now, but believe me this time next year, you will be grateful. Let me explain. This shorter eighteen-month posting is because from today onwards, you will be classified as being on Active Service, in line with the rest of our troops serving with the British Commonwealth Forces in the Korean theatre of war. This also means that whether you are on or off duty, you will at all times wear uniform. The only exception to the rule is when visiting the Officers' Club, which is just a short walk from the Mess.'

After a dutiful 'Yes Ma'am', we were instructed to collect our belongings and to follow our senior officers out onto the deck and down the gangway for the last time. There two official cars were waiting to transport us, along with a type of jeep called a Tilly for our heavy baggage.

The Kure dockyards were huge, sprawling and very ugly. However, the sun was shining and it was a glorious spring morning. It was not long before we drove through the dock gates and out onto a narrow hilly road, climbing gently upwards until we drove into an untidy-looking town. At a junction of what appeared to be the main street, we turned on to a dusty side road, which was little more than a long potholey track and from where we continued to climb up a steep-ish hillside, leaving the remnants of the town behind us. Ahead I caught a glimpse of a line of craggy hills, in the middle of which there was a solitary, sparse, but impressive-looking mountain.

Minutes later our driver turned left into a gravelled drive and pulled up beside the long, low, whitewashed single-storey building of the Women's Services Officer's Mess, Kure. Alighting quickly, we had our first exciting glimpse of Japan, as on the forecourt we saw an attractive wooden handcart overflowing with the most beautiful and brilliant display of spring flowers. There, standing beside it, dressed in a dark brown kimono, with a large tortoishell comb decorating her jet black hair, was an oriental lady who on seeing us smiled widely and said something pretty in Japanese.

'Pinch me!' I said to Pat, 'as I still cannot quite believe that we really are here.'

After depositing our khaki caps on the hall table, we were shown into the ante-room, which to our amazement was vast in comparison with anything else we had experienced. This was a huge low-ceilinged room, lit by numerous large windows, furnished with comfortable chintz-covered armchairs and matching settees attractively arranged in groups around the highly polished coffee tables. Suspended at intervals from the squared, beamed ceiling, I noticed three large electric fans.

However, it was the two enormous floral arrangements on separate stands which made the biggest impression. Large white, oval pottery bowls magically filled with tall, upright displays of deep blue irises, golden chrysanthemums, scarlet peonies with a sea of chalky white blossom, transforming the immense room into something of a florist's shop.

'Come and sit down, the girl-*san* will bring us coffee and afterwards I will take you across to your quarters. You must be glad to be on dry land again,' Home Sister remarked as she bustled off to organise the coffee.

'Phew! This all looks quite luxurious,' observed Georgina.

'And I have a feeling this posting is going to be fun,' added Pat.

'But however many Mess members are there do you think, because this is such a colossal ante-room?' remarked Helen, just as Lucy the Major-Ma'am reappeared with Matron. The latter, overhearing Helen's remark, replied, 'Yes, this is an unusually large Mess, but as part of the British Commonwealth Occupation Forces in Japan, we also have an unusually large number of staff to accommodate. Approximately, there are eighty members, comprising about thirty sisters from the Royal Australian Army Nursing Corps, a smaller attachment of Canadian Naval nursing sisters, thirty-three QAs, plus a handful of radiographers, physiotherapists, some ladies from the Red Cross and two members of the Women's Voluntary Service. Rather a fluctuating number but normally there are just over eighty women living here.'

Staring sternly at us over the rim of her spectacles, she continued, 'Now a timely word of warning to you less experienced and young ones. You will be unaware that we members of this Mess are the only European women living here, in this large garrison of Commonwealth troops. So please be warned and behave impeccably at all times. That is all for now, so enjoy your coffee.'

'What on earth does she mean by that, Jilly?' muttered Pat as we dived over to the trolley.

'I don't know but it all sounds rather exciting and quite cosmopolitan.'

'Heavens! Just look at the cream on the coffee,' gasped Georgina, as we gazed in disbelief at the pretty cups extravagantly topped with thickly whipped cream.

Home Sister smiled and sitting down with us said, 'Don't get too excited because it's only evaporated milk, but the Australians prefer to take their coffee this way. 'Incidentally the dining room is through the double doors on the left and meals are at the following times: breakfast at 0700hrs before you start duty at 0730hrs. Lunch is between 1200hrs to 1330hrs depending on your off duty. Dinner is earlier than at home. Again this is an Australian innovation, served from

1700hrs to 1830hrs depending whether you are on duty or finishing at 1730hrs for the evening.

'You will also find that there is always a trolley of tea, sandwiches and fruit cake left in the ante-room for you at 2100hrs and if perchance you have friends popping in to see you they are welcome to share this.

'Finally, you will have girl-*san*, that is a house-girl, to share between two of you. She is responsible for your personal laundry, care of your uniform including the polishing of brass buttons and shoes. And provided you give advanced warning when you are off duty, she will bring a tray of afternoon tea to your room and when you have your day off, breakfast in bed.' Before we could purr with delight, she concluded briskly, 'Now, if you have finished your coffee I'll take you over to the living quarters. Hopefully your trunks will arrive soon so that you can start unpacking.'

Putting down her empty cup, Matron stood up and spoke to us again. ' Oh yes, I should have told you that today will be counted as your day off for this week, and as tomorrow is Sunday, you will take the morning off so that you can attend the special service in the nearby garrison church, to commemorate the Golden Jubilee of the foundation of the QARANC. And this will be celebrated afterwards, with a cocktail party in the Mess. However, you must all be ready to commence duty in the hospital promptly at 1300hrs, your individual ward allocations are displayed on the notice board in the hall, and I shall arrange for you to be individually escorted over to the hospital, which is about a ten-minute walk from here.' With a pleasant nod, she dismissed us.

The four of us left the Mess with Home Sister who showed us the short cut up a steep, short flight of stone steps, passing a lone Jacaranda tree and on into some quaint Japanese gardens. These were situated in front of two large, whitewashed two-storey living quarters built at right angles to each other, with a surprising backdrop of steep, craggy hills which included the impressive sparse looking solitary mountain.

Some time later, whilst I was struggling to sort out the untidy chaos of unpacking, there was a quick tap on my door and in burst Pat, flopping excitedly onto the bed, amongst a jumbled miscellany of uniform, underwear, stockings and books.

'Jilly, guess what? I've just had a phone call from Charlie. The good news is that he, Fergus and David are still here at the transit camp and they have invited you, Helen and me to the dance at the Club this evening. The bad news is that they are flying to Korea tomorrow night.'

'Oh Lord, what are you going to do? Quite honestly the last thing in the world I feel like doing is to go out tonight, as everything is in such a Mess! But on second thoughts, if they really are going to the front tomorrow, maybe I ought to, as I've already got that nasty wartime feeling of "here today and gone tomorrow".'

'You know I feel exactly the same, and to be honest I have accepted for you both, remembering how awful we felt that time seeing Peter, Rob and Paul disembarking in Pusan. I wonder how they are?'

'Incidentally Pat, how did you get on with the others at lunch? Did you get the same impression as I did, that some of the sisters, especially one or two of them, were doing their best to dampen our enthusiasm?'

'Yes I did, in fact I felt that several of them weren't too happy to be in Kure at all. It's a bit deflating!'

'What struck me, was that apart from sounding somewhat homesick and dispirited, they all looked really tired. Maybe that's what Matron was trying to warn us about this morning. But I think in any case, we must be positive and make the most of everything.'

'In that case, Jilly, let's ditch the unpacking and dash out for a break now. After all, it is our first day in Japan!'

'Brilliant idea, I'd love to as I'm dying to see what Kure is like, just give me five minutes and I'll be ready.'

We left the quarters soon after, turning right at the main gates to walk down the hill to Kure. Although it was only late March, it was baking hot and the dusty, dry, deeply rutted road seemed long and never ending. All along it there were dozens of potholes, some partially filled with sharp stones which, despite wearing beetle-squashers, were particularly hard on one's feet. On the way down we passed several little dwellings and then we came to a large stone archway to our right. Pat said she had been told that in Japanese it was called a *torii* and this was the gateway to the temple lying directly behind our quarters, and that during festivals we should hear the beating of gongs and strange music!

Ten minutes later, we arrived in the outskirts of Kure where to our relief the road was properly paved with a collection of unimposing buildings scattered around. This opened on to what was obviously the main street, called the *Hondori*, and was flanked by mainly small untidy looking shops on either side of the wide thoroughfare, which extended for a considerable distance.

On the road a modern single-decker bus flashed past us, with its brightly painted Japanese slogans glinting in the sunshine, but otherwise there seemed to be little traffic, apart from a British Commonwealth military convoy rumbling slowly through.

'Which way?' I asked.

'Let's try the shops on this side of the road, to start with.'

There were a few Japanese about, some dressed in Western style, others traditionally attired in richly embroidered kimonos, clip-clopping along on what appeared to be wooden platform-soled sandals.

Dodging in and out of the small and rather shabby shops as we progressed up the road; disappointingly there was little to enthral us. Further on, however, suddenly we were overwhelmed by loud and sensuous music blaring out from a scruffy, small, square building, from which there emanated a strong smell of beer. Standing across the entrance, we observed a large, fat Momma-*san*, her arms akimbo, obviously searching for her prey.

'My God,' exclaimed Pat, 'I bet that's a real den of vice!'

Pointing upwards, I said 'See that sign, it's a beer hall and I'm sure I've heard somewhere that these are out of bounds to the troops, though she looks as though she is waiting to pounce on some innocent lad straight out from home. Come on, let's go.' And off we dashed and into the safety of a nearby, more prosperous looking, china shop.

'This looks more like it, especially as I've promised to send my mother a pretty tea-set,' as I showed Pat an exquisitely hand-painted cup and saucer.

Hearing our voices, a pleasant looking Japanese gentleman smartly dressed in a dark lounge suit, emerged from within; smiling politely and bowing, he enquired in perfect English, if he could be of any assistance.

After admiring his fine collection, I explained that, regrettably, we had insufficient time to choose a tea-set but promised to return soon as I wanted to send one to England, and was this possible?

Reassuring me that this was not a problem and adding that he personally would supervise the safe packaging, we parted company with much bowing on both sides.

Checking the time, we realised that if we left the town then, we should be able to have afternoon tea at the Club, before returning to the Mess. So, retracing our steps we toiled back up the long dusty road, feeling uncomfortably hot and weary in our serge battledress and sensible thick khaki hose, somewhat disappointed with our first encounter with Kure.

Happily, in contrast to the shabby dusty little town, the Club when we located it was situated on a cool hillside and set in lush gardens with tiny rock pools of brightly coloured fish. Arranged invitingly on the grassy green lawn were a number of chintz armchairs and sinking gratefully into the nearest, we ordered tea and sandwiches from a pretty Japanese girl-*san*.

Late that evening, after bathing and changing into something feminine, Pat, Helen, and I returned to the Club with the three boys, dancing until midnight to the quaint rhythm of a local Japanese band.

Sunday 30 March

Feeling somewhat insecure and knowing few if any of the seemingly vast number of staff, guests and VIPs thronging the teeming ante-room, I was more than grateful when someone tapped me on the shoulder and said, 'Hallo, you are one of the new ones aren't you? Anyway, I'm Kathy and I don't suppose by any chance you have been allocated to the officers' ward?'

'Yes I have and I'm Jill, but most of my friends call me Jilly.'

'Oh good, because I've been told to take you across to the hospital now.'

'That's a relief, as my other three colleagues, have already been collected.'

'You look fine, Jilly,' Kathy said reassuringly as I hastily checked my uniform. 'But I should bring your long grey cloak with you, as it could be chilly when you finish duty at 2000hrs'.

It was a pleasant walk over to the rear of the hospital, crossing the road outside the Mess and through a large open gate which boasted a small but unoccupied guard house adjacent to it, then on to the narrow, unmade hospital road with dusty fields on either side. After several minutes, in the distance, I saw the outline of a number of large whitewashed buildings, surrounded by lovely tall trees.

'Is that the hospital compound over there, Kathy? It appears to be an enormous set-up'.

'It's pretty big, with about 1,000 beds, divided into different wards. Did you know that it was built by the Japanese before the Second World War as one of their naval hospitals when Kure was a huge base for the Japanese Navy? Apparently the harbour here is still full of wrecks.'

She continued, 'While there's time, I'd better give you the gen on the lay-out. The first thing you will see is that the wards are well spaced, with few having more than two floors, a sensible precaution in an earthquake zone. The busy surgical station is the one exception with four floors. The operating theatres are at ground level, and there is an eighty-bedded casualty ward above. Believe it or not, this particular building has been built on rollers, to withstand any damage. But since I've been here we have only experienced the occasional earth tremor, although that in itself is quite an odd sensation.'

'How long have you been stationed here, Kathy, and do you like it?'

'Just about fifteen months. I really love my nursing duties because the patients are great, and very brave, with some horrendous injuries, while others can be very ill too, from medical nasties. For example, hepatitis seems to be quite prevalent. But to answer the rest of your question…'

Kathy paused for a moment before replying thoughtfully, 'Living in Japan is still quite exciting and from what little I've managed to see of it, it's a beautiful country, although to put it mildly, Kure itself is a bit of a dump. But to be truthful, living in such a huge Mess does have its drawbacks with over eighty women cooped up, and the inevitable petty jealousies that can occur. On the whole the atmosphere tends to be rather artificial, mainly because there are so few women here in comparison with the huge numbers of servicemen. Many of them are married men, and therefore unaccompanied on active service. This can cause problems and sometimes one has to tread warily, to avoid any silly complications.

'But don't let me put you off, although it's only fair to warn you.'

By this time we had arrived at the entrance of the principal administration block, from where Kathy showed me the main front entrance of the hospital, before taking me down a long corridor to the officers' ward.

'This is it, Jilly. Good luck and don't let the senior dragon bully you!' And with those comforting words she dashed off. Taking a deep breath, I pushed through the swing doors to report to the sister in charge. Leading into the ward there was a short corridor and off this was Sister's office, closely situated to two side wards and opposite the treatment room and a pantry.

Hours later, walking at a snail's pace back to the Mess, as a kaleidoscope of images flashed through my weariness, for a short spell I was grateful to be alone in the cool of the quiet night.

Luckily for me, there had been no dragon in charge but instead a kindly deputy standing in, and about half an hour before we were due to finish duty, she called me to the office, remarking unexpectedly, 'Poor thing, you look dreadfully tired and I think you should go off duty now. All is quiet and I can manage until the night staff take over.'

'No really, Sister Shaw, I can easily carry on until then but thank you.'

'It's only because you haven't had time to acclimatise yet,' she continued as I protested. 'You see it's rather a shock to one's system and I can well remember my first day on duty in Japan and how utterly weary I felt by the end of it. In any case, the patients are all comfortably settled and there shouldn't be any more emergencies tonight.

'So off you go now Hall and get a good night's sleep, as I've just heard on the grapevine, that there has been a bit of a push in Korea, and we can expect a Cas-Evac convoy of wounded in tomorrow. Good night and thank you.'

The ward was long, light and airy, and almost full, with twenty-five of its twenty-eight beds occupied, the majority with young patients and several of these were far from well. But despite suffering from some shocking wounds, they seemed mostly in good heart and with an unquenchable sense of humour. This was embarrassingly demonstrated when I entered by a cheeky lad whose legs were obliterated by enormous plaster casts, brashly announcing, 'Just look at what we have here – a positively brand new, blue-eyed, pink-cheeked sister straight out from home!'

After several hours on duty, the patients to me were still a sea of young faces, where only a few names had really stuck, although some of the injuries were unforgettable. The second lieutenant in bed six was the youngest, his left leg amputated above the knee. His bloodied stump bandage needed changing and this was my first job. When I pushed the dressing trolley between the screens to attend to this, the boy in the next bed leaned over and whispered that Toby had been one of the best rugger players at school.

The screens were permanently around bed thirteen, which was nearest the door and close to Sister's office.

'Sister Hall, will you give the flight officer in bed thirteen his high protein drink please; he can just manage to take it through a bent straw – and don't forget to record his fluid intake.'

Quietly drawing back the screen, I was ill prepared for the severity of the burns of the New Zealand airman, lying passively between the crisp white sheets. His badly disfigured arms extended, immobilised on waterproof pillows, his distorted face deeply encrusted by a mass of blistered sores and starkly framed by a shaven scalp.

Gulping a 'Hallo', I said, 'I've made this drink especially for you, so may I help you please to take it?'

His patient eyes flickered in response as he tried to croak his thanks. Gingerly, I rearranged his pillows, before gently passing the straw through his cracked and swollen lips. And very slowly, with many pauses, he managed to swallow the strengthening fluid, until the feeding cup was empty.

Whilst marking in the ounces on the fluid chart, I suddenly heard Sister Shaw calling urgently, 'Over here quickly, Sister, and bring some screens.' Her voice was anxious. Grabbing the nearest set, I hastily dragged them across to bed six. Pushing them into position, I looked in horror at Sister Shaw's blood spattered dress and crimson sheets and, with admiration, as her hands expertly secured the thick red rubber tourniquet around the spurting stump, to arrest the haemorrhaging artery.

'Now, take over, exerting all the pressure you can, whilst I ring the surgeon and alert the theatre staff.'

My hands slid down over the sticky, bloody, bandage, automatically checking the lifesaving rubber and at the same time I smiled at the chalk white face and said, 'Don't worry Toby, we'll soon have you fixed up again. This sort of thing always looks a lot worse than it really is.'

'Hope so, Sister, because I'm beginning to feel a bit woozy, my feet are so cold and I can't stop shivering', he murmured through chattering teeth.

'Hang on, you are doing splendidly, I'll put this chest blanket over you,' clutching it from the bedside chair with one hand, whilst I pressed on to the bleeding stump with the other.

Urgent footsteps sounded in the corridor and in rushed a Medical Officer.

'Hallo young man and what have you been up to?' he enquired, swiftly assessing the gravity of the situation.

'Right it's the theatre for you my lad, where we'll get this little lot stitched up in no time.'

As he spoke, two green-gowned theatre orderlies entered the ward, pushing a trolley.

'Here we are then,' one of the two stalwart lads said as they gently lifted Toby and deftly lowered him on to the mattress, whilst I steadied his bloody stump.

'The tourniquet is holding well. Good work, Sister Shaw,' called the Medical Officer as he left.

Stripping off the badly stained sheets, I left them soaking in the sluice-room at the far end of the ward, before re-making bed six into an operating pack, in readiness for the patient's return.

All through the afternoon we had been short staffed, with only the two of us on duty, plus a couple of Japanese orderlies who were limited in their medical training. There were at least half a dozen dressings to be done. After each, to avoid cross infection the dressing trolley had to be washed down with disinfectant and the instruments thoroughly cleaned and sterilised by boiling for twenty minutes. Drugs and medicines were stringently checked before being administered and promptly at 1800hrs the lifesaving penicillin injections were given, using the new type of plastic syringes, which again had to be thoroughly cleaned, boiled for twenty minutes and cooled before re-use. Last of all twenty-five temperatures had to be taken and recorded prior to Sister's serving of supper.

Toby, our young amputee, returned safely from theatre soon after 1830hrs and I was detailed to sit with him until he had fully recovered from the anaesthetic. He looked a better colour due to the blood transfusions, which drop by slow drop replaced the loss from his recent haemorrhage.

Poor brave lad who, at only nineteen, had had to survive yet another ghastly ordeal.

As my feet scrunched slowly along the grit of the road, I greedily inhaled the fresh night air. Ahead, I could faintly see the bulky shape of the distant mountain where, on its summit, I noticed the warm red glow of an aircraft warning beacon.

Soon the lights of the Mess twinkled invitingly. Oh for a strong cup of tea, I thought, wondering at the same time what sort of duties Pat, Helen and Georgina had survived, since this first long day of ours had begun.

CHAPTER FOUR

FROM CASUALTIES TO HONEY POTS

IN KOREA, DISCUSSIONS REGARDING REPATRIATION OF PRISONERS OF WAR. UN DELEGATION INFORMS COMMUNISTS THAT ONLY 70,000 OF 132,000 POWS ARE WILLING TO RETURN HOME.

By mid-April 1952, we were far more acclimatised – geographically living in Japan and professionally occupied as junior members of the large nursing team at the British Commonwealth General Hospital. Working and living with several different nationalities was a wonderful experience and I found it fascinating to hear the contrasting accents on the wards and also in the ante-room. Within the first week the Major-Ma'am had been elevated to the post of Deputy Matron. Pat, Helen and Georgina were all on night duty, whilst to my surprise I remained on day duty, and unfortunately, because of the size of the hospital, I had seen little of them.

The situation in Korea continued in something of a stalemate regarding any progress with the peace negotiations and sadly few of us were sufficiently informed enough to understand the whys and wherefores of the ongoing war. However, just being in close proximity to our patients we were made well aware of the continuing conflict, as I discovered when admitting my first three patients from the Cas-Evac convoy. These lads, with a number of other wounded soldiers, had been transported by airlift from Korea to the Australian Air Force Transit Base at Iwakuni, then on from there by ambulance train for the forty miles or so to Kure Station and then driven up to the hospital in a fleet of ambulances.

On arrival, most of them were exhausted and generally coated with a penetrating layer of white dust, often caking their hair into a thick matt. More than once I had to shampoo their hair soon after they had been admitted. Wearied from their journey and ill from their injuries, they would sink gratefully between the crisp white sheets, asking, 'Do you think we will get our mail here from home, Sister?'

To each one of us mail from home was of the utmost importance, and it didn't matter whether it was a glossy advertisement or an unwanted bill, as long as there was something in one's pigeon-hole on a mail day! Dependent on the weather the UK mail was usually flown out three times a week. Parcels, newspapers and packages were sent by sea-mail and took up to six weeks to arrive, whereas an air-letter took only six days. Everyone serving with the British Commonwealth Brigade was issued with free, buff-coloured Forces Letters and could also send ordinary letters via airmail at the concessionary rate of 3d. Our families, providing they marked the envelope 'On Active Service', had the concession of sending airmail by the cheaper rate of 6d.

Another bewildering aspect of acclimatisation was learning to live with two different currencies. Soon after our arrival we were informed that whilst living in Japan we should only be allowed to draw two thirds of our salaries, the remainder being paid directly into our UK bank accounts. When in need of some cash, we went to the Pay Office situated in the hospital compound and filled in a form to draw BAFVs (British Army Forces Vouchers), used for buying goods in the NAAFI, drinks in the Mess and for meals at the Club. Apart from this paper money, one of the coins in use was the distinctive Australian penny with a large kangaroo on the reverse side. In the local shops and elsewhere we used Japanese Yen, with the rate of exchange at 1,018 Yen to £1.

The difference in climate was another new experience with variable fluctuations of temperature, often hot and oppressive by day, dropping to near freezing at night. Rumour had it that summer officially began in mid-May when the change into tropical kit would be published in Orders. One odd phenomenon, which Pat and I had observed in some of our colleagues during our first day in Kure, was a general feeling of weariness.

This too was starting to affect us, partially due to the climate, the heavy nursing and long hours, being on duty from 0730hrs until 2000hrs, with a three-hour off-duty break either from 1000hrs to 1300hrs, 1300hrs to 1730hrs or finishing duty at 1800hrs, plus a Sunday half day and one whole day off per week. Our quarters, although basic but with the additional luxury of a shared house-girl to cope with our personal chores, were really quite comfortable.

The Mess was issued with Australian rations, and my first cooked breakfast was a real surprise when I was presented with a plateful of two huge scraggy lamb chops, topped by a glassy looking fried egg! Unlike in our UK Messes, meals in Kure were quite informal and eaten – usually in something of a rush – in the large dining room. On the whole, the food was reasonably good, mostly imported, with the additional purchase of some local fresh fruit and vegetables.

However, the sheer delight of living in Japan, with its strange sounds, quaint smells and exotic eastern sights, made life very absorbing. From our hillside position we could glimpse the beautiful Inland Sea, which on a clear day appeared a deep sapphire in contrast to the customary pearl grey haze. Practically encircling us, there were the high sparse hills, some partially and some prettily wooded on the lower slopes although these mainly were neatly terraced for cultivating crops and rice. Occasionally, when in the Mess, we heard the curious sounds of high-pitched twanging accompanied by the booming of gongs emerging from the old temple situated below us.

So far, the few Japanese that I had encountered were immensely polite and helpful, particularly our little house-girls who always addressed us as Sister-*san*. On the whole, the men, for some strange reason, seemed to be less trustworthy than the women, most of whom were so attractive looking with beautiful jet black hair – unless of course they had tried to perm it when it looked frizzily disastrous. Not far from the hospital, there was a large junior school. This was full of happy young children, with lovely almond shaped eyes, peach coloured cheeks and shining dark hair. All the children were smartly dressed in a neat navy school uniform, clean white socks and polished shoes.

Since my initial disappointing shopping encounter on the *Hondori*, with perseverance I had discovered that despite their unimpressive appearance, a few of the shops did sell attractive goods and even one or two luxuries. Otherwise, most of them were in the more lucrative business of selling souvenirs such as the popular and particularly gaudy, crimson coloured tea-sets with ferocious orange painted dragons prancing around the teapot, bamboo mugs and trays by the dozen, cheap and cheerful china, shoddy silk scarves and hundreds of tiny coloured glass animals, given in the Japanese tradition after purchase, as 'present-os'. Already, I had collected a clutch of pretty green ducklings with bright red beaks. The best china shop did indeed resemble an Aladdin's cave with an amazing variety of choice, from exquisitely hand-painted tea-sets in either a traditional pink and gold cherry blossom or in the green black and gold bamboo design, with tea cups of delicate egg-shell china, and I arranged for a cherry blossom tea-set to be packaged home to my mother.

Lying parallel with the *Hondori*, although some distance away, was the *Nakadori*, another busy but much narrower street with little market booths and situated in the older part of the town. There was practically no vehicular traffic, just a few hand carts, and a couple of Japanese men cycling along, wearing their black Trilby hats and kimonos, their wooden sandals pedalling away amongst the numerous pedestrians. Several of the little shops there looked quite spooky and one in particular caught my attention. This was fronted by a small grubby window stacked high with glass jars, each filled with slimy black objects. After closer examination, I was convinced that most of these were pickled snakes, with possibly a toad or two! Far more attractive were the pottery stalls set up in the street in market fashion, with colourful plates and bowls, oddly shaped pots and pretty vases. These were exactly right for arranging the masses of spring flowers, always available to buy from the nice Momma-*san* who daily visited both the hospital and the Mess.

Sunday 14 April was brilliantly sunny and the small garrison church – conveniently situated in the hospital grounds – was packed with servicemen for the traditional Easter Day service. St Peter's was a modern building with elm-coloured pews, whitewashed walls and large windows which caught the sunlight, thus adding an ambience of warmth and light over the abundance of beautiful flowers decorating the church. During the familiar responses, I noticed that several of the congregation were affected, just as I was, by an unexpected surge of homesickness, as we remembered families and friends, many thousands of miles away. Regular church services were held for all religious denominations and there was one resident Padre to visit the hospital sick.

Sundays in Kure were usually mail delivery days and looking in my pigeonhole after church, I found a bundle of letters and amongst these a long one from Miles. His news was somewhat upsetting because, after being examined by several eye specialists, he had been told that as a result of the accident he would not recover the partial loss of sight in his left eye. He was still on sick leave and could not commence his course until he had had a medical board. And with the damage to his eye confirmed, I realised this could seriously affect his career as a regular soldier.

Reading hospital orders, I saw that I was due to commence night duty on 21 April for fourteen nights, after which I should be due for five nights' leave. Unfortunately, Betty, an Australian nursing sister from the Royal Australian Army Nursing Corps with whom I had become friendly, was on day duty, so there was no hope then of getting away on leave together.

A few days later when I was on duty one evening in the Mess as Orderly Officer, I had an urgent plumbing problem to cope with as the drain from the 'Ladies' adjacent to the ante-room had a blockage. This was the only available WC there, so I had to raise the duty plumber promptly; easy enough by telephone. The difficulties only started when a pleasant, portly Japanese gentleman arrived whom I discovered to my embarrassment could speak no English! After spending about ten minutes together in a very confined space, with a totally inadequate explanation on my part and inscrutable politeness on his, in sheer desperation I began to mime the situation. He immediately burst into smiles and with much hissing through many teeth, exclaimed, 'Ah so! *Benjo – Benjo!*' and, bowing politely, quickly set about his business.

The Japanese employed by the hospital authorities were on the whole very helpful and obliging, especially my house-girl Shindo-*san*, for whom nothing was too much trouble. Sometimes when I crawled off duty, she would appear as if by magic, relieving my aching feet of their beetle-squashers and insisting on brushing my hair – a wonderful, relaxing and unaccustomed luxury. Something of a problem in Kure was to locate a hairdresser. Already I'd made two mistakes in trying to get my hair trimmed: once in the town by a Japanese girl and secondly by the Australian hospital barber. The first venture would have been alright had I been Oriental by birth and the second, if I hadn't been a Pommy!

On duty the wards were busy as the turnover of patients was fairly rapid. Towards the end of the month our young amputee had sufficiently recovered to join the homeward-bound Medical Air-Evac convoy. We were sorry to see him go but equally delighted to know that he was well on the way to rehabilitation. Likewise, our poorly burns patient was almost ready for repatriation to New Zealand, where he would get the best possible plastic sugary. Others thankfully had recovered, but almost daily new lads would be admitted.

Not only were we expected to work hard but at the same time take an active part in the round of social duties which varied from the somewhat boring and obligatory Mess functions, to the much more enjoyable Scottish country dancing at the Club and an large organised picnic by small boats, to see the famous cherry blossom on a beautiful tiny island in the Inland Sea. This was so pretty with small sandy coves, a few little houses and masses of cherry trees enveloped in such a captivating abundance of pale pink and white flowers, that from a distance there appeared to have been a heavy snowfall.

One of the significant changes to take effect was from 28 April, when the Allied Forces ceased to be the Occupation Forces and we ourselves became part of the British Commonwealth Forces in Japan. For us this meant removing our shoulder badges and sewing on the new square badge with the Crown and British Commonwealth Forces inscription on a blue background.

'Make sure that Private Green in room twelve does actually drink his high protein feeds at 2100hrs and 0630hrs. You see, if you don't watch him, he'll try to dispose of it. Poor lad, he's far from well and I'm worried that if he doesn't soon gain some weight, he won't be fit enough to go home, let alone stand the long trip by sea next month.'

'I will, thanks for warning me but why doesn't he want to go home – most of the lads can't wait to get away. Is it because he has tuberculosis?'

'It could be and he's probably worrying about a girlfriend's or even his family's reaction to the news. Anyway I must be off now, hope you will have a quiet night.' Smiling at me as she picked up her cloak, Day Sister left the ward.

This was my seventh night on duty and already I was halfway through my stint, which so far had been a busy one. For twelve hours each night I was in charge of a Medical Block of three wards which were separated by pretty little gardens. The isolation ward with twenty-eight beds, the smaller psychiatric unit and a medical ward of thirty beds which was full, mainly with patients suffering with infective hepatitis, an illness which unfortunately seemed prevalent in this area of the Far East with the classic symptoms of jaundice, accompanied by loss of appetite, nausea and vomiting. These patients were always quite poorly, although after several days' rest and nursing care they began to perk up and were soon complaining bitterly about the urgent need to stick rigidly to an unappetising fat-free diet and a strict abstinence from alcohol, absolutely essential for their recovery.

On each ward there was at least one RAMC nursing orderly to care for the patients' primary needs, whilst it was my overall responsibility to look after them. The RAMC lads, who were mostly young, some just doing their eighteen months' National Service, were usually caring, helpful and hard working.

Later that night I crept around the dimly lit isolation ward, quietly checking each patient. All were sleeping peacefully, until I got to room twelve, where a crumpled heap of bed clothes made me somewhat suspicious.

'Are you okay, Private Green, or can I make a hot drink for you? I whispered but there was no response; even his breathing was subdued. Persisting, I continued, 'Is there anything I can help you with? I know how rotten things must seem for you right now. You are a regular soldier aren't you, how long have you been a fusilier?' The blankets moved and very slowly there emerged a head of tousled hair above a gaunt young face, an anxious expression in the dark encircled eyes. With some effort, the lad raised himself up onto his untidy pillows, his breathing rather rapid and shallow.

Gently I rearranged his pillows to prop him up comfortably, when after a long pause he blurted out, 'It's my old man, Sister, he's going to kill me if I go home in this condition; he'll never forgive me for getting TB and worse still if I have to be boarded out of the Army.' He coughed noisily, paused to get his breath, then whispered with a sob, 'God I don't know what I can do – He'll just never understand it.'

'But why shouldn't he, surely your Dad must realise, that in no way was it through any fault of yours that you caught TB while serving in Korea. In fact, I think he should be very proud of you.' Quietly pulling up a chair I sat down beside his bed.

'You don't know, Sister, you couldn't. You see my Dad was a sergeant in the Army with over twenty years' service; he just lived for it and never had a day off sick. He has no time for sickness of any kind. And when I left school he was determined that I should become a regular soldier like him, and now I'm going to let him down by being so ill.' He gulped. 'Why did it have to be me to get TB? I haven't even told me Dad that I'm in hospital, let alone with that. And then if I'm boarded out of the Army for medical reasons, oh God!' Sobbing again he started to slip down the bed.

'Look, let me make a quick cup of tea for you and while you are drinking it, I could tell you what happened to a QA friend of mine, who just like you, was in hospital with TB.' Plumping up his pillows again, I quickly settled him and dashed off to the ward pantry. Returning with the tea, he looked a bit brighter and asked, 'Do you mean to say that one of your lot actually got TB?'

'Oh yes she did – this can happen to anyone. Fortunately, the last time I heard of her she had almost recovered and that she would soon be discharged from hospital with a clean bill of health.'

'Can you really be cured, Sister? I thought that once you got TB it was with you for life.'

'Well to be honest you will probably have to be quite careful for some long time. You see it could take several months to a year before your cure is completed but during your convalescence you will become stronger and stronger.

'Please drink this as I made it especially for you and while you do, I will try to explain how everything should work out for you.' Leaning back on his pillows he slowly sipped the hot sweet brew and listened.

'Has anyone here explained to you that to become fit and well again you will need to really co-operate and follow the medical regime closely? This means resting as much as you possibly can and eating all the extra specially nourishing food which is given to you. Then quite soon you will begin to gain the extra weight you need, to be well enough to enjoy the voyage home as a patient in the ship's hospital. And once you arrive in England you will be transferred to either a military hospital near to your home for treatment, or you might go to the special TB Sanatorium at Midhurst in Sussex where my friend was treated.'

'That sounds really hopeful, Sister, but what about my Dad – he's not going to be very pleased.'

'Don't worry any more about him. With your permission I can ask Day Sister to get the Medical Officer to write a letter to your father explaining everything clearly to him, without you yourself having to be involved. All you need to do now, Private Green, is to put all your effort into beating your illness, which I know you can do. Don't forget, too, that next time you see your Dad he's going to be so proud of you and your two new gongs.'

'What's that, Sister? Oh, I know, you mean MacArthur's pyjamas!'

'That's it, the blue and white striped ribbon of the United Nation's medal and better still the British Korean service medal – you wait and see, your Dad will be bursting with pride when you get home.

Yawning and smiling happily for the first time, he said, 'Phew! That's a weight off my mind, 'cos I'll make it work, and I might even get to sleep now.' And sliding down comfortably as I tucked the blanket around him, he sighed sleepily, 'Thanks, Sister, you're great.'

Flagging wearily towards the end of my fourteen nights, as well as suffering the agony of a vast number of huge mosquito bites, it was a relief to escape for a couple of hours one morning with Cynthia, a QA friend who was also on night duty.

After walking some distance from the town we found our way to the small and deserted Karuga beach. This was a pretty place where we lazed for a while in the warm sunshine, idly watching an army of bright red land crabs invade our space, as they marched in a dignified but sideways fashion across the sandy strip of beach. Close in shore and shimmering in the shallow water, we saw large numbers of jelly fish flattened on the shingle, lying in wait to sting any unobservant wader.

'Let's walk back through the hills,' suggested Cynthia.

'Okay by me, just as long as we don't meet any snakes!'

Gathering up our few belongings, we clambered over the steep sand dunes to the top of the rise. There to our amazement, growing in wild profusion, we came across banks of beautiful purple and white azaleas.

As we rounded the corner of the track to join the road up to the Mess, suddenly an ancient wooden handcart lurched straight into our path. The rickety contraption being pushed along by a venerable but shabbily dressed Oriental gentleman, holding a long, large and slimy wooden ladle in his right hand.

'My God… What a pong and look at those disgusting buckets!'

Glancing over at the cart, I saw six or seven bulky wooden pails tightly lidded, bar one from which the stench was emanating.

'Gosh see that horrid stuff slopping about in there, it looks just like human faeces!' continued Cynthia, as pressing our hankies to our noses whilst the old cart wobbled past and exchanging a polite '*Konichiwa*', or 'Good Day', in Japanese.

'I've got it, Jilly, he must be the Honey Pot Man, you know, the one that empties all the little cesspits and privies for the locals. Actually, I remember now overhearing someone in the Mess laughing about the type of medieval sewage system, in certain parts of Japan.'

'That's okay, Cynthia, but the big question is exactly where does he dispose of it?'

'Ah! Just give three guesses, though I'll give you a clue. Don't eat the local vegetables unless they have been scrubbed and always avoid any lettuce!'

'Hi! Are you coming over to the Mess now for breakfast or dinner or whatever our meal is meant to be at this ungodly hour? Because afterwards we could walk over to the hospital together,' Cynthia enquired as she poked her head around my door, adding kindly, 'Heavens you look a bit worried – are you okay, or couldn't you sleep today?'

'Yes thanks, I'm almost alright, apart from these wretched mossie bites, which I'm praying will clear up before I go on leave in a couple days, as I feel such a mess.'

'Poor you, though I'm sure that by Sunday they will have subsided. But what do you mean by "almost"?'

'Oh Lord, I'm pretty sure that I've blotted my copy book this morning, by accidentally disobeying orders. Have I time to tell you about it now?'

Flopping onto the only chair, and shaking her dark curls in disbelief, Cynthia chuckled, 'I can't believe this – not you, Jilly – but we've a good ten minutes, so fire away.'

'Well, this morning I discovered that I had run out of writing paper, so I nipped down to Kure to get some but when I got to the outskirts of the town, I thought that things seemed strangely quiet, because although it was after ten o'clock there were few people about. Imagine my surprise as I turned into the *Hondori* to see masses of people there forming into what appeared to be a large parade, with a smaller crowd of spectators lining the pavement.

'Initially I was dumb enough to try to walk on to the *Nakadori*, stupidly not realising what was happening. But as the crowd continued to gather, it began to block my way and it suddenly dawned on me that there was no traffic, no sign of the familiar Military Police jeeps, or even any of the military vehicles which are usually around. The crowd was increasing rapidly and everywhere was jam packed with people. Observing them more closely, I noticed that many of the Japanese men were waving little red flags and only then did I realise that they must be Communists and remembered to my horror, that the date was 1 May!

'Immediately the atmosphere became quite eerie, with the realisation that I was the only European in the street, conspicuous in my khaki uniform and by which time not only was I hemmed in, but also getting some sly looks from the crowd. Fortunately for me, within a minute or so, the marchers began to shuffle off, chanting in a desultory fashion and waving their dreary little flags. My first thought was to disappear post-haste, which I did by shoving my way through the crowds, managing to get back to the Mess unscathed.

'Then recovering there over a much-needed cup of coffee, I wandered over to the notice board to read Orders, where I saw to my dismay that due to the May Day celebrations Kure was Out of Bounds to all Commonwealth Forces for twenty-four hours starting from midnight. Help! What can I do? Because as sure as God made little apples, the Major-Ma'am will have had her spies out and you know the penalty for not reading Orders.'

'Oh Jilly! Even I knew that we weren't allowed out today, but never mind, do you think anybody saw you go?'

'Not to my knowledge, but I'll know soon enough when we go over to the Mess.'

Despite my pessimistic outlook, my Good Fairy must have been watching over me because as we walked into the ante-room I practically collided with the Major-Ma'am, who was standing beside the letter racks. Swallowing hard to greet her, she interrupted with, 'Oh there you are, Hall, the sea mail has just arrived and there is a parcel for you in the office.' And to my immense relief she actually smiled at us both, before leaving the room.

Sunday 4 May ultimately materialised, and after saying farewell to my patients, most of whom I felt quite sad to leave and in particular Private Green who at last was beginning to make progress, I was free to go on leave to Kobe for the next five days. This had been arranged through the kindness of an ex-QA called Emma, who had served in the QAIMNS during the Second World War, subsequently marrying an international banker and now lived in Kobe. Apparently Emma had persuaded her friends in the British community – for their war effort – to provide accommodation for tired QAs, granted a few days leave, by generously opening their homes to them.

Five hours later, the three of us, who had just finished night duty and destined to spend our nights off as Emma's guests in Kobe, were rattling along on the Forces Leave train, with several hours travelling yet ahead of us.

From my dusty window seat, I glanced at my companions, neither of whom I knew too well. Major Ann Brown had until that morning been Night Superintendent in charge of the hospital, a heavy responsibility but one that had not hassled her, so that she always had time for a kindly word when doing her rounds. Jane Greenhead, another young lieutenant, was a quiet dark haired girl with a good sense of humour. The one thing we all had in common whilst bumping along was the sheer fatigue which always superseded night duty, and I was also plagued by the intense irritation from the mosquito bites on my arms and legs.

The old steam train rumbled on at a snail's pace, stopping occasionally at a station to pick up more men and kit-bags. It was exceedingly long, with a shabby interior and windows engrained with many miles of dirt.

'How much longer do you think we shall be stuck in here, Ma'am?' Jane enquired sleepily.

Glancing at her wristwatch, Major Brown smiled, 'Just over a couple of hours I imagine, as we left Kure at 1345hrs and it usually takes about seven hours to get to Kobe. Incidentally, whilst we are on leave, can you both drop the Ma'am bit – it's much too formal. It's Jane and Jilly, isn't it? And I'm Ann,' she added kindly, then asking, 'Heavens! Can either of you remember what time we were allocated our evening meal, as it must be quite soon?'

Pulling out a crumpled ticket from the top pocket of my battledress I said, 'It's okay, mine is stamped for dinner at 1830hrs, that's if we can ever find the dining car.'

It was quite a feat to stagger along the swaying corridors, crowded with American GIs and British servicemen, their eyes lighting up as we lurched our way through, frequently followed by an appreciative wolf whistles. Finally we made it to the dining car where we were seated at a reasonably clean table by the attendant, who handed Jane a somewhat dog-eared card, saying 'Menu, Ma'am.'

Glancing quickly at it as she handed it over to Ann, she exclaimed, 'Gosh, I'm starving and that looks good with several choices on it.'

'This is great and I think I'll go bust and have all three courses as it's such a long time since we've eaten,' said Ann. I added, 'Me too.'

After sometime the Japanese waiter returned but as we began to order, he politely interrupted us asking, 'Please to show your meal tickets.' After scrutinising them, he said to our dismay, 'Ah so sorry, you have British Commonwealth meal tickets – one course only! So sorry, what you like please?'

'This can't be true,' I moaned. 'Just take a peep at those GIs at the table over there, I've been watching them and so far they've bulldozed their way through at least two courses and are just about to start on their third!'

Major Ann interjected quietly, 'To be perfectly fair, I have just noticed that our tickets are a different colour to those of the Americans and I'm afraid this means that we shall have to make do with only the main course, girls.' This was our first introduction to some of the inequalities which existed then amongst the Forces of the United Nations.

Just after 2100hrs the train rumbled slowly to a halt at Kobe Station. Thankfully we pulled our suitcases down from the luggage rack, tried to smooth the wrinkles from our khaki skirts and feeling rather like tired zombies, staggered out on to the platform.

'Thank God I'm not going on to Tokyo, as I couldn't stand another hour – let alone another eleven,' remarked Jane, just as a well-dressed, attractive lady stepped forward to greet us.

Smiling warmly, she introduced herself as Emma, and said 'You must be the little party of QAs we are expecting. Welcome to Kobe and may I say on behalf of everyone, we are so pleased that you could come.' Shaking hands, we introduced ourselves to Emma, a petite brunette, probably in her late thirties. She continued, 'But before we all climb into the taxi, I must explain, that unfortunately I am unable to put you up myself as I had originally promised – however, please don't despair because some good friends of mine are absolutely delighted to stand in and best of all they also live quite close to me. Oh, and something else I should just mention, is that the Hunts are actually away until tomorrow but their servants will make sure that you are comfortable and of course I'll be round in the morning to arrange our day.'

An ancient taxi took us to our destination, which was a large Western-style private house, situated in the quiet and elegant suburbs of the city. After disgorging ourselves and saying an appreciative good-night to Emma, we made our way into the hall of the house, where the servants greeted us kindly, picked up our small suitcases and showed us to our rooms.

Ann was given a pleasant single room, whilst Jane and I were shown into a palatial double bedroom. The little house-girl smiled at us again, this time pointing to the push button bell just above the twin beds and said to our delight, 'Please to ring when you like breakfast and I will bring.' Then, showing us where to locate the bathroom, she continued, 'This has only Japanese bathtub but very good when you are very tired. You like bath now please? I run for you. Yes?'

'Oh yes please,' thinking it might relieve the wretched irritation as, by that time, I was beginning to feel quite groggy. Minutes later, there was a tap on our door, 'Bath ready now for you Missie.'

'You go first, Jilly, because you look absolutely whacked, while I unpack,'

The bathroom, which by normal standards was large, had to my astonishment a huge square wooden bath tub, raised on a small platform in the centre of the room, from which impressive spirals of steam rose. This being my introduction to the customs of Japanese bathing, through my abysmal ignorance, I ignored the small basin of water beside the hot tub and plunged straight into it, flopping exhaustedly into the blazing water, too tired to care whether I scalded to death or just suffered acute burns. The first five minutes were the worst, after which I began to feel an immense sense of relief as, due to the intense heat, the irritation miraculously stopped.

After sleeping blissfully for twelve hours and breakfasting luxuriously in bed, we were up, dressed and feeling much brighter by the time Emma arrived. We spent the rest of the morning with her before driving by taxi to Osaka – a huge city about two thirds the size of London and not a great distance from Kobe.

There Emma took us to visit a glass factory, where it was fascinating to watch beautiful bamboo designs incised on to wine and brandy glasses. Already that morning, I had spent some time admiring our hostess's lovely collection of similarly patterned glassware and at the factory was thrilled to make a modest purchase of half a dozen sherry glasses, for just 5s!

Then it was on to see Osaka Castle, an impressive, moated edifice built in the pagoda style. Emma explained that although the castle was destroyed by fire a long time ago, it had been rebuilt during this century. An unexpected bonus for us was the Trade Fair exhibition in the castle, with a remarkable number of interesting Japanese goods on display. This was crowded with people. Although several were in Western garb, they were mainly wearing traditional dress, whilst some businessmen dressed in black kimonos, carrying leather briefcases, also wore the ubiquitous high platformed wooden sandals. These, Emma explained, were called *Geta* in Japanese and were very practical to wear in the rainy season.

Afternoon tea was last on the day's agenda and this we had in a hotel, exquisitely served and frightfully expensive. Something else I had discovered since living in Japan was that food – especially Western food – was always costly but at least it was not rationed as it was in England. Indeed it was still an unexpected joy to buy unlimited amounts of biscuits or chocolate in the NAAFI.

'Shall we go to Kyoto tomorrow?' asked Emma, as we sipped the refreshing tea.

'Is it far and how do we get there?' enquired Jane.

'No, from Kobe it's only just over an hour's ride on the electric railway. It is also such an old and interesting city, having once been the capital of Japan. So we really should try to see as much of it as we can. I think if you are agreeable, we ought to make an early start, and leave about 9 a.m., is that okay?'

At dinner that evening we met our generous hosts, an exceedingly kind couple, both of whom were intensely aware of the ongoing hostilities in Korea. At the same time, they were almost overwhelming in their efforts to make us feel at home in their beautiful house.

The following morning the smart little suburban train deposited us in Kyoto, where in the environs of this ancient city, we spent a long and absorbing day with Emma, our perfect guide.

Two silk factories were our first ports of call and after all the dreary business of rationing and utility clothes, it was enchanting to see real silk again, in such vast quantities and with such a rainbow of colours.

Working the heavy looms were a number of tiny Japanese women, some of whom skilfully wove the intricate patterns forming the rich brocades. As we passed by, they peered shyly at us, giggling together at the sight of four fair-skinned foreigners walking in their midst. During our tour of the second factory, we were intrigued by the story related to us by one of the Japanese guides, how long ago certain of the highly accomplished workers were instructed to grow their fingernails to a specific length, in order to weave the complex and delicate designs commanded by the Royal Household.

Next on our itinerary was the old Imperial Palace, situated in an enormous park and surrounded by the most heavenly gardens. This building was long, low and constructed in a traditionally oriental style. Touring through some rooms of the palace we followed a lengthy crocodile of navy blue uniformed schoolgirls, whose exemplary behaviour much impressed us. Leaving behind the somewhat oppressive splendour of a bygone age, we rested for a while in the royal gardens, landscaped to perfection. There, with some amusement, we observed the clever camouflaging of the concrete branch-like fencing surrounding the lake, coloured in an earthy brown to blend perfectly with the gnarled trunks of the many ancient trees encircling the water.

Feeling hot and dusty in our khaki and by then quite ravenous, Emma suggested that it must be lunchtime, and skilfully guided us to a well-known Japanese restaurant in the city. There we were courteously welcomed by the manager who, bowing low, showed us into a comfortable lounge where we sank gratefully into deep armchairs and perused the large menu cards, written in Japanese and translated for us by Emma. Within minutes of our arrival, to our surprise we were served with small cups of hot green tea. Jane and I both found the bitter, thick pea green coloured liquid distasteful, although both Emma and Ann assured us it really was an acquired taste.

Ten minutes after ordering, the manager reappeared and personally escorted us to a pleasant window table in the spacious Western-style dining-room. Shortly after this, our lobster arrived on an enormous silver salver carried by two little waitresses who placed it reverentially in the centre of the table, bowing gracefully as they left. Neither Ann, Jane nor I were prepared for such extravagance as we gazed in utter disbelief at the magnificent arrangement lying in front of us. Towering over the lobster, intricately sculptured in ice, stood a colossal eagle with folded wings and nestling on a bed of crushed ice between its talons, lay our large pink crustacean, superbly decorated with heads of pretty pink and blue cornflowers and a few sprigs of fresh parsley. Just for a moment, we were utterly speechless.

During the delicious meal, I noticed various Japanese families coming into the restaurant and was amused to watch the grand entrance of one particular couple, at least that of the husband. Important looking and expensively dressed, he strode imperiously ahead of his downcast little wife, attired in an unusually drab kimono and shuffling several paces behind him. And this, I thought, is 1952…

Much refreshed, we set off again to visit some antique shops full of exquisite china, embroidered silks, oriental paintings and old pottery, sadly well beyond our reach. From there we visited the *Heian* Shrine, or Red Temple, with its huge and impressive gateway at the entrance. Emma referred to it in Japanese as a *torii*, explaining that it was the symbolic gateway of a Shinto shrine and represented the division between the everyday world and the divine world. Surrounding the shrine were some lovely gardens including several large ponds. One of these was full of the most enormous carp, their brilliant colours flashing in the sunlight as they swam lazily past.

We crammed in a quick visit to a lacquer factory – yet another treasure house of elegantly lacquered objets d'art – gold rimmed black coffee sets, imaginative red powder bowls with silver tasselled lids, tall slender wine glasses with golden interiors and so much more!

'Let's take a taxi now, as your poor feet must be killing you,' said Emma, as she expertly waved down a passing cab. A mile or so later we disembarked at the top of a hill onto a twisting narrow lane, crowded with small shops, their windows stacked with brightly coloured pottery. From there the view over the old city was incredible with its multitude of ochre tiles merging down the hillside, forming into a glinting, golden mass.

'This is called Tea-pot Lane. Isn't it fascinating – shall we have a quick look?' Emma suggested. Glancing at the other two, I realised that like me they too, were feeling the heat of the late afternoon.

'Tea, do you think we could possibly find a cup of tea somewhere, soon, please Emma?' I asked, and seeing our tired expressions she replied with concern, 'Of course – I know just the place and it's only around the next corner.'

We climbed up the steep wooden stairs to the top floor of the tea-house only to find that it was packed with Japanese. But a kind waitress came to our rescue, saying 'Ah so, *dozo*, you come,' and found us an unoccupied table.

'Please takee.' Looking up I saw another waitress holding a steaming tray in front of me, full of strange, white sausage-shaped objects. Hurriedly looking at Emma, she nodded asking, 'Haven't you come across hot towels before?'

'No, what do I do?' Mystified, I gingerly took hold of the extremely hot flannel roll.

'Just unwrap it, hold it to your face, and then wipe your hands with it, it really is refreshing, try it!' And it was, as the intense heat from the small towel drew the dusty weariness from my pores, thoroughly cleansing my face, hands and even my neck, from the grubby discomfort of my khaki collar.

Wednesday was our final day of leave and so Emma kindly drove us out of Kobe into the beautiful wooded hills surrounding the city. It was a perfect drive past lush green fields and on through refreshing avenues of tall pines where the air was crisp and cool and in complete contrast to the dusty, parched and sometimes depressing atmosphere of Kure.

That evening Emma took us to a local cinema to see the English film *The Tales of Hoffman* (with Japanese sub-titles) which we all thoroughly enjoyed, before taking us to her home to meet her husband over dinner. Trying to thank them adequately for giving us such a wonderful holiday was really difficult, as Emma brushed away our heartfelt thanks with the simple explanation that, apart from being delighted to have met us, she was still proud of her past connection and continued association with the QAs, and very much hoped that we should all visit her again whilst we were in Japan.

CHAPTER FIVE

SUMMER HEAT AND ISLAND MAGIC

IN KOREA, FIGHTING CONTINUED, AS DID THE STALEMATE ON BOTH
SIDES REGARDING THE PRISONER OF WAR ISSUE. 12 MAY, GENERAL
MARK CLARK SUCCEEDED GENERAL MATHEW RIDGWAY, AS UN
SUPREME COMMANDER.

Summer was officially decreed in Orders on 15 May, when we thankfully stowed
away our battledress and changed into khaki drill. On ward duty we wore grey
dresses with just the epaulettes from our tippets. Having also been warned that
the wet season would soon start, I took the precaution of investing in a large pink
waxed paper and bamboo Japanese umbrella for cover, whilst dashing to and from
the hospital.

Life continued apace and on duty I was one of a team working on the eighty-
bedded and hectically busy casualty ward. Our patients were a grand bunch
of mixed nationalities, amongst whom there were a Filipino, two Chinese,
Australians, Kiwis, Canadians, one French Canadian and a large number of British
lads. Many had suffered dreadful gunshot wounds, with painful dressings, and
others had badly fractured limbs encased in heavy plasters. However, the boys
were all so cheerful that it was a joy to look after them. Although, I felt sorry for
one poor lad tucked away in a corner bed, who apart from his injuries was also
suffering from shell shock when at times he seemed to be very withdrawn and
quite unable to respond to the general banter. One of the cheekier patients had
nicknamed me Smiler; another wanted to tattoo my likeness on his chest!

Socially my feet had not touched the ground since returning from Kobe, aptly confirmed by Cynthia, who remarked when we finally met in the ante-room, 'Do you realise, Jilly, that for over a week now, the only evening you have been in, was when you were Orderly Officer and that was two nights ago! What have you been up to?'

'Oh this and that! I've had so many invitations to go out that I'm dying to tell you about it, as I really could do with your advice.' Leaning forward, I whispered, 'Life's a bit awkward at the moment, as I seem to have acquired no less than four boyfriends – so what on earth can I do?'

'Is any one of them particularly special?'

'No, they are all pleasant boys and I am just amazed at my sudden popularity, although realistic enough to know that it's most probably due to the shortage of females here.'

'Yes, there is that, possibly coupled with the uncertainty of life these lads must experience. You know what I mean, Jilly, a sort of "here today and gone tomorrow" feeling. But to change the subject, what do you think about the set-up here? Because having been here longer than you have, I myself think that it's not a particularly happy one.'

'Personally, I think the reason for this is that we are living in an artificial situation, created by being on active service and affecting each one of us differently. I mean, have you noticed how much more some people seem to drink here than they would at home? Is this because the booze is so much cheaper? Or because of this wretched war?' Cynthia nodded appreciatively.

'Sometimes when I'm tackling yet another ghastly gunshot wound – and you know what those particular dressings can be like – I feel quite upset, so whatever can it be like for the poor lad lying there, with his stinking, suppurating wound? I try to conceal my feelings but that's not always so easy. So maybe this is the reason why a few of the older QAs have several whiskies when they are off duty in the evenings, remembering too that most of them would have served through the last war.'

'And this one is bad enough,' added Cynthia. 'But to change the subject again – where were you last night?'

'Guess – no – okay, I was on board HMS *Unicorn*.'

'How?'

'With Betty, she has a friend who is one of the ship's officers and they invited me to make up a foursome.'

'Wow! That must have been great.' Noting a slight tinge of envy, I hastily added, 'It was, but in any case you were out with James and he is your extra special.'

'But how did you get to the ship? Isn't she anchored well out in the harbour because of all the explosives on board?'

'Ah! We skimmed over in the ship's launch. It was a lovely, fine evening and we had a super dinner in the ward room. Afterwards, we were escorted down to a gigantic hanger which doubles as the ship's cinema, where we sat with the rest of the ship's company and watched an old Bing Crosby film. Did you know that *Unicorn* is nicknamed "the grey ghost of the China seas" because, despite being such a colossal aircraft carrier, she manages to slip in and out of port, quickly and quietly.'

Feeling weary after finishing duty later than usual one night, I decided to go straight back to my room, only to hear as I opened the door an ominous scuffling sound inside. Switching on the light disturbed the scuffling, when to my horror I saw that on my bedside mat there was an enormous black rat, staring straight at me with beady little eyes, baring its jagged teeth.

'Help!' I yelled, and grabbed the nearest weapon – which happened to be my new pink umbrella! Realising that I was about to have a swipe at it, the offensive rodent shot off at great speed and led me a merry dance. After an exhausting chase, I eventually shoved it through the door into a passage way leading into the garden.

That was nasty, I thought, as I walked over to the ante-room to report the incident because although I had heard stories about the rat population in the hospital compound I had not so far believed them!

Day by day the weather became increasingly hotter and, as predicted, the much heralded wet season began in the middle of June. This made life uncomfortable, as there was little coolness with the rain which was always heavy and with the level of humidity intensifying, we all felt constantly damp and sticky; even our uniform brass buttons were dull with verdigris.

Monotonously, for five days out of every seven the rains came down so that we expected to get soaked at sometime or other. Frequently the hills were obliterated, either by sheeting rain or a blanket of black clouds. Everything was affected by the weather, especially the roads with vast new potholes appearing daily. This made walking down to Kure (practically our only means of transport) something of a problem, trying to avoid the deep puddles. Also, it had been established by the Duke of Wellington long ago that umbrellas would not be carried when in uniform!

However, in spite of the overall dampness, the overriding humidity and general lethargy which affected us, life still continued at a gallop. Once again I was on the officers' ward, only this time a little higher up the echelon. We were busy with small convoys of patients arriving at frequent intervals, mostly young lads suffering from a variety of gunshot wounds, usually treated first at a Field Dressing Station before transferring to the BCGH Kure, dusty and exhausted.

Recently my parents had sent me a large packet of *Picture Post* magazines which I took over to the ward, where they were rapidly devoured. I wrote to my mother and asked if, as a sort of war effort, she could send me a supply of old newspapers, or any other reading material, that I could pass on to the patients. Apart from the *Japan News* which was a typewritten roneoed news sheet of just one or two pages, produced at the base camp for the British Commonwealth Forces, there was a great dearth of UK papers and magazines, although we did occasionally get hold of some from Australia. Luckily, we could also listen to the local forces radio programme, broadcast from somewhere near Kure.

Despite the rain, the semi-social whirl continued with a lavish party given by the Pay Corps to celebrate Empire Day, with such sumptuous food that it could only be described as a banquet, whilst I remembered guiltily the meagre food rationing at home.

At the end of the month our Mess was to hold an important event. This was the Jubilee Dance to celebrate the fiftieth anniversary of the foundation of the QAs. This would be a combined British and Australian venture, with an expected 300 guests. For this occasion I desperately needed a new dress, but without any suitable shops in Kure my only hope was to find a local dressmaker to make up my Colombo sari. Jess Milton, a QA captain, an attractive brunette with a keen sense of humour who had by then had been stationed in Kure for some time, kindly rescued me, patiently explaining the whereabouts of her own reliable dressmaker.

Miraculously, the next afternoon was fine and clutching my sari plus a crumpled sketch of an off the shoulder evening dress, torn from an old *Vogue* magazine, I set off to find the location of Jess's dressmaker. This was not easy and after getting lost in the back streets of Kure several times, I eventually found my way through a warren of narrow passageways to a tiny house. Timidly, I knocked on the door, which was opened by a small Japanese lady dressed in a pretty kimono. She bowed politely as I tried to explain that Milton-*san* had sent me to her for making special dress please.

'Ah so, *dozo*, please…' and invited me in. The doorway was extremely low and I almost had to bend double to get through it to the small room beyond, where several young girls were sewing industriously. As I entered the confined space, they looked up and stared. Hastily, I removed my khaki cap to give an impression of femininity; however, the staring continued and was now accompanied by a soft giggling. Glancing at them again, in a flash I realised that it was my feet which had caught their attention which, shod in size six big black beetle-squashers, must have appeared Amazonian to these dainty little women.

'Please… Shoos … take off,' the lady in charge blurted out. Mortified, and pink with embarrassment, I removed the offending articles, apologising profusely.

'Please to sit down,' when my next gaff was to look for a nonexistent chair. Dawning slowly that it was meant to be the floor, I slid down as gracefully as my tight uniform skirt would allow, tucking my knees beneath it.

The actual negotiations with regards to the style and size of my dress were relatively simple and thirty minutes later, after much bowing, I left with the promise that the gown would be ready in two weeks.

'Have you got a minute, Jilly? You see I've been trying to get hold of you for the last few days,' said Rachel, one of the two British Red Cross ladies attached to the hospital, as she caught up with me on the way over to the Mess.

'Of course, I'm off duty now but what can I do for you?'

'Well that's just it … do you think that you, perhaps with a friend, could possibly take on the job of doing the flowers for the garrison church?'

She continued hastily, 'You see it would only involve you once every three weeks and we know that you do go to St Peter's whenever you can.'

'Crumbs! I'm not at all sure that flower arranging is my métier, as I've never really had the opportunity to try it,' I said, hopefully stalling for time.

'But Jilly, you must have arranged the flowers on the wards hundreds of times, so of course you'll be good at it – in any case it's only a little church and not a big cathedral!'

'Okay, I'll do it, but when do you want me to start? Only I'll have to persuade Betty to help too. What exactly should I have to do?'

In actual fact the duties were simple enough, because there was always an abundance of beautiful flowers available from the visiting Momma-*san*; intuitively I knew that I should love to take on this little task.

There must have been a big push in Korea, as latterly we were rushed off our feet and had recently admitted five stretcher cases from the Air-Evac convoy. All were weary and poorly lads, their khaki battledress coated with the familiar white dust. That evening I was shocked to discover that one of them was actually a friend of mine from the *Empire Trooper*, David from the Penny Regiment. Thankfully his leg injury, though bad enough, was not too severe and he soon settled into the ward routine. For me, however, it was the first time that I had nursed a friend whilst on duty and this I found was somewhat disconcerting.

Another victim of this relentless war was a very sick lad suffering from badly suppurating multiple burns, and sadly these were not healing well. One hot and humid morning when I was dressing his extensive wounds, suddenly the sickly sweet smell of pus enveloped me and before passing out – just for a moment – I had to make a quick dash for it. Poor, poorly lad and I felt dreadfully embarrassed on returning to complete my task.

The majority of gunshot wounds (GSW) which we nursed (and these could affect any area of the body), especially flesh wounds, usually healed well. Unfortunately, however, there were always just a few, particularly if badly infected or associated with a compound fracture during battle, which responded painfully slowly to the surgical treatment of daily cleansing, changing of dressings and four hourly intramuscular injections of penicillin. On other rare occasions a soldier would be admitted to a surgical ward with a self-inflicted GSW – usually having shot himself through the foot.

The war to us seemed to be thoroughly nasty, especially when for most of the time we felt cut off and miles away from home with poor communications, creating the impression that few people there had any idea of the horrors of the war in Korea. It was depressing too to realise that probably, apart from the wives and families of the troops involved in this forgotten war, few others cared much about it; when writing to my parents I frequently mentioned this.

Possibly due to a shortage of sisters, I was promoted to second-in-command of the officers' ward. The extra responsibilities were more than rewarding and I felt that perhaps at last I was doing something worthwhile. The main goal for most of us was to get over to Korea but this remained frustratingly blocked by those at the top.

Once a week, instead of Matron's daily round during the morning, each ward suffered an awe inspiring cavalcade of matrons, when all must be exactingly tidy – patients, wards and staff. The matrons entered the ward in order of seniority, with our British Lt-Col Widger in the lead, followed by her Australian counterpart and catching up in the rear of the procession, the pretty senior Canadian nurse. It was the duty of the QA sister in charge (properly dressed with her sleeves rolled down neatly into her scarlet cuffs) to escort these good ladies around the ward, starting at the first bed and introducing each patient by their rank, name, diagnosis, general condition and concluding with a brief prognosis. The whole visit could be lengthy and was one which required swift preparation when the buzz swept around the corridors: 'Watch it – they're on the way!'

An unexpected and welcome diversion from the downside of casualties and war, presented itself in an invitation to Betty and me to join the Green Room Club. This was run by the Dramatic Society which held its meetings in Kure House, the Forces Recreational Club, situated on the *Hondori* in one of the few substantial buildings in Kure. On the ground floor there was a well-stocked shop selling mainly good quality Japanese goods, whereas the upper floor had a large hall for functions. Betty and I were asked if we would take part in the next production, *The Tinsel Duchess*, a one-act play by Philip Johnson. Neither of us was too confident about our acting ability but again, because of the shortage of women, we were as always in great demand.

High summer came with a vengeance; the temperature rose into the eighties, the humidity increased to 100 per cent and the wet season continued for several more weeks. The constant whirring of fans both on and off duty yielded some relief, but by the end of June, the date for the Jubilee dance, most of us were too bushed to enjoy it.

Somewhat cooling and something of an advantage for us, there was in the hospital grounds a small swimming pool, no larger than a static water tank – in fact, it was exactly that. The disadvantage was that it was positioned in full view of the officer's ward, where it was not only one's swimming prowess that was at stake! It was, therefore, seldom used.

In spite of the heat, whenever we had time on a dry day, Betty or Cynthia and I would walk up into the hills behind the Mess. This was a stiffish climb but worth it for the illusion of freedom and spectacular views across the hazy water to the little islands dotted around the Inland Sea. Japan, intriguingly different as it was from our own Western culture, had me spellbound, and these lovely hills were full of wild flowers, and huge great blue and variously coloured butterflies, some almost the size of tiny birds.

Living only a short distance from Hiroshima, some people at the BCGH were of the opinion that the Atom Bomb had been meant for Kure which then was a secret Japanese naval base and where they had built two of the largest battleships in the world. These were both sunk and were then still lying on the harbour bottom. Around the hillsides there were also a number of fortifications to be seen.

The war machine ground on and we were continuously busy with a higher ratio of patients suffering from gunshot wounds than normal on the officers' ward, where we even admitted two South Koreans. Pleasant as they were, the lack of language did present some difficulties.

There were many dressings to be done, stitches to remove, plasters to support and, as always, one or two amputees to watch over. Already, in the relatively short period I had been there, I had nursed three young men each of whom had lost a leg, and at times found the futility of it all more than depressing.

It was some relief to change wards when my turn for night duty came round again in mid-July. This time I was in charge of two single-storied medical wards and, although I had far more patients to look after, there was not the sense of urgency associated with the numerous casualties on day duty. And after seven nights on duty, when the majority of my patients slept soundly, I myself began to feel less fraught. Even Cynthia remarked that I had lost my apparent wanness, of which I had not been aware. She was also on night duty, and in charge of the busy casualty ward situated on the top floor of the tallest building in the hospital.

However, things were not always so tranquil because two nights later, at about 1 a.m., Cynthia and I had something of a fright. Having just completed my ward rounds checking that my patients were sleeping comfortably, I settled down at my desk to read. Suddenly I experienced a strange sensation beneath my feet when my chair started to rock, the windows rattled noisily and finally, for a moment or two, the ward shook. My immediate thought was 'Earthquake… Help!' by which time, fortunately, the tremors were subsiding and stopped soon after.

Nevertheless, it had been a peculiar experience, feeling as if a giant hand had gently shaken the whole building. Quickly I did a round of my wards to check that all was well but the boys were snoring peacefully, none of them disturbed by the recent shakes. The telephone rang, 'Are you okay, Jilly?' Cynthia enquired breathlessly. 'I was just going to ring you. I'm fine thanks but what about you, are you alright?'

'It was quite a nasty feeling being right up here, because for a few moments the entire building actually seemed to sway, so that it's a jolly good thing that it was built on rollers, although I really didn't believe this, until now'.

'Do you think it was a strong earth tremor?'

'I expect so, though it's the first I've ever experienced. I'll have to dash – see you at breakfast, Jilly. Take care.'

No one else in the hospital knew more than we did that morning, but when we were up again late that afternoon, news had emerged throughout the day of an earthquake in Osaka which sadly killed seven people, also causing numerous injuries and considerable damage.

Two nights later there was another scare, as after giving me the day report, Sister casually remarked, 'Oh just be careful, Hall, when you are cutting across to Ward Five tonight, because I must warn you that somewhere in the bushes between the wards, there is a snake on the loose, and it could be a poisonous one!'

'That's all I need,' I thought, as I checked my torchlight to find to my dismay the battery was waning, with no hope of a replacement until the NAAFI opened next morning. By the time I was ready to go over, the wretched thing flickered once and passed out. So my only defence that night was the microscopic light from an auriscope which I borrowed from the ward. Each time I ventured out into the darkness and through the undergrowth, I trod very warily, hoping that I would not have the misfortune to stumble on the unsuspecting reptile. Thankfully we never did meet but by the time I had finished my spell on night duty, rumour had it grown out of all proportion, to 14ft with the additional configuration of purple and gold stripes!

By this time the weather during the day was extremely hot, making sleeping difficult, but luckily I was allocated an electric fan for my room, which I left running all day. Persistently, for days on end, one's face and arms, and every crevice of one's body, glistened with rivulets of sweat and as a precaution against heat exhaustion, we were instructed to take salt tablets regularly at each meal. Often, when on my way over to the wards in the middle of the night, I would pause for a moment or two, longing for a breath of fresh air but even in those early morning hours the humidity was so high that the atmosphere was disappointingly stale and heavy.

Regardless of these discomforts, being on night duty in Japan had unexpected privileges, such as perceiving a midnight sky bursting with luminous stars, the brilliance of an early morning sunrise and, later, the diffused radiance of a spectacular sunset silhouetting darkly wooded hills. In addition, just outside Ward Four there was an intriguing old gum tree which I soon discovered literally started to hum at about 0430hrs every morning. Investigating this noisy twanging, I found that the tree was teeming with flying beetles, obviously using it for a dawn conference. Beetles appeared almost everywhere, particularly at night, in all shapes sizes and varieties, from those that just walked, to the hugely heavy flying stag beetles.

Just before completing my two weeks, I received a packet of UK newspapers from my mother, and I gave one of my patients the local Hastings paper, knowing that he was from Sussex. Unfortunately, I did not realise what a mistake that was, until I did my late round when I found him unable to sleep after having a bad bout of homesickness. Poor lad, he was miserable but hopefully talking about it may have relieved the situation, though I doubted this, as he told me that he still had another two years to serve in Hong Kong after being discharged from hospital.

Homesickness was very real and something from which even the most hardened suffered occasionally. Hitting one with a sudden longing to pop home for a day off, or to drink a glass fresh milk – at that time there were no dairy herds in Japan – or perhaps even to glimpse a green field. However, with the numerous distractions surrounding us it would pass, and we would count our blessings, especially if the UK mail had arrived on time and there were letters in our pigeon holes. Although Miles had written recently with the good news that he had passed his medical board and was now away on his course, I had also detected that things between us were changing, although at the time I was really too tired to be concerned.

Permission was granted for Cynthia and me to spend our night duty leave on the island of Miyajima, where we could be accommodated for only three nights at the Leave Hotel there. This was part of the convalescent and leave centre for all serving members of the British Commonwealth Brigade, and as this was one of the most popular leave centres, it was not surprising that our visit had to be curtailed. Since the signing of the Peace Treaty with Japan on 28 April, several changes had occurred and the important one which had affected all of us was the gradual handing back to the Japanese of most of the original leave centres.

Miraculously, since Saturday 26 July it had ceased to rain – exactly when the wet season officially ended. Monday dawned brilliantly fine with a lovely hot sunshine burning away the early morning mist as we left the Mess by jeep en route to the RASC jetty in Kure, with Mary, another QA who had also just finished night duty. The three of us were in high spirits as we boarded one of the work-boats, which the RASC (Royal Army Service Corps) ran as an essential ferry link, to transport troops and stores between islands and the airport on the mainland at Iwakuni. Seemingly small, they actually held quite a considerable number of passengers on deck and in the cabin.

Settling ourselves on a bench seat in the bows amongst a number of convalescents and a handful of troops on leave, with a jolt I saw a familiar face grinning at me from the opposite side of the boat. 'David! What on earth are you doing here? How are you?'

'I've managed to wangle some sick leave. The leg is a lot better thanks and nothing that a few days of swimming and relaxation won't fix.'

'That's great news, but have you met Cynthia and Mary? This is David.'

'And these disreputable characters from my ward are Monty and Jim; incidentally, Jim is from Canada,' explained David as he introduced the two tall lads sitting beside him.

'Right! Is everybody on board now, who should be?' called out the NCO in charge of the boat, at the same time swiftly counting heads. 'Okay then, we're off.' He started the engine while the other crew member pulled the mooring ropes on to the deck, and we started to chug out of the harbour, gradually picking up speed. Breaking the comfortable silence of quiet anticipation, one of my convalescent patients from Ward Five shouted raucously, 'Hey Sarge, how long will it take to get there? Will we be in time for dinner? 'Cos I'm starving now!' Replying good-naturedly, the NCO quipped, 'About two and a half hours, laddie, and there's no buffet car on board, so you should have eaten up your breakfast like a good boy.'

The deep blue waters of the inland sea whooshed past as we sat there, lazily watching the stunning coastline slip by. Spiky, sparsely vegetated hills swept down to the water's edge, some on the lower slopes with neatly terraced rows of rice. Sporadically there were little fishing boats, elderly in appearance and usually moored alongside ancient jetties. Huddled near them were small clusters of tiny stone cottages, shaded by a few wind-blown pines.

Once or twice during the trip, we noticed collections of large neat frames or fences, situated in the water but always some distance away from the shore.

'I think those may well be oyster beds,' said David, as I looked inquiringly at him.

After a couple of hours or so, the hazy outline of Miyajima emerged, to give us our first glimpse of this beautiful island. Gradually we observed that it was exceptionally wooded and hilly, with one particular high hill or small mountain rising well above the others. Closer inshore, we noticed several pretty little sandy coves.

The work-boat bumped gently against the stone walls of the jetty and gathering up our few belongings we disembarked, calling out 'Goodbye, have a good time', to the lads as they made their way to the convalescent leave centre close by the beach. Then the three of us, with David, Monty and Jim, clambered into the waiting jeep for the short drive along a sandy track to the hotel.

This was a large and very attractive three storied building, constructed in a typical oriental style and situated in a superb position close to the waterfront, where it nestled amongst ancient maritime pines, their huge branches casting cool shadows round about it.

'Gee, what a wonderful place. See here, we've even got our own beach, right there.' Jim said.

'Heavens! Just look at the architecture, this truly is real Japanese, with all those delicately curved roofs,' exclaimed Cynthia.

The staff were welcoming as they allocated rooms; Cynthia and I were given an enormous bedroom to share on the first floor, complete with a balcony with French windows which we immediately threw open.

'Goodness, what a stunning view – look you can see the mainland in the distance, Cynth, just how lucky can we be!'

'I'm feeling tons better already and we haven't even had lunch. Let's change quickly because I should think that it must be pretty imminent.'

Unpacking rapidly, we consigned our crumpled khaki drill to the back of the big ornate Western-style wardrobe, in the joyful knowledge that we should not have to suffer it again until late Thursday afternoon. After flinging on a bright sundress each, we dashed down the stately old staircase in search of the dining room.

There were several other guests staying at the hotel but because the six of us more or less knew each other we tended to stick together as a group for the precious few days we had on Miyajima, spending much of our time in and out of the lovely warm, buoyant salty water. After an initial foray to the local shops which, in reality, were just an untidy collection of wooden shacks, the boys returned armed with a variety of water pistols, which they used with great precision…

It was truly beneficial to unwind in such quiet and relaxing surroundings. Stretching out on the warm sand after a long swim, under the cool pines emanating their pungent aroma of hot resin, was magical. And for Mary, Cynthia and me, it was blissful to be relieved from the strict timetable of routine. We imagined too, for the three convalescent boys, having now escaped from both the constraints of the hospital and the rigours of war, this must have been a dramatic change.

Miyajima, we found was quite a sizeable island, about eighteen miles round, reputed to be one of the most beautiful locations in Japan and frequently referred to as Shrine Island because of the number of shrines both large and small established there. For that reason it was also respected by the Japanese as the Sacred Island and legend had it that even then in 1952 no person was allowed to be born or to die on the island. However, as we observed whilst we were there, Miyajima was certainly not over inhabited and the only transport available on the island then, apart from one or two old wooden carts, was the single jeep belonging to the Forces stationed at the leave camp.

The most famous landmark was the ancient and huge offshore *torii*, the sacred gateway through which the fishing fleet passed for their annual blessing by the priests at the huge Itsukushima Shrine. Due to its close proximity to the water, this shrine gave an illusion of floating, with its wooden-piered platform, extending well out over the water. It was the magnificent *torii* which enraptured me, rising majestically from sea-level to approximately 50ft and built towards the end of the last century from massive tree trunks of camphor wood, once painted bright red but now weathered to a soft, rosy pink. At low water it was possible to wade out through the muddy sand to appreciate both its enormity and culture.

From the hotel there was a pretty sandy path stretching for some distance beside the shore and placed at intervals along, it surrounding the bay, there were numerous large stone lanterns, which we were told were lit by candles on special festival days.

Practically the whole island was covered with a luxuriant growth of different species of trees, and close to the hotel there was an abundance of Japanese maples, their small and delicately shaped leaves, guaranteeing a stunning array of autumn tints.

During our short leave we explored a considerable area, taking the most of one day to scramble to the summit of Mount Missen – the highest hill – where I spent some of the time looking out for the wild deer that were supposed to roam freely through the woods, but most of it trying to avoid hidden snakes! Another afternoon we sailed right around the island by launch. Cynthia and I spent our last morning walking to the tiny village to buy souvenirs for our families – hand-carved wooden merchandise for which Miyajima was famous.

Returning to the hotel we stopped along the way to admire the old pagoda, reputedly of the seven sorrows. This beautiful building had already intrigued us, painted red, with its five-tiered gabled roofs curled up towards an azure sky, and with aura of calm surrounding it. Disappointingly it was then closed to visitors.

Lying lazily in bed, savouring the prospect of breakfast on a tray, each morning we heard the pleasant phut-phut sounds of the little fishing boats of Miyajima as they returned to base after a night's toil. Again in the late of the evening they chugged slowly away from the harbour.

Rehabilitated by good food and much sleeping, not even the ghosts of the Kamikaze pilots could waken us. We had gleaned from the local legends how these unfortunate young men had traditionally spent their last night in this same hotel on the sacred shrine island before speeding off on their deadly missions. Nevertheless, Miyajima was enchanting, timeless and healing, with its calm, pearl grey waters, superb scenery and vivid sunsets: the perfect location for the convalescent war weary.

August in Kure was almost unbearable, its stifling heat and intense humidity affecting the whole hospital. Working on day duty, we were all weary of glistening skin and the monotonous dripping of sweat, reaching saturation level after the slightest exertion. By the time we had completed just the early morning routine on the wards our grey dresses were soaked from rivulets of sweat, constantly running down our backs. If perchance we were fortunate to sit down whilst on duty, on rising we would find we had stuck to the chair!

The wards were full and everyone was working flat out. By the end of our duty, as we staggered back to the Mess, conversation was both lethargic and monosyllabic, as we thought longingly of a cool shower and yet another clean dress. Even our white QA veils hung limply, despite conscientious starching by our house-girls. Trying to avoid pungent odours and to keep oneself smelling sweetly was quite a challenge, with the demand for 'Mum' in the NAAFI at a premium. Just to add to my misery, I had had a dose of prickly heat, when for several days the irritation had been intense.

'It's no good, Jilly, you will have to report sick. You look awfully pale and you must be feeling rotten.'

'But I can't, Cynthia, I've only just come back from leave and everyone's so busy on the wards, and you know how sarcastic the Major-Ma'am can be. Though I must admit I do feel a bit lousy because my cervical glands are aching and rather swollen.'

'You really must go now: shall I come with you?' Cynthia offered kindly.

'No thanks, I'll muster up the courage and in any case I'll be back in a jiffy.'

Less than an hour later, I was tucked up in bed in a cool airy room in the Sisters' Sick Bay, having just been diagnosed with the symptoms of glandular fever. The treatment was rest, which I appreciated immensely and after a week or so of calm and much kindness from both the hospital staff and my friends, I felt much recovered. When our Commanding Officer, Colonel Meneces, visited me with Matron during the ward round, he kindly explained that although I was to be discharged from hospital on the following day, he considered that as I was not quite fit to return to duty yet. He recommended to Matron that, to ensure a complete recovery, I should be sent to the leave centre at Miyajima for three days' sick leave. This unexpected bonus I could scarcely believe, as I stammered my sincere and heartfelt thanks.

An hour or so later there was a quiet knock on my door when, to my astonishment, in walked David, bronzed, fit and without any trace of a limp.

'David, how lovely to see you, but how on earth did you know I was here?'

'Jilly, I've only just this minute heard that you've been ill. I'm so sorry because I really would have visited you before now but I've been so tied up with re-training at the Battle School – which is way out of Kure – that until today it has been impossible to contact you. Anyway, how are you feeling and what has been the matter?' Pulling up a chair, he sat down beside my bed.

'It's okay, David, please don't apologise. I've only had a mild attack of glandular fever, and guess what? Our kind CO is sending me to Miyajima the day after tomorrow, to recuperate for a few days. Isn't that lovely? But what about you? What's your news?'

'That's why I'm here. As you can see, my leg is fine now and I've just passed my fitness test. So like you, I'm on the move the day after tomorrow, flying back to Korea.' After pausing for a moment I said, 'Oh! I am sorry David, as I'd hoped you might have had a bit longer to get over your injury but are you pleased, or is that a silly question?'

'Yes, I suppose that I am, as from what I've heard they are pretty short in the battalion, and it's much better to get on with the job. But what I am really pleased about now is: did I understand that you are being discharged from here tomorrow?'

'Yes that's right.'

'Good, but what time do they let you out?'

'After lunch, but why?'

'Excellent, then we can have a quiet dinner together at the Club; that is if you feel up to it?'

'Thanks a lot, that would be terrific and a great start to my so called convalescence.'

'What time does he fly out today?' Cynthia asked, as we sat in a shady spot in the Mess garden for the hour or so before my ferry transport was due.

'Oh Jilly! I am sorry, because you always seem to meet the nice guys who are forever on the move.'

'You can say that again! But for David's sake I'm rather relieved, as he told me over dinner that he is only returning to Korea for another six weeks, after which he leaves with the rest of the battalion for Hong Kong. So it's great to know that he won't have more than a few weeks to do on Active Service. And after all, Cynth, we were truly, just good friends.'

'You know, you do look better but still a bit off colour, so I'm hoping that the Miyajima magic will really buck you up again.'

'I'm quite sure it will, only this morning I had a letter from Miles and that threw me a bit.'

'Miles? Oh I remember, you've known him since you were in Aldershot and he was quite keen about you?'

'Yes, perhaps he was, only at the time I wasn't too enthusiastic as I wanted to stay in the QAs and travel for a while. Miles is also a Regular like me, and now that he has recovered from his eye injury is obviously destined for a bright career. However, we have continued to correspond quite frequently since I left the UK last February. But this time his letter was surprisingly short and somewhat curtly written, telling me that he has recently become engaged to the daughter of his mother's best friend. Adding that, understandably, he would no longer continue with our correspondence and concluding with the vague hope that I was still enjoying life in the Far East.'

'That's a bit tough for you, Jilly, especially just now.'

'Not really, but thanks for listening. Actually, I've most probably had a narrow escape as Miles was inclined to be a bit stuffy and he wasn't exactly the sort you could push into a puddle!'

'In that case he's bound to put his career first and might even end up as a red-nosed general,' remarked Cynthia cheerfully.

History later proved Cynthia's predictions to be correct, although neither of us could be sure about the red nose!

Seventy-two hours of complete relaxation – on what was fast becoming my favourite island – restored the roses to my cheeks and more importantly a sense of well-being, and it was with a much lighter step that I returned to duty. This time Matron had kindly designated me as a relief sister, on light duties for the next two or three weeks.

CHAPTER SIX

VIPs AND HIROSHIMA SHOPPING

7 SEPTEMBER, GENERAL WEST SUCCEEDED GENERAL CASSELS AS
COMMANDER OF THE COMMONWEALTH DIVISION. THE FINAL
OFFER ON THE PRISONERS OF WAR QUESTION WAS REJECTED BY
THE COMMUNISTS AND AN INDEFINITE RECESS WAS ANNOUNCED.
17 NOVEMBER, INDIA PROPOSED A COMPROMISE SOLUTION.
18–19 NOVEMBER, SECOND BATTLE OF THE HOOK FOUGHT
BY THE BLACK WATCH

Since returning from the magic of Miyajima at the beginning of September, I had found that Kure was depressing, with a shabby squalidness of beer halls and ill-reputed brothels; it was quite often referred to as a den of vice! There had also been vague rumours of a penicillin racket, although nothing was ever confirmed to substantiate this. It was not surprising, having so many temptations, that some of the lads stationed there went off the rails. This was brought to my attention when as a relief sister I was sent to work on the bolted and barred detention ward. In this ward there were several offenders in my care, mostly young alcoholics, and after much locking and unlocking of doors I began to feel like a jailor, finding it altogether a cheerless scene.

'Hi Jilly, have you heard the news?' Betty whispered over coffee in the ante-room.

'No, what have I missed, is it important?'

'It could be.'

'Come on, what is it?'

'Well, I've just heard on the grapevine, that quite soon, a handful of sisters, British, Australians and Canadians may be going to Korea as part of a medical team to set up a small hospital somewhere over there.'

'Crikey! Is that for real?' Betty nodded.

'When can WE go?'

'I think that if the powers-that-be really do get this off the ground, with a bit of luck we might have a good chance.'

It was about six weeks later when two nursing sisters from each force flew to Korea to establish the small British Commonwealth Zone Medical Unit situated somewhere in Seoul. Due to the rough conditions and general lack of facilities, they were to be stationed there for two months only.

On the morning of 11 September the retiring Commander-in-Chief, General Cassels, visited the hospital and, because the senior sister on the medical ward whom I was relieving was off duty, I escorted him around the ward introducing him to each of the patients. The general was charming, handsome and much younger than we had expected. After his necessarily brief visit, with so many more patients and staff to meet, we felt quite uplifted, principally because he seemed to think that we were all doing a good job.

We had been warned that the typhoon season began in September. This was heralded by days of torrential rain and thankfully an appreciable drop in the temperature.

'Whoops, just look at that, Sister!' Glancing towards the windows, I saw exactly what Private Jones, the RAMC orderly on duty with me, meant. For several hours the heavy rain had been continuous until, suddenly, the heavens had opened with a cacophony of walls of water, sheeting noisily down onto the gravel path outside.

'Are you going off duty now, Jones?'

'Yes Ma'am.'

'Would you like to borrow a waterproof? There's a spare one in the cupboard.'

'It's okay thanks, as I've got mine here, though I think that a life raft might be an easier way to get back to the barracks; if not I'll swim!'

After duty that night, Betty and I were due at the Green Room Club for the dress rehearsal of *The Tinsel Duchess*. The play, having suffered a considerable delay, was now being produced with two other one act plays, before an invited audience at the small theatre in Kure House four days later. Despite the inevitable downpour we managed to get down to Kure by taxi, one of the local and extremely shaky motorbike taxis which, due to a paucity of wheels, was predictably both wobbly and unstable. By the time we arrived at the rehearsal, none of us could remember our lines and somehow during the next few days, these I had to commit to memory as well as knitting a night-cap for my husband, the Duke!

On our return to the Mess, we discovered from the newly published duty roster, that to my utter dismay I had been detailed to start night duty on Sunday 14 September, two nights before the production of the play! Thankfully, as Betty suggested, I found some kind soul to relieve me, until midnight on the Tuesday evening.

Night duty was a definite disadvantage as far as *The Tinsel Duchess* and I were concerned. However, in spite of feeling bog-eyed after a restless day's sleep, I managed to surface just before 1700hrs. Three hours later, I was unrecognisable in my costume, with my face concealed beneath my grandmother's widow's veil and a homemade pearl tiara perched on top of my head. The excitement was exhilarating as we, the cast, peeped nervously through the slit in the heavy curtains to catch a glimpse of the audience sitting in the front row, their various bits of 'scrambled egg' and gold braid glinting in the footlights.

The stage manager gave the order, the curtains were raised and we were on! The props were good, the costumes (although homemade) were authentic and, marvellously for us, the dialogue flowed freely as we settled into our unaccustomed nineteenth-century roles. At the end of the performance the applause was generous as the guests appeared genuinely appreciative of our combined efforts.

After my modest blaze of glory, things seemed to be rather flat on night duty; however, my patients made up for this as they were all such pleasant lads of mixed nationalities, including one from the USA and, unusually, two others from South Africa. One of the minor annoyances of this particular night duty was that my office on the medical ward was at times infested by cockroaches. These would suddenly appear in the middle of the night and start marching up the walls in small platoons. Their habits were nauseating, as I was to discover when leaving some laboratory blood slides – which I had just taken from a patient – in the treatment room whilst I was called away. Returning a few minutes later to despatch them to the lab, I found to my horror that several fat cockroaches had invaded the slides and were busily devouring the samples of blood.

Friday 19 September was a tragic day for the Japanese people in Kure when, during a salvage operation in the harbour to recover a sunken submarine, its torpedoes unexpectedly exploded and killed many of the men.

Due to a shortage of staff, for one night only I.was assigned the extra and unexpected duty of Orderly Officer. At 2330hrs I left the hospital compound by jeep to drive over to the Mess, where my duties were to lock approximately fifty windows and to turf out the residents of the ante-room – which was easier said than done – and switch off all the lights, before finally securing the doors.

My brief reward (as a lowly lieutenant) was when the guard at the gate saluted both times as I was driven through!

During the afternoon of my last night on duty, after meeting Betty for tea at the Club, we walked over to St Peter's to do the flowers. On this occasion we had chosen huge sprays of scarlet and golden gladioli, with some small button chrysanthemums, to blend with the well-polished altar brass. I loved this tranquil little task which, by then, we had continued to do for some months.

Later that day, when listening to the news, we were all devastated to hear that the beautiful old Miyajima Hotel had on the previous night been destroyed by a blazing fire.

My five nights off were a blissful break and gave me time to catch up with lost sleep and other pressing tasks, such as resurrecting my winter kit from mothballs and retrieving my grey cloak to sew on the United Nations and Commonwealth badges and shoulder flashes which I had collected during the past months. I had started my collection in Aldershot, after admiring one of the senior sister's cloaks where, in the scarlet lining, she had sewn an impressive patchwork of Second World War emblems. At the same time, she advised me that this practice was usually frowned upon by the top brass, adding that although it was a fair risk, to make sure that my cloak was buttoned up if Matron was in the offing. Otherwise, it might mean the purchase of a new cloak, which at the cost of £10, could become an expensive hobby!

(Back then, in 1952, it was beyond the bounds of my imagination to conceive that in 1988, in an exhibition at the National Army Museum to commemorate the Korean War, my own QA cloak displaying its lining of illicit badges would be exhibited in a glass cabinet next to the one presenting the uniform worn by Private Speakman VC when he made his heroic stand on Hill 355.)

Another more important job was to complete the parcel of canned and dried food which I had collected over the past few weeks, to send home to my parents in time for Christmas. Food rationing continued and my mother in a recent letter had mentioned that the cheese ration per person per week was still only 1oz. Cheese would be impossible to send home but tinned Australian butter was available in the NAAFI, along with many other canned goods.

'Come in, if you can get in!' I called out, simultaneously trying not to lose the darning needle wedged between my teeth. Cynthia, popping her head around the door, exclaimed, 'Heavens, Jilly, what ever are you doing?' Removing the needle I checked to see if it was still threaded, whilst saying:

'It's lovely to see you, Cynth, but please bear with me and hold this corner while I finish stitching it up. Oh and mind the shavings!'

'I can hardly avoid them considering they are all over the floor!' Chuckling loudly she hung on to the calico, whilst I shoved the blunt needle through the tough material, with punctured bloody fingers.

'Thanks a million, you've just saved me, as I've been struggling for the last two and a half hours to pack up this parcel. Thank God it's finally done.'

'It's so big, what ever is it?'

'Oh, it's only the Christmas food parcel for my parents and you know I've got a horrid feeling that it's well and truly overweight even for sea-mail.' Handing her the bulky package, I asked, 'What do you think – could it be more than 22lb? 'Cos that's the maximum allowance to send.'

'I don't think so but I'm not sure, Jilly. Get it weighed in the mail office to make certain.'

'I suppose I shall have to anyway, but I just can't face unstitching it, then having to re-pack it and worse still, having to sew up the whole blasted thing again. My fingers would never stand it!'

'What are you sending them?'

'Tinned, bacon, sausages, fruit salad, cream, fruit juice, you know, Cynth, all the things that are rationed. Oh and yesterday I was so thrilled, because I managed to buy six packets of Sun-Maid raisins, my mother's favourite and which have been impossible to get at home. And guess where I found them?'

'In the NAAFI?'

'No, in Hiroshima!'

'You actually got there, Jilly, well done, because either you were very brave or very naughty! I bet you travelled there unaccompanied, and by that I mean by yourself!'

Replying somewhat defensively, 'Well you were much tied up with James, Betty was on duty and yesterday was my only free day. But I did ask for Jess's advice, as I knew that she had been there more than once and she was very helpful saying that as long as I wore my uniform and was sensible, I should be alright and she even told me where to catch the local bus. I can understand why the powers-that-be don't like us to travel singly. But it was essential that I did my Christmas shopping then, to be in time to catch the sea-mail.'

A gentle tap on the door interrupted us when in walked Susie-*san*, my new treasure of a house-girl, carrying an afternoon tea tray, with sandwiches and cakes.

'Me have brought you two cups and more cakee for other Sister-*san*, shall I put here?' she said pointing to the only spare bit of space on my trunk which, through necessity, stood in for a table.

'Thank you, Susie-*san*, that was very thoughtful of you.' Smiling warmly at us both, she withdrew from the room as quietly as she had entered.

'Gosh, Jilly, you are so lucky to have her. I'm just green with envy, as my wretched girl has lost at least one of my QA veils, which are both difficult and expensive to replace.'

'That I am! Because my other one lost a uniform dress which was also a good six guineas down the drain, but Susie-*san* really is a dream. But you know, Cynth, I do feel sorry for her and for many of the other Japanese girls working here, as I've noticed that things appear to be quite difficult for them and costly too. This was brought home to me the other day when I chucked my old evening sandals with a broken strap, into my bin and the next day was very surprised when Susie-*san* came to find me, holding the shoes, asking if she could have them because they were so pretty, adding that if she cut the tops off then the sandals would fit her.'

Whilst Cynthia poured the tea, I continued, 'But compared with her delicate little feet mine are like boats, so I've written to my mother and asked her to send me a similar pair but several sizes smaller, so that I can give them to Susie-*san* for Christmas.'

'She will be thrilled, but thinking of Christmas, please tell me all about your visit to Hiroshima as it must have been quite an adventure.'

'Well it's quite a long story! Luckily it was a lovely crisp autumn morning when I got up early to hoof it down to Kure Railway Station. There I caught the 0900hrs bus which, surprisingly, was a single-decker, modern, streamlined Japanese bus and absolutely jam packed with locals but I managed to get a seat and do you know, my return ticket only cost seventy yen!'

'That's only about 1s 5d! Go on.' She urged, as I grabbed a mouthful of cake.

'The route hugged the coastline all the way and you can imagine how lovely the scenery was, with a cornflower blue sea, bright green terraced hillsides, some high pastures on the hills and along most of the way, there were the steep over-hanging barren cliffs.

'I can't remember how long it took to get to Hiroshima, probably an hour and a half before I disembarked into a huge, bustling city.

'Oh Cynth, I was absolutely astounded, having heard so much about the cata-strophic devastation caused by the Atom Bomb – which after all, is only now, just over seven years ago. Suddenly there I was standing in the middle of what appeared to be a totally re-built city, surrounded by many tall, modern buildings, with numerous little wooden shacks propped up between them.

'Feeling disoriented, I surveyed the busy street, then seeing a large shop in the distance I made a bee line for it, which luckily turned out to be one of the big department stores.

'If only you could have seen it, Cynth. A real Aladdin's cave, chock full of won-derful goodies, as were all the other large shops that I eventually found. In fact the last one I discovered was the best and sold everything from cuddly teddy bears to exquisite kimonos, so it was there that I did most of my Christmas shopping. And would you believe it, on the top of the large roof of this store, there was a children's playground, with a lovely miniature railway train chugging around on a circular track, with its little carriages full of happy, laughing children.

'Actually, it was from that particular roof top that I spent some time, gazing in sheer amazement at the panorama of the new city of Hiroshima which sprawled far away into the distance. This also gave me a sense of relief, as well as the inevitable feeling of guilt. Can you understand just how dreadfully mixed up I felt, Cynthia'?

'Poor you, Jilly, because I know that I'd have felt exactly the same way about things, as you did then. And perhaps that's one of the reasons why I haven't been to Hiroshima yet, let alone gone on one of those organised visits to the Japanese hospital there, to meet some sick survivors of the radiation. I've found that it has been upsetting enough, on the few occasions when I've actually come face to face with a badly crippled survivor, wearing a cardboard placard and begging in the street.'

'I agree, and quite honestly feel we are dealing with so many injured and sick here in Kure, that I just couldn't cope with much more.'

'Did you actually see the site where the bomb dropped?' Cynthia asked with interest.

'Yes, I managed to, because I had deliberately set aside an hour or so for this before catching the bus back to Kure. So, gathering up all my packages, I set off in the early afternoon to make my private pilgrimage to the place where the atomic bomb fell on Hiroshima. By this time the temperature had much increased and the streets were crowded with people but somehow I found my way through the strange straggling city and after a long walk down a hot, dusty road, suddenly I was standing in front of the remains of what had once been an impressive building. This was called The Industrial Promotions Hall, which is now no more than a domed memorial of twisted steel and broken masonry.

'Standing there beside the wreckage, it was unusually quiet, the nearby river flowing noiselessly and even the birds were silent. Only a handful of Japanese walked past, tiptoeing through, and like me, pausing to give homage to the massive dead. Later, I took a snap of the simple memorial in front of the ruined building. This was a fair-sized concrete wall with PEACE engraved in huge letters at the top and inset to one side of it was a painting of the building in its original state.

'And that was that! I trekked back to the bus station laden. The return journey went without a hitch and I was safely back in the Mess by about 1700hrs, feeling positively knackered.'

'That was incredibly interesting, well done, but what about the rest of your nights off?'

'Not much, just mainly sleeping and I did go to Scottish Dancing a couple of nights ago, when we actually danced to two pipers. This was great fun although rather spoiled for me because I was chased by a chap in a kilt. He was very persistent and although I managed to shake him off then, he has rung me several times since!

'But to completely change the subject, Cynthia, tomorrow evening there is a meeting of the Green Room Club, when a new play is being discussed. Would you like to come with me? As we are desperately in need of new talent and although I can understand why you aren't too keen to take on anything extra while James is around, this could be just the thing to keep you occupied whenever he's away from Kure.'

Reporting for day duty on 3 October, I was again posted to the officers' ward, this time with the dubious honour of being in charge until a senior sister was available. That evening, after admitting the last convoy of wounded, we were extremely busy with almost a full house, and it was rewarding to see that however exhausted and ill these lads were on admission, normally it only took them twenty-four hours to respond to the ward routine. Even the really poorly ones usually began to perk up after a day or so of treatment, which included several of our special high protein egg-flips.

Sandy, a nineteen-year-old, had shown great fortitude throughout his extended stay. The poor boy had such a multiplicity of gunshot wounds and fractures, that practically the whole of his body was encased in plaster of Paris. The huge cast, extending from the cervical area of his neck to just above his toes on both feet (excluding a small toilet area), included his left arm from shoulder to wrist. Never before had I nursed anyone in such an immobilised condition and although through sheer necessity young Sandy's body was more or less inactive, his razor-sharp intellect and wicked sense of humour kept us all on our toes. One of my first duties on the ward was to remove no less than seventy-one stitches from his face and a tiny area just visible on his chest. During this delicate procedure, I had much difficulty in keeping a steady hand, let alone suppressing my giggles.

Appearing in Orders during the previous week was some important information regarding the imminent arrival of the Australian DAG, General Sir Kingsley Norris, who was scheduled to inspect the whole of the day staff – both medical and nursing – on the parade ground opposite the hospital at 0715hrs on Monday 6 October. So, for several early mornings prior to this, we had had to practise assembling on parade before commencing duty. This inspection also meant that a certain amount of our off-duty time was spent in attempting to dye the brown leather chinstraps on our Quarter Master issue khaki caps black to match our black beetle-squashers, and these had to be polished until they glittered!

The big moment came at 0700hrs when the entire day staff of RAMC, QARANC, Australian and Canadian medics and sisters had been neatly lined up. By this time Cynthia and I were feeling somewhat giggly, as we realised that our

Matron (who was in charge of us on parade) had probably had even less training in military drill than the rest of us. In this respect we were correct, because, although she brought us to attention just in time for Sir Kingsley's inspection, with her final order to dismiss, added under her breath, 'And you had better get on duty straight away…'

The General was a dear old boy and during the afternoon I had the pleasure of escorting him around my ward. He was charming and really interested in each of the patients, to the extent of finding out whom they were and from which particular Commonwealth country they came.

This appeared to be the visiting season, as the First Sea Lord was also supposed to be in the vicinity. Another VIP visitor in Kure was the well-known comedian Ted Ray, with his ENSA party, when the female performers were accommodated in our Mess. Cynthia was lucky enough to meet him when he entertained the patients on her ward.

Meetings at the Green Room Club recommenced with the casting of three one-act plays. These included GBS's *Dark Lady of the Sonnets*, in which Cynthia was suitably chosen to be the dark lady, with her lovely dark eyes and excellent pronunciation of the olde worlde English. In one small leap I inadvertently climbed the social ladder from Duchess to Queen!

Socially, the occasional game of hockey had replaced tennis, with a few of us playing in the All Ranks mixed team, in which our nice CO had offered to play Goalie. Scottish dancing also continued at a pace but there, unfortunately, I had been unable to shake off some Scot – resplendent in a bright tartan – whom I dubbed the Kilt, and who persisted in chasing me through the reels, as well as ringing me several times a week, despite my adamant refusal to meet him!

On 13 October, all of us who were off duty that evening had to attend the All Ranks' dance held especially for the lads at Kure House. Despite the inevitable chore of polishing the brass buttons on my No.1 dress for that evening (having recently changed into winter kit) it was more than worthwhile and the dance was fun. It was good to see some of our hardworking RAMC nursing orderlies relaxing when, after sinking a pint or two, they would pluck up the courage to invite the WVS and Red Cross ladies and some of the QAs to dance. Towards the end of the evening, when I was dancing with rather a shy young lad, to our mutual surprise, we won the elimination waltz. My prize was a pair of earrings but he, poor boy, was so embarrassed he bolted off as soon as the presentation was made!

Recently a new senior sister had taken charge of the officers' ward and so I reverted to junior sister again. This I did not mind a bit, although I often wished that even if she did have the exalted rank of Major, that she wouldn't take such a delight in bossing me around…

The previous Wednesday was a Japanese national holiday which I discovered when, after walking down to Kure, I found the town was crowded with people of all ages, most of whom were in traditional dress. Set along the roadsides there were numerous attractive stalls, selling everything from bright balloons to odd-looking sweetmeats, with many families enjoying a day out together. As always, there were lots of excited little children running around, all of whom looked so sweet with their chubby smiling faces, peach-coloured cheeks and shining jet black hair. In fact, everyone appeared to be having a wonderful time, chattering away and enjoying the local goodies such as dried baby octopus legs which they seemed to chew like old fashioned liquorice sticks, whilst others contentedly flew their gorgeous kites of golden carp, which danced and whirled above us in the autumn sunshine.

Passing the temple grounds as I returned up the hill, I heard the chanting there of many voices and caught a glimpse of some of the worshippers tying paper prayers onto the bushes beside the building. Everywhere that afternoon there had been laughter and happiness; later I found out that this particular national holiday was appropriately called a Happy Day.

Latterly, several of the hospital staff had been afflicted by heavy colds and mine, annoyingly, was exacerbated by my annual TAB inoculations. Coupled with this, I felt somewhat anxious about one of our patients, an Australian recently admitted after unexpectedly developing gangrene of his right foot and lower leg – possibly caused from a circulatory problem. He was only twenty-seven and, ironically, had just been promoted to major. Now, through some obscure tragedy, he would have to face up to the inevitable amputation. Poor chap, somehow I imagined that it might have been easier for him had he suffered a gunshot wound, but he was being very philosophical and hopefully would otherwise make a good recovery.

Sister had really been on my back, nit-picking over this and that… Fortunately, in less than a week's time, Betty and I had been granted seven days' R&R leave, when Emma had kindly arranged for us to stay with friends in Kobe. However, before making my escape, in my off-duty time I had promised to make the Beefeater costumes for the two boys in the *Dark Lady*, provided I could beg some plaster muslin for the Elizabethan ruffs. Rehearsals went well and we were all becoming quite attached to this little play.

Saturday 1 November was a red letter day for the Japanese shipbuilding industry and for the privileged few invited to attend the launching of the first oil tanker to

be built in the Kure yard since the Second World War, which, at the time, was the largest tanker in the world at 38,000 tons. With two of my colleagues and several of the senior medical and nursing staff, we drove down to the dry docks on a chilly, dull, grey morning. There we were seated on a huge stand, which even at that quite early hour appeared to be filled with people of several nationalities.

Fluttering above us against an overcast sky, there was an impressive show of colourful flags including the Rising Sun, the Stars and Stripes, our own Union Jack and others, plus the Liberian flag (presumably under which the new ship was to be registered). Stretching out way down below us, and blanketing the full length of the dry dock, we saw the expansive shell of the newly constructed ship.

Our initial excitement soon subsided as we sat passively during the seemingly long periods of waiting and interminable speeches taking place before the launching actually began. This was performed by a young Japanese princess, the newly married daughter of the Emperor, but unfortunately from where we were sitting it was impossible to see more than a smudge of her, although we did hear her name the ship: *Petro-Kure*. Following the naming it seemed to take forever for the water to whoosh into the dock and for the ship to float, until eventually and very cautiously its huge bulk slid slowly out to the harbour. At the conclusion of the ceremony we stood to attention through four different national anthems, with each being played right through to the end...

Escaping on 2 November for our first R&R leave made all the difference to Betty and me, and we felt much refreshed after having a complete change and a much needed rest in Kobe. This time Emma had arranged for us to stay with a delightful young Scottish couple, who not only showered us with kindness but also treated us as part of their family by sharing their home. This in itself was immensely beneficial after surviving months of institutionalised living in Kure, where sometimes homesickness could be a real problem. We both fell deeply in love with their baby son Hughie, who gurgled handsomely at us each time we played with him.

For me it was lovely to return to Kobe and to meet up with Emma again and for Betty it was an exciting first visit with much to absorb, especially as Emma had arranged lots for us to see and do – some of the places I had already visited, whilst others I had not. By far the most exciting was a trip to the famous Takarazuka Theatre, situated some distance from Kyoto.

Setting off quite early one morning, we travelled by electric train to the special station which had been built close to the opera house. Emma warned us that because of the length of the performance the matinée started at sometime between 11.00 and 11.30 a.m.! She explained that by tradition all the actors of the Takarazuka company are women – there are no male performers – and that the roles are played only by these female actors who have undergone years of highly specialised training to cultivate the rich deep, throaty voices of the male characters, adding that many of these women were literally born into their profession, carrying on family tradition through many generations. Emma also mentioned, that in Tokyo, there is another eminent theatre called The Kabuki, where the pattern is reversed into an all-male cast of actors.

The theatre, which was large and of a somewhat modern design, was packed solid with a lively Japanese audience, all of whom were noisily appreciative of the forthcoming programme which consisted of two complete operas, lasting for over six hours. It did take a while for us to become accustomed to the strange oriental music and the constant plucking of the *shamisen*, with its high pitched twanging tone. This provided the plaintive background music throughout both performances, with an atmosphere that was absolutely fascinating and utterly unlike anything we had experienced in the Western world.

The first opera, *The Mad Woman of Chaillot*, was rather heavy going as it was a Western story but sung and narrated in Japanese. Personally I did not care for this, mainly because I felt that East and West did not mix well. However, the scenery and stage effects were spectacular, where everything looked authentically Parisian.

During the interval, whilst those sitting around us delved happily into their bamboo *Bentos* (picnic boxes), from which exuded some pungent odours, Emma thoughtfully suggested a walk in the theatre gardens, before having coffee in the bar.

After several hours of solid concentration, it was something of a relief to escape from the stuffy atmosphere into the lovely garden and as we admired the beds of beautiful chrysanthemums Emma explained these were *Kiku* in Japanese, and were also the national flower of Japan.

The second opera was superb and based on an ancient legend from the Tales of Genji – reputedly over 1,000 years old. This was traditional Japanese at its most excellent and although the whole score was sung or monotonously chanted in an unfamiliar language, it was so poignantly acted that I clearly understood the plight of the little princess, the main character in the play. She was exceptionally beautiful but, of course, destined for a tragic fate! Again, running through this opera was the haunting strain of the *shamisen* which, as the story unfolded, was enhanced by the narrator. Dressed inconspicuously in black and sitting cross legged on the stage, he recited the dialogue in a twanging tone. The scenic effects surpassed all expectations, with thunderous dragons puffing out real flames, an underwater scene alive with floating fishes and the grand finale of a forest of softly shaking cherry blossom, their delicate petals falling as silent snowflakes in homage to the dead princess.

We spent our last afternoon with Emma at a sort of United Nations tea-party held in a large hall somewhere in Kobe, where a number of ladies of mixed nationalities had gathered to serve their equivalent of the English afternoon tea. This was fun. After a warm welcome, we visited each table to try the different beverages. The American ladies served aromatic coffee from antique silver pots, with generous helpings of strawberry shortcake. The little Japanese ladies fluttered around in their beautiful brocaded kimonos, serving small, delicate eggshell china cups of green tea, with tiny cakes of seaweed. The British were present too, with thinly sliced cucumber sandwiches, buttered scones and lashings of hot strong tea.

An uneventful train journey found us back safely in Kure, Betty to report on night duty and for me – once again – it was the officers' ward. Fortunately, this time without the presence of the dragon sister – she having been replaced in my absence by a congenial colleague.

No sooner had I returned to duty when two totally unexpected events overtook me. The first was much less exciting than the next but, nevertheless, one for which I was unprepared. This was written notification informing me that I had been co-opted onto the Board of Examiners, to examine the RAMC Nursing Orderly candidates in the November examinations. My instructions were that I was to examine them orally and also assist with the marking of the written papers for the qualification of Nursing Orderly Class One – an equivalent rating of a third year civilian nurse. Therefore, a high standard would be required from both candidates and examiner!

The list of examiners was daunting, the Board being presided over by the senior medical specialist; a lieutenant colonel in the RAMC, with the Sister Tutor in charge of the school of nursing; a senior major in the QARANC; plus a medical officer; an RAMC captain, and most junior of all – me! This unexpected duty meant some hasty revision in medical nursing and I quickly made my number with Major Mary Innes to find out exactly what was expected of me. Meeting her professionally for the first time, she was kindness itself and throughout the weeks preceding and during the examinations she was always helpful and encouraging.

Whilst I was recovering from the shock of reaching such giddy heights, I was also battling along in my off duty, trying to design and sew (by hand) most of the costumes for the *Dark Lady*, and at the same time struggling to learn my lines. On the ward we were rushed off our feet with a full house, having admitted an unusually large number of wounded officers from the Black Watch after the battle of the Hook. And recently I had been press-ganged into playing in a hockey match...

The second unexpected event was when Matron suddenly sent for me one morning. I felt bowled over, wondering – as usual – what misdemeanour I had inadvertently committed. Looking up from her desk as I entered, she said, 'Oh yes, Hall, I wanted to tell you personally that we have now decided who shall relieve the two QAs due to return from Korea just after Christmas, and we are sending you and Lieutenant Macdonald to replace them.'

Whilst catching my breath, Matron continued, 'And you, Hall, will take over the duties of senior nursing officer in Seoul. This is a big responsibility, as you will be representing the British sisters in the small Commonwealth Unit there. As you are already aware, there are only six sisters serving in the hospital, two Australians, two Canadians and our own two QAs.' She smiled encouragingly, and at that moment – having just digested this astonishing news – I really felt that I could have hugged her!

'Thank you, Ma'am, I will do my very best, but when exactly could I expect to...' Waving her hand, she stopped me by saying, 'I'm not at all certain Hall, but most probably early January.' Continuing kindly, 'Remember too, it will be bitterly cold over there, so you must get yourself well kitted out.' Then, looking over her spectacles she added sternly, 'There is also one important aspect which I must impress upon you, which is, due to security reasons, it would be inadvisable for you to mention this new posting to anyone other than your closest friends and only tell your immediate family at home. But don't worry; this is only until the details of your posting to Korea are completely cleared. Right, I will give you more information when I receive it. Thank you, Sister, that is all.' And with a nod, I was dismissed.

The excitement and near disbelief remained constant for the rest of the day and I was dying to get off duty to tell Cynthia, in certain knowledge that I could trust her silence. And having heeded Matron's dire warnings regarding the perils of frostbite, I realised that I must write to my long suffering mother, inveigling her into stocking me up with Chilpruffe vests and thick long johns...

However, before I caught up with Cynthia – who was on late duty – I bumped into Betty in the ante-room.

'You are just the person I wanted to see, Jilly, but I have to go straight back to my ward now. So when can we meet?'

'Is it urgent?' She nodded.

'Would it help if I walked part of the way with you now?'

'Thanks a lot, that's great,' adding mysteriously, 'as I don't think we should be overheard on the way.'

No one else was in sight as we scrunched our way along the gravel track, even so Betty moved a little closer, before posing the question – 'Are you going too?'

'Going where?' I replied blankly.

'To Korea, of course!'

'Why do you ask?'

'Because – well... I AM – and what's more, I believe that you are too, because our Matron told me that your Matron and she have decided to send us there together!'

'Oh Betty that's wonderful – but I had no idea – and it will be lovely to go with you. In fact I can hardly believe it, can you?'

With only five weeks to go before Christmas, time was really flying past and at lunchtime the day before the Sister Tutor had handed me a heavy, large, brown envelope containing the written answers for the examination papers for Nursing Orderly Class One, requesting me to read them through and to add any pertinent comments. Marvellously she had already completed the marking proper, but reading them all kept me much occupied in my off duty for the next few days. Major Innes also reminded me that I was examining in the Orals the next Tuesday – 25 November – and hoped that I had my questions well prepared.

Although this was my first attempt as an examiner, the actual procedure was not as daunting as I had anticipated. However, by the time I had examined fourteen candidates for ten minutes each, I began to feel somewhat bushed as it was a baking hot afternoon which dramatically increased the temperature in the schoolroom, thus resulting in a number of the RAMC boys to sweat so profusely that I could not decide whether this was due to the weather, me, or general nervousness! Despite this, they all seemed to be bright lads and keen to get on. Surprisingly too, I had enjoyed my new role and even the allocation of marks was not the big problem I had envisaged.

Shortie-*san*, Cynthia's boyfriend's diminutive house-girl, called to see me and brought me a lovely bunch of flowers which she skilfully arranged in my best vase. James was away on duty in Korea and before leaving he had asked Shortie-*san*, in his absence, to look after Cynthia and apparently because I was her friend, I was also entitled to the same loyal treatment.

Christmas was really creeping up on us and two days previously the church choir had recorded a Christmas carol for the BBC, to be included in their Home Service programme entitled *Carols From Around the World*. Social life continued apace, as throughout this time we were desperately trying to fit in rehearsals for the *Dark Lady*, which thankfully, had been postponed until early December.

Sweet little Shortie-*san* completely saved my bacon when she popped in to see me one day, with yet another pretty bunch of flowers. Entering my room she had to struggle through a sea of materials, plus a huge roll of plaster muslin powdering the floor, because for the last two hours I had been trying to finish off the two Beefeaters' costumes. These were somewhat complicated, consisting of cloak, doublet and hose, hopefully to be complimented by deep white ruffs and cuffs – of plaster muslin!

Swiftly assessing the untidy mess, she said sympathetically, 'Ah so, Sister-*san*, you makee dresses for the Sister-*san*'s playee, yes? You have too muchee to do, yes?' And taking a small piece of damp, irregular sewing from my hand, she added very kindly, 'Me helpee you please.'

So with a considerable amount of sign language and many smiles, after a while she persuaded me to let her take the unfinished costumes home where she assured me that she and her mother – who had a sewing machine – would be pleased to do them. What an absolute gem Cynthia's James had for his girl-*san*, and what a wonderful relief for me, most especially as the dress rehearsal was scheduled for the following week.

Thursday 27 November was one of those hectic, non-stop days, with three significant VIP visits to the hospital, which also meant three processions of Matrons, senior medical officers and entourages accompanying each visitation. So we were frantically busy all day long, trying to keep both the wards and the patients tidy!

The first to visit our ward was a Canadian general – whom I missed, being much occupied with a dressing behind a screen. Pleasant though he was, he was but small fry compared to the next VIP.

This was the Hon. William McMahon, the Minister of Naval and Air Defence for Australia. He was very quiet and hardly said a word to anyone as he toured the ward. However, when leaving, he gave me a limp handshake, adding, 'Well, you seem to be looking after them fairly well.' A remark which somewhat surprised us…

The last visitor was our own young General Mathews, who in complete contrast was handsome, lively and very amusing, immediately hitting it off with all the patients. Stopping abruptly when he was halfway around the ward, and peering quizzically at me from a great height, he thundered out for all to hear, 'Sister, do you have much difficulty in controlling these young officers?' Utterly embarrassed, my reply was unintelligible. Grinning broadly, he swiftly continued, 'I bet you have a deuce of a time!' And with that succinct remark, all the patients roared with laughter and even the three matrons managed a smile.

The General's assumptions were partially correct, especially when the ward was full of spirited young subalterns. The next day, I retaliated whilst blanket bathing one of the really cheeky ones by hiding some ice cubes at the bottom of his bed, which was something of a change from the inevitable dose of Andrew's Liver Salts concealed within a urinal! Expecting a speedy reprisal, I steered clear of that corner of the ward until I went off duty.

1 HMT *Empire Trooper* in February 1952.

2 The main entrance to the British Commonwealth General Hospital (BCGH), Kure, Japan.
(Courtesy of New Zealand Kayforce Public Relations Section, 1953)

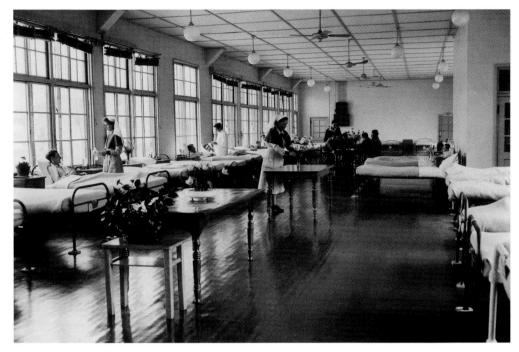

3 Medical ward, BCGH, showing, centre, Captain Mary Knowles QARANC, Sister-in-Charge. (Courtesy of New Zealand Kayforce Public Relations Section, 1953)

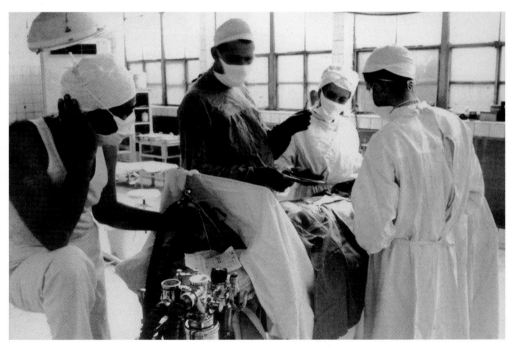

4 War surgery, BCGH, Kure. Left to right: Lt-Col McNally, Royal Canadian Army Medical Corps, Anaesthetist; Capt. Webster, Royal Army Medical Corps, Assistant Surgeon; Lt Betty Crocker, Royal Australian Army Nursing Corps, Theatre Sister; Lt-Col Wright RAMC, Surgeon. (Courtesy of Mrs Betty Lawrence OAM)

5 The ante-room in the Women's Services Officers' Mess, Kure. The author can be seen in indoor uniform, ready to go on ward duty, reading a newspaper. (Courtesy of New Zealand Kayforce Public Relations Section, 1953)

6 Royal Australian Army Nursing Corps Quarters, Kure. (Courtesy of New Zealand Kayforce Public Relations Section, 1953)

7 Lieutenants Georgina Johnson and Helen Strachan, off duty and wearing battledress, outside the Queen Alexandra's Royal Army Nursing Corps Quarters.

8 Captain Daphne Watts and Lieutenant Cynthia Gould in the hospital gardens.

Above: 9 Pat Fitzgerald (left) and Georgina Johnson relaxing in garden of the Officers Club, Kure.

Right: 10 Lieutenants Mary Hynes and Betty Crocker, Royal Australian Army Nursing Corps, freezing in Seoul in January 1953. (Courtesy of Mrs Betty Lawrence OAM)

Above: 11 Susie-*san*, my kind and helpful house-girl.

Below: 12 The waterfront of the Officers' Leave Hotel, Miyajima Island.

13 The Leave Hotel, Miyajima,
tragically destroyed by fire in 1953.

14 The site of the atomic bomb, Hiroshima, October 1952.

15 The simple memorial to victims of first atomic bomb in Hiroshima.

16 The Green Room Club, Kure House, in September 1952, with the cast of *The Tinsel Duchess*. Left to right: Cpl B. Karlsburg; Lt J. Hall; Pte J. Beaumont; Lt B. Crocker; Sgt P. Byrne.

17 G.B. Shaw's *Dark Lady of the Sonnets* in December 1952. Left to right: Pte J. Beaumont (William Shakespeare); Lt C. Gould (The Dark Lady); Lt J. Hall (The Lady (Queen Elizabeth I)).

18 St Peter's Garrison Church, Kure, Christmas 1952.

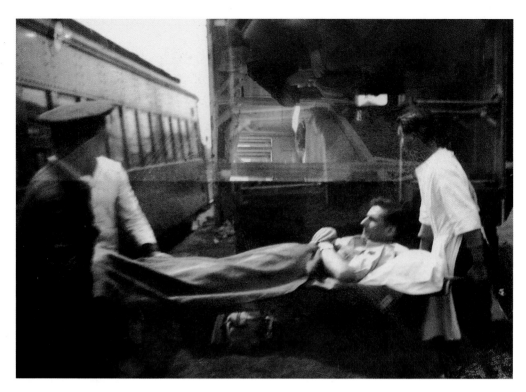

Above: 19 Kure Station showing a patient being carried by Japanese orderlies from a hospital ambulance into the ambulance train.

Below: 20 Interior of the sixteen-litter 'ward' on ambulance train.

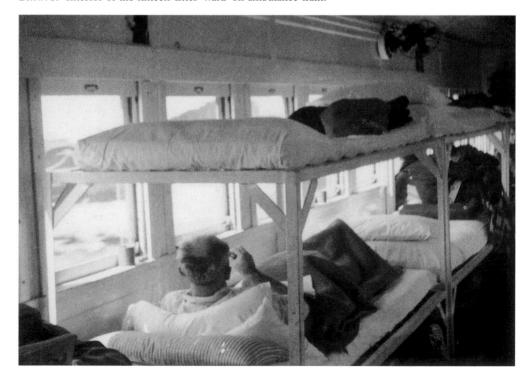

Right: 21 Main entrance to the British Commonwealth Zone Medical Unit (BC Z MU), Seoul, Korea. 1953

Below: 22 Officers' Mess, BC Z MU, Seoul.

23 Jess, Gay and Jilly outside 1940's Olympic Stadium building on Coronation Day, 3 June 1953.

24 Anne from the British Red Cross Society with her driver, en route to visit injured British troops in the American Hospital in Seoul.

Right: 25 Our French Canadian armed guard, somewhere outside Seoul.

Below: 26 The children of Myung Jin Orphanage, some distance from Seoul.

27 The sweet little orphaned girl who danced for me.

28 Large numbers of the 'Unification or Death' demonstrators passing the BC Z MU hospital entrance.

29 School girls demonstrating through the bombed city of Seoul.

30 Lt Irene Chesters with an admirer at Inchon.

31 Gay with Minnie the kid at the Royal Australian Air Force base some distance from Seoul.

32 The double gangway onto the Danish Hospital Ship *Jutlandia* at Yokohama in September 1953.

CHAPTER SEVEN

DECEMBER BLUES

The UN General Assembly adopted the Indian
compromise solution to the POW issue – no forced
repatriation of POWs.

30 November was warm and sunny and after finishing duty at 1300hrs, the rest of my Sunday was much occupied, beginning with a strenuous hockey match against the HQ staff of BCFK Kure, which left me somewhat bruised and battered. A hot shower worked wonders and a couple of hours later I was on board HMS *Unicorn* with Betty and her friends, where after a delicious dinner we saw *The Card*, an excellent film with Alec Guiness.

For me, it would have been an enjoyable evening if we had not made such a late arrival into the hangar, just as the film was starting and by which time the lights were out. Consequently, I had some difficulty in finding my seat. Stumbling along in the dark and trying to avoid row after row of legs with whispered apologies, I mistakenly grabbed at what I thought was a vacant seat, when at the same time practically fell into someone's lap. To add to my confusion and embarrassment, the someone said in a recognisably deep voice, 'Good evening, Jilly, how lovely to see you!' Cringing visibly as to my dismay I realised that the someone was the Kilt, whom I had only recently managed to shake off! With that I fled – dragging my partner up through another long row of seats, until I found two safe ones at the end of the line. Later that evening, and to my great relief, I discovered his ship was sailing on the following day!

The dress rehearsal for the *Dark Lady*, was reasonably successful. The Beefeater costumes fitted and looked authentic, and the two boys were delighted. These talented young lads were both national servicemen, serving their time in Kure as part of the British Commonwealth Brigade before going up to Oxford on the completion of their two years.

Cynthia and I had concocted our own costumes; she out of necessity had to be well cloaked as the Dark Lady. With a stroke of genius, I altered my new crimson silk evening dress by attaching the embroidered stole to the bodice and converting it into regal sleeves, adding a large and prickly plaster muslin ruff to give it an Elizabethan appearance. The jewelled coif was more of a challenge, but with a bit of ingenuity I botched this up out of a mix of black velvet and some faux pearls.

By 2000hrs on Saturday 6 December, the small theatre was packed. Peeping through the chink in the curtains we saw the front row had its usual quota of VIPs. Fortunately our play was billed last, therefore giving us time to acclimatise to the familiar tension and excitement.

The programme commenced with act one of Ben Travers' farce *Banana Ridge*. This was followed by some entertaining short sketches before the interval, which then gave time for the stage manager to set the scene for our presentation of George Bernard Shaw's *The Dark Lady of the Sonnets*.

In stark contrast to the raucous laughter and noisy applause which had followed the previous acts, the moment the curtains parted, a sudden hush fell upon the audience, as the moonlit courtyard of Queen Elizabeth's palace was just visible. In the play there were only four characters, the warder, the man – who was really Shakespeare – the Dark Lady, and the lady – Queen Elizabeth in disguise. When rehearsing, we had looked upon this little play as an amusing and earthy comedy, as when Shakespeare unknowingly addresses the Queen: ''Tis no fault of mine, Madam, that you are a virgin.' My blushes were many!

However, halfway through the performance, we began to realise that the audience was responding rather unexpectedly and after the final word had been spoken, there was an endless, deathly pause, until suddenly a spontaneous eruption of applause broke surface, with much cheering and clapping. Later, some of us wondered whether because the *Dark Lady* was such an English subject, that it had inadvertently touched on a raw nerve of homesickness; especially as many of us would be spending our first Christmas thousands of miles from home.

During the next few days, Cynthia and I were amazed at the amount of publicity which followed us in the wake of the play. We were both warmly praised on our individual performances to such an extent that we felt that we should go down to posterity in our acting roles, rather than our nursing careers! Several of the hospital staff had seen the production, including both the senior medical and surgical specialists and I was completely blown off course when after finishing the morning ward round with the medical boss (Lt-Col Peter Brown) we returned to Sister's office, he quietly asked me if I would be his partner at the RAMC dinner party and Christmas dance at the Club, on 27 December. I was so taken aback, that I automatically stood to attention, and stammered – 'Yes Sir, I should love to come!'

Two days later, whilst still feeling rather puzzled, I bumped into Mary Innes who mentioned that she too was invited and I realised then probably the reason for my invitation was that only last month we had all been on the same Examining Board. Prudence had to be my watchword during the next week or so, because young and inexperienced as I was, I also knew that if the news leaked out, the proverbial cat really would be amongst the pigeons, since the Colonel – as well as being one of the senior doctors in the hospital – was tall, dark and handsome, and although somewhat older, one of the most eligible bachelors around.

Matron confirmed that Betty and I would be flying to Korea on 3 January 1953 and at the same time I was told to commence night duty on 14 December. This, I calculated to my dismay, meant that my very last night on duty would inevitably be Saturday 27 December – the night of the dinner dance – just my luck! Hopefully I should be able to persuade some kind soul to relieve me, although like Cinderella, I would have to miss most of the ball.

By mid-December, there was a dramatic change in the weather and it was incredibly cold. For the first time ever, I resorted to wearing my heavy Crombie greatcoat over my uniform when walking over to the hospital. Jess reckoned that the piercingly bitter winds were blowing straight at us from Siberia. At the same time, due to some blasted regulation, the heating in our quarters was on for only two hours each evening, which meant that the early mornings were absolutely perishing.

Three days before I was due to start night duty, I had a surprise call from David, who had unexpectedly flown in from Korea (en route for Hong Kong) and we managed to meet for dinner at the Club. It was good to see him and especially to know that this time he had left the battlefield unscathed. Conversely, it was odd to realise that I myself should soon be in Korea.

The following morning the bombshell dropped and afterwards I waited impatiently in my off duty through the afternoon, until I could reasonably disturb Cynthia's precious sleep, before knocking urgently on her door.

'Cynthia, it's me Jilly. Look I'm really sorry to wake you but please if you are, please can I have a word?'

After a few muffled sounds, the door was opened by a sleepy looking Cynthia, exclaiming anxiously, 'My God, Jilly, whatever time is it? Have I overslept again?'

'No. No not at all. It's all my fault because it's only 4.30 p.m. and I really am dreadfully sorry to wake you early but I just must talk to you; please…'

'Jilly, you look awful, come and sit down. I'll creep back to bed and keep warm, while you tell me what on earth has happened.'

'Oh Cynth, I'm desperately afraid that my Korean posting will be cancelled now. You won't believe this but when I was on duty this morning, Lieutenant Colonel Wright – you know the surgical specialist – happened to be in Sister's office and said he would like a word with me. At first I thought that it affected one of the patients, but no, it was about me.'

'But whatever could he have said to you? Your nursing care is always of the best.' Cynthia interrupted indignantly.

'Well, leaning across the desk, he completely floored me by saying – "Sister, Matron and I have noticed recently, that you have been walking with a pronounced stoop and we are both concerned that you may have something radically wrong with your spine." Then looking at me sternly, he enquired if I had ever suffered from backache or any pain in my lumbar region?'

'Of course I denied this, because apart from feeling dead tired after a session on the wards – and who wouldn't! – I don't! I also explained that I've never had a perfect carriage, saying somewhat limply, that I was probably a bit tired at the moment.

'Colonel Wright then said that he would feel a lot happier if I had a spinal X-ray, to see if there is a problem. Finally concluding with a cheerful – "You see Sister, you could possibly be suffering from a TB spine!" – which as you can imagine, has given me a bit of a jolt.

'Pulling myself together, I said that I wasn't sure whether I should mention this to him in confidence, but I had recently been posted to the new unit in Korea and was due to go over there early next month. Adding pleadingly that at this late stage, I really couldn't bear anything to prevent me from going.

'Smiling kindly at me, he replied, "Lassie, yes I did know, because you were recommended for the job, but at the moment your health is more important. So come along and be a sensible girl, have the X-ray and we can take it from there." And then after almost patting me on the head, he picked up the telephone to ring the radiography department.'

'Poor Jilly, what a dreadful shock, especially just now. But I'm so glad that you've told me and believe me I am truly sorry.' Smiling encouragingly, Cynthia continued, 'Let's look on the bright side. You see if there really is a problem – which I personally think is unlikely – at least you are in the right place to get it mended. And I'm sure too, if the worst happened and your posting was cancelled, then I'm pretty sure the powers-that-be would send you to Korea once things are sorted.

'At least you wouldn't have to suffer the additional worry of frostbite! And to be perfectly honest, Jilly, one or two people in the Mess have noticed your little lean and remarked that you must be feeling a bit weary. I tell you what, if you like and if I can, I'll come to the X-ray department with you.'

'That's great, because my appointment is at 1000hrs tomorrow... Bless you Cynth, that's a wonderful help and you really are a true friend.'

The X-ray resulted in the diagnosis of a partial Spondylolethesis, showing part of my fourth lumbar vertebrae was partially misplaced, which caused me to stoop when overtired. Colonel Wright prescribed an immediate course of intensive physiotherapy to strengthen my muscles, but as I was to go on night duty the following day, he wisely decided to postpone the treatment until after Christmas.

I was much relieved by the verdict, which could have been considerably worse. Although all was not finished until I saw Matron the next morning, when sounding genuinely sympathetic, she explained that under the circumstances, she could not risk sending me to Seoul at present, but if possible promised to do so later on. Her last remark, I am afraid, I took with some disbelief.

Cynthia was a tremendous help, as the bitter disappointment was deflating and for a short period a feeling of tired depression crept over me. Having already completed one week of her fortnight's stint on night duty, she generously asked Matron if she could remain on for an extra seven nights, so that we could be on duty together over Christmas. When I tried to dissuade her, feeling certain that James would wish to take her to the many parties to which we had all been invited, she assured me that during that period he would be away with his boss in Korea, and so she was more than happy to remain on night duty.

Night duty proved to be exceptional, because I was given charge of the main surgical/casualty ward. This tended to be a fast-moving scene with some urgency, especially as we could accommodate up to eighty-four patients. Even the geography was different from the other wards, utilising the whole of the top floor of the tallest building in the hospital.

The ward was divided into three large bays, all similar in design and each bay had about twenty-seven beds with the usual offices of sluice room, lavatories and bathroom. These bays were connected by a lengthy corridor, off which there were three small side wards where seriously ill patients could be quietly nursed. Sister's office and the all-important treatment room were further along, plus the entrance to the wide lift where stretcher cases arrived, and were later transported to the two operating theatres situated on the floor below. So, all in all, it was quite a trek from one end to the other.

Despite continuing to feel flattened by the cancellation of my Korean posting, I very soon settled into my new duties and loved every minute of it. Although my initial reaction to the plight of the patients was one of deep sadness and in a letter to my parents at the time, I wrote, 'It is pitiful to go into the ward, seeing all those young faces drawn with pain – legs and arms in plaster, amputation stumps, bandaged eyes – oh, their poor mutilated bodies – God only knows what it is all for?'

However, I swiftly realised that I was looking after an amazing crowd of patients, whose average age was about twenty. They were indeed a great tonic;

because however painful and serious their condition might be, without exception they were conspicuously bright and cheerful.

My first night on was not quite so busy, with only sixty-nine patients, although in the early morning I did have sixteen lads to prepare for the operating theatre! This procedure began by fixing a small notice above the patient's bed – NIL BY MOUTH – and starving him from midnight.

Early in the morning each was requested to produce a specimen of urine for testing, then before being anaesthetised, his temperature, pulse and respiration rates were recorded, as a rise of temperature could indicate infection. Preparation of the area of his anatomy on which the surgeon's knife would fall was of the utmost importance as a large region of the skin surrounding it had to be thoroughly cleansed and shaved to remove all offending hairs. Then, under sterile conditions, after swabbing thoroughly with an antiseptic solution, a sterile dressing was secured by a bandage. Finally, the patient was dressed in a white cotton theatre gown, with its somewhat embarrassing full-length back opening, tied by three sets of tapes – which the hospital laundry frequently chewed off in transit – plus a matching cap and knee-length, thick, woollen bedsocks!

Usually I had one RAMC nursing orderly to help me and sometimes two if I was really lucky. These nursing orderlies were good and invariably very kind and patient when looking after the injured boys.

Our patients were from many different parts of the Commonwealth, with lads from as far away as South Africa, New Zealand, Canada – two of whom were French speaking – Australia and, of course, a large percentage were our own British soldiers. But no matter what nationality they were, without exception, each one reacted with the same great sense of humour, however grim their personal situation might be.

Many had broken limbs due to gunshot wounds, where shrapnel had shattered the bones. These fractures were generally encased in heavy plaster casts which remained in situ for several weeks, frequently causing not only an unpleasant smell but also an uncomfortable skin irritation, particularly as the wound healed. 'Got a knitting needle, Sister? So I can have a good scratch,' was a frequent request… At times, some severe wounds were rested on a half plaster cast to give maximum support to aid healing. And to prevent further infection, either four-hourly or six-hourly penicillin injections were prescribed or, occasionally, some form of Sulphonamide drug.

Others had had amputations, and quite often following this type of surgery some poor lad might suffer from agonising phantom pains from his amputated foot or even itching between his non-existent toes – of which one of my previous patients had complained. Because of the bitter Korean winter, cases of frost bite were not uncommon, usually where digits or parts of digits were blackened and needed amputating. There was also one little lad who was much bandaged with an eye injury.

Another, Billy in bed seven, was a sweet-tempered Maori of immense proportions, who had been hospitalised for several weeks and was firmly attached by his right leg to a Thomas's splint. His prized possession – from which he could not be parted – was a Spanish guitar, propped up beside his locker. Whenever he was able he would reach down for it, playing and singing softly to everyone's delight.

There were some nights when the majority of the patients seemed to be wakeful and I wondered then if they were missing their families and friends at home. Then, I spent a long time going around the ward with hot milky drinks, in the hope that this might help them to get to sleep.

By the evening of 22 December, the day staff had decorated the ward with brightly coloured bunting, and slowly but surely the Christmas spirit was beginning to affect the boys. When doing my early rounds I noticed that some of the near convalescent patients were more skittish than usual, but imagined this was due to the impending festivities

Just after midnight, when I was creeping past their beds to check if they were sleeping, suddenly and from beneath my feet, there was an almighty bang. Stifling a shriek, I stood motionless in the darkened ward, but as no one stirred I moved on cautiously. Seconds later there was another loud crackle which I ignored, but as I moved on a little further there was a third ear-splitting detonation, and I shrieked – followed instantaneously by muffled sniggering and much laughter as several tousled heads popped up to survey the scene. It was only then I discovered that somehow or other, the wretches had laid a trail of Chinese crackers in my path! As it was, I nearly killed them until they said contritely, 'Oh go on Sister, it was just a bit of fun, 'cos we only wanted to see you jump!'

Actually, they were such a super bunch, so that however rushed I was to get through all I had to do before the day staff took over, these boys were always willing and helpful, busily making wise cracks even at that early hour. Once, when in the middle of doing a sick lad's extensive dressing, he suggested that he should show me how to play Postman's Knock on Christmas Eve! And every morning as I dashed from bed to bed, I seemed to be showered with compliments, including a proposal of marriage from an eighteen year old! From another, there was the gift of a small bar of English chocolate – this I really should not have accepted but I knew that it would be too hurtful to refuse it. On another rushed morning, with an endless list of pre-operatives to prepare, one of the lads as I flew past him with my laden trolley, unwittingly lightened my day with, ''Ere Miss, you don't half look 'andsome this morning...'

Apart from the age-old expectancy of Christmas and all that it meant, for the past few days the whole hospital had experienced something of a rough time, due to the recent strike action taken by the large numbers of Japanese staff employed there (approximately 1,500 in various capacities as theatre and ward orderlies, engineers, plumbers, civilian guards, porters and servants). For several days things were quite chaotic, with no hot water or heating in our quarters whilst the weather was freezing. Far worse, on duty I had seventy-four patients in my care, with very little hot water, few facilities and precious little heating. Adding to our already heavy duties, we had to take our turn at washing-up and cleaning. However, with all of us 'mucking in' with the extra chores, we just about coped.

Thankfully, on the morning of the fourth day of the strike the Japanese decided to return to work – without the monetary increase they were demanding. For us to have unlimited hot water again was pure bliss and for me a lucky escape, because had the strike continued, I had been detailed to clean the bathrooms and lavatories in the quarters during my nights off!

Despite being in the thick of winter, the cockroaches still plagued us, emerging from the cold of the night into the warmth of the wards and even settling down comfortably in my office to the extent of crawling over my desk. Horror of horrors, one fat wretch actually dropped from my cap onto a page of the night report.

After duty on 24th, with some other volunteers, I helped to decorate the garrison church during the morning and by the time we had finished it looked very pretty with masses of fresh flowers.

Amongst the batches of Christmas mail that most of us had received was news of heavy snow falls at home. With fuel rationing still enforced there, we felt that perhaps even in the perishing Japanese winter we were the more fortunate, especially with the prospect of a much earlier and warmer springtime. With Christmas upon us, our thoughts automatically turned towards our families and friends at home and I suspected that even the most hardened felt a qualm of homesickness, which from time to time, affected us all in various ways. For me personally, it was simply a longing for a glass of fresh chilled milk with a slice of brown bread and butter, and after the parched months of a Kure summer to see a green field again.

Missing my family and friends was tempered by mail from home, something much looked forward to by everyone. So far, to avoid causing them concern, I had not told my parents of the real reason for my cancelled Korean posting but instead, had written just a brief note telling them it had been postponed. By Christmas, a long letter from me was overdue.

Women's Services Officers' Mess,
British Commonwealth General Hospital
B.A.P.O.5.
25th December 1952.

Dear M and D,

　　Having just completed my ward rounds and checked that all my patients are flat out – after what they have described as being a really good day – I'm free to scribble a quick line to you.

Here in Japan it's almost midnight and Christmas Day is coming to a close, but with the nine hours time difference, I imagine that at home in Sussex you are recovering after a lovely Christmas Dinner.

Many, many thanks for your greetings cable, which I have stuck safely on my dressing table mirror – I hope too that mine turned up – and also that you have had and are still having a really super day.

Understandably, my Christmas Day has been a quiet one but nevertheless enjoyable. After duty this morning, I walked down to St Peter's for the choral communion service (beautifully sung) then dashed back for breakfast before rushing over to my room to open my parcels – which somehow I'd managed to keep intact until this morning! Never ever, had I felt so utterly spoiled, because simply everyone but everyone at home had remembered me this Christmas, and I felt quite overwhelmed.

Changing into battledress, I returned to the ward to have coffee with the Day Staff, prior to going on to church with Cynthia and other friends. This time the church was absolutely packed and the service was taken by the Senior Army Chaplain, who gave a touching and sympathetic sermon. This left many of us more than a little dewy eyed, especially when singing the national anthem and thinking of those much loved, and far away at home.

Sleeping for the rest of the day, I got up in good time to shower and get dressed (in indoor uniform) before going over to our Mess Christmas Dinner. The large and usually impersonal dining room, was prettily decorated and we had a really enjoyable traditional meal with lots of good food (for a change!). The tiny Father Christmas I've enclosed, was from my place setting and which after dinner I pinned to my Tippet, to cheer up the boys when I went on duty.

This time last night things were not quite so peaceful on the ward, and I had some difficulty in settling them all down. Perhaps this was because it was Christmas Eve, as there was a definite air of excitement even amongst the toughest of the NCOs. Eventually after producing a sea of Horlicks and buckets of tea, I managed to get them to settle quietly at the same time promising that I would do my best to get Santa Claus to call, but only if they went to sleep straightaway! And privately praying that the good ladies of the Red Cross would stand in for him, because they, as far as I knew, would be distributing small gifts to every patient in the hospital, later on.

Soon after midnight when the last of my patients had fallen asleep and I had finished my immediate tasks, I sat at my desk for a short break, where, for a brief moment or two, I was suddenly overwhelmed by an acute sense of isolation. This induced me to feel somewhat sorry for myself, in the realisation that I was missing the many Christmas Eve parties and dances that would be in full swing.

Opportunely, my transient spell of self pity was abruptly broken with the surprise arrival of Mary Innes and Col Wright, who having just returned from a dance, crept into my office to wish me a Happy Christmas, bringing a small gift. I was much touched by their kindness, which immediately vanquished my self inflicted misery!

Half and hour or so after they had left, when I was back once again in the office, I heard an odd shuffling sound coming from the corridor outside. Looking up I was horrified to see one of my patients, a young lad recovering from severe frostbite of both feet, hobbling on crutches through the doorway. My initial reaction was to blast him for being out of bed, however remembering that it was Christmas Eve, I bit my tongue, smiled sweetly and asked 'What is wrong Private Goodson, can't you really get to sleep?' The poor lad appeared to be overcome with embarrassment, his crimson blushes clashing violently with the roots of his ginger hair. Then leaning heavily on his crutches, with great aplomb he plunged his right hand into the bosom of his pyjama jacket, and pulled out a box of gaudily coloured handkerchiefs. Handing these to me, he said 'Happy Christmas Sister!'

Feeling completely overwhelmed by his generosity and before I could open my mouth to thank him, he rushed on, imploring me 'Not to tell the other boys, 'cos they'll only brass me…' from which I gathered, they would pull his leg! After reassuring him, and saying that I should treasure his lovely gift, I saw him safely back to bed. Then bolted back to my office, before giving way to the tears that were prickling hard. At the same time thinking how little most of these young lads actually have in their lives, not only in their pay (approx £1-12-8d per week for national servicemen!) but in every way, and yet they are always prepared to give so much.

Going about my rounds on Christmas morning I tried not to appear to be too rushed (luckily there were no emergency pre-operatives) in order to give me time to wish everyone a Happy Christmas. I found too, that I was being stopped by practically every patient, each of whom gallantly tried to press something into my hand. Individual chocolates, an odd fag here and there and many handshakes. The two nice Canadians were sweet as they shyly thrust a brightly coloured scarf at me, explaining with some embarrassment that they had clubbed together to get it.

Finally I feel, that although it was somewhat discouraging of Ma'am to postpone my Korean posting at the last minute, working on this heavy casualty ward, and caring for these brave bright young and badly injured lads has more than compensated for any initial disappointment. Realising too, that perhaps here in Kure, we are looking after those who need to be nursed, just as much as those who are in Seoul.

Tomorrow afternoon, I'm playing in a hockey match entitled 'Belles-v-Beaux' and on Saturday evening another QA is kindly relieving me until midnight, so that I can go to the Ball!

So glad the food parcel has arrived in time, please let me know when you would like another.

Wishing you both a very happy 1953. With all my love and all my thanks for everything,

Jilly.

'Let's have a coffee in the ante-room before going over to the quarters; there's a free table behind you, Jilly.' Sitting down, Cynthia sighed, 'Isn't it blissful to have finished night duty?'

'Poor Cynth, you must feel absolutely whacked, having just done that extra week for my benefit. You know I can't thank you enough, as it made all the difference to me, especially as I've now got over the hump of not going to Korea.'

'I can't believe that I have the whole week off and better still that James has just got back from Korea, though I do wish that he wasn't returning to the UK so soon.'

'When does he leave Kure?'

'He thinks about the end of next month.'

'Oh Cynth I'm sorry, as I didn't realise that it's only a matter of weeks but then how much longer do you have to do, to complete your eighteen months?'

'About another six, as I'm due to go home in June, which seems such an age to be separated. But Jilly, I'm bursting to tell you – guess what – we are now unofficially engaged. James gave me this for Christmas when he got back late yesterday afternoon – whilst you were preparing for your big date!' Deftly retrieving a slim gold chain concealed beneath her grey uniform collar, she proudly showed me the lovely pearl ring attached to it.

'That's beautiful Cynth and I'm so very happy for you both,' I said, giving her a quick hug. 'That's the best news I've heard for ages. Oh and I've just thought of something! After James has left for the UK, why don't we put in for some R&R leave together, and then really try to see something of Japan whilst we have the opportunity? How about going to Tokyo? What do you think?'

'I might; it's an idea. But tell me Jilly, how did it really go last night? Because so far you haven't said a thing about it. Was it okay? And did you get relieved alright?'

'Yes to the latter question – as to the former – it was a pleasant evening, if somewhat daunting…'

'Tell me.'

'Well, it was quite marvellous to go to my first Christmas party and I suppose, to be honest, half the fun of it was dressing up beforehand, though I must admit that I felt pretty bog-eyed after sleeping throughout the day.

'Briefly, there were eight in our party, seated at a special table at the Club. This had been beautifully arranged down to the smallest detail, with a lovely corsage of flowers for each lady present, the menu was superb and had obviously been hand picked.'

'But what about the Colonel – was he as shy as he is supposed to be; how did you get on?'

'To be truthful, Cynth, it wasn't an awfully easy evening. You know that he is a somewhat quiet person – probably, I should imagine because he is an ex-Japanese

POW – and you know too how stupidly shy I can be. So at times the conversation was a bit sticky. Although he was kind and courteous, as were the rest, apart, of course, from dear Agatha.'

'My God, she wasn't with you, was she? Poor you, you wouldn't have stood a chance with her breathing down the back of your neck.' Lowering her voice, she continued, 'You know too, that she is absolutely hooked on him, but then I suppose she is much more of his age than you are Jilly.'

'Too right! She was just like a protective dragon, positively showing her disapproval of me most of the time, as obviously in her eyes I had no right to be there, being far too young and very junior to boot!'

'How on earth did you cope? As it couldn't have been much fun.'

'Most of the evening, Major Aggie seemed to be trying to attract his attention from me, with her clever and acid remarks, which succeeded in making me feel gauche and uncomfortable. However, after dinner, we managed to have a couple of dances or so, before it was time for me to do my Cinderella act. But wait for it, Cynth, watching me closely as I gathered up my evening bag and wrap, with great aplomb, she rose up from the table and announced to her acquiescent partner that as it was time for Jillian to leave, they would walk Peter and Jillian back to the Mess, so that Peter could then return to the dance with them!'

'She didn't!'

'She did! And not only did they escort us, but dear Aggie clung to Peter's other free arm all the way up the hill and back to the quarters! Actually thinking about it now, it seems so comical, as I tried in vain to thank him for a lovely evening but even this polite gesture was interrupted. So giving in gracefully, I smiled, shook hands and dashed off to change into uniform, before reporting for duty at midnight.

'Damn! I've just remembered that tonight of all nights I am on duty as Orderly Officer – how's that for a restful first night off? Perhaps I should try to have a little kip now.'

'Never mind, at least Susie-*san* will bring you breakfast in bed tomorrow morning.'

'Oh Gosh! I've forgotten to tell you that she has gone! She suddenly left about two days ago but I can't find out what has happened to her. In fact, I did feel quite upset as she was such a good little house-girl, even more particularly because I've just received the pretty pair of shoes which my long-suffering mother kindly sent out to give her for Christmas. Unfortunately, no one has any idea of her whereabouts and I suppose that it's possible that she may have left Kure.'

'What a shame, Jilly What will you do with the shoes?'

'Actually, I was thinking that it would be a nice gesture to give to give them to Shortie-*san*, as she is much the same size as Susie-*san* and she was so helpful in making the costumes for us; what do you think?'

'That's a great idea and I know that she will be thrilled to bits.'

❖

The next five days flew past, merging comfortably into a blurred memory of much sleeping and the luxury of two new novels by Neville Shute to read – my father's Christmas gift which, when finished, would be passed on to the Red Cross Hospital Library. Despite the bitter winds constantly howling around and rattling the ill-fitting windows of our quarters, the complete rest was beneficial.

Since the advent of winter, the state of the roads had become diabolical and I had to invest in a new pair of duty shoes. As usual, it was impossible to buy a pair of black regulation shoes in my size (6), so I had to compromise with a pair of Australian NAAFI beetle-squashers. These were not only half a size too big but were also brown leather, which meant that I had to dye them black. Adding insult to injury, they cost almost £3. In contrast to the gloom of the new shoes, I arranged with the two kind physiotherapists to commence my remedial course as soon as I had returned to day duty. This time, unbelievably, I was to be given charge of my own ward; in Kure one was seldom granted this responsibility below the rank of captain.

On Wednesday, two days before she left for Seoul, I saw Betty to wish her well. I would be sorry to see her go, especially without me, although latterly she had become more involved with her own Australian friends.

For all of us at the BCGH, the final days of 1952 were tragic, with the very sad and premature death of one of our own RAMC nursing orderlies who, despite expert treatment from both medical and nursing staff, died suddenly on 28 December from an undiagnosed disease. Poor little lad, he was only nineteen and everyone was devastated by his swift and untimely death.

New Year's Eve passed quietly. Who was to envisage what 1953 held or what lay ahead? I, with so many others, hoped that it would bring peace.

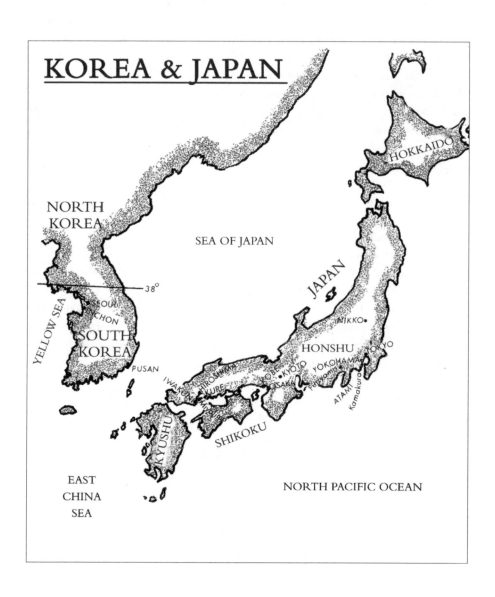

KOREA & JAPAN

NORTH
KOREA

SEA OF JAPAN

HOKKAIDO

JAPAN

— 38°

SEOUL

YELLOW SEA

CHON

SOUTH
KOREA

NIKKO •

HONSHU

TOKYO

PUSAN

KOBE

KYOTO

YOKOHAMA

IWAKUNI

HIROSHIMA

KURE

OSAKA

Fujinomiya

ATAMI

Kamakura

KYUSHU

SHIKOKU

EAST
CHINA
SEA

NORTH PACIFIC OCEAN

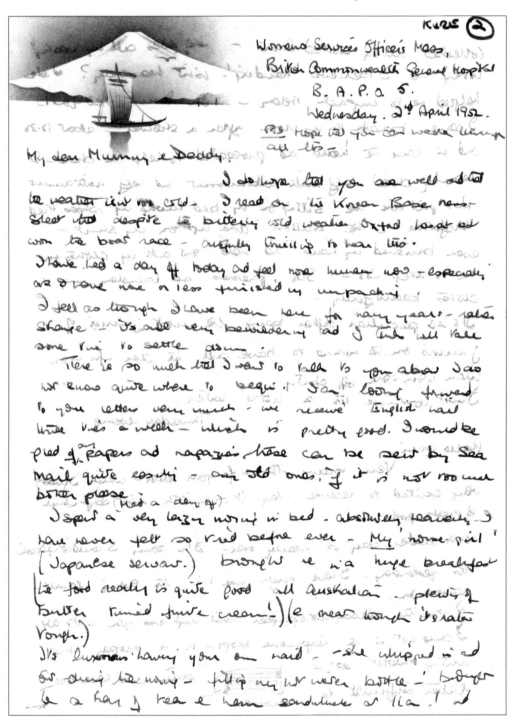

Womens Services Officer's Mess,
British Commonwealth General Hospital
B. A. P. O. 5.
Wednesday. 2nd April 1952.

PS Hope that you are well among all this!

My dear Mummy & Daddy.

I do hope that you are well and that the weather isn't too cold. I read on the Korean Base news-sheet that despite the bitterly cold weather Oxford boat had won the boat race - awfully thrilling to hear this.

I have had a day off today and feel more human now - especially as I have more or less finished my unpacking. I feel as though I have been here for many years - what a change. It's all very bewildering and I think will take some time to settle down.

There is so much that I want to talk to you about I do not know quite where to begin. I am looking forward to your letters very much - we receive English mail twice weekly - which is pretty good. I would be pleased of any papers and magazines these can be sent by Sea mail quite easily - only old ones, if it is not too much bother please. (Had a day off)

I spend a very lazy morning in bed - absolutely heavenly. I have never felt so tired before ever - My 'house-girl' (Japanese servant.) brought me in a huge breakfast (the food really is quite good all Australian - plenty of butter tinned fruit & cream!) (a near though it's rather rough.)

It's luxurious having your own maid - she whipped in and out during the morning - filling my hot water bottle - brought me a tray of tea & ham sandwiches at 11am. & at collected all my soiled linen — she does all my washing, ironing and I believe mending'. Isn't heavenly? She helped me to unpack today — Oh I must tell you — I came back to my room after a shower — about 12.30 — and in came the maid and proceeded to help me dress — I nearly died half with embarrassment and half with amusement. Just picture me sitting on my bed having my shoes tied on for me and the buttons done up on my shirt — even brushed my hair' and held out all my clothes for me to step into — She presses and launders my clothes beautifully.

It's so peculiar after being the most junior of juniors on the ward to have all this done for you when you come off duty.
I must continue this a 'little' later.

Thursday evening.

Hallo again',

Very many thanks for your letter — which I was very excited to receive today — it only took eight days which is pretty good.

Well another day is nearly over — I'm sorry I couldn't finish this yesterday — I have much more time this evening, so will ramble on.

I hope this classy notepaper will impress you — it's all I could get in the Japanese shops — on a proper Jap writing tablet so — Later difficult to narrower. which would have been

2   There is an ~~another~~ archway just
like this to a Jap. temple
just below us - I have been
in it several times, quite
fascinating & weird - with a
peaceful atmosphere.

I must describe Kure to you - To be honest it is not
an impressive place by any manner of means - the
harbour is quite large - the docks are rather grim -
with shocking roads - terrible holes - all the road
around here are in an awful state, though apparently
far better than they were when this hospital first opened.
Everything is dusty and the dust seems to penetrate everywhere -
The town is fairly large - all little (mud streets) more or less of
wooden shops - most of them look as though they
would collapse very easily! Kure is surrounded by
very high hills - and one view of it is rather similar to
that of Hong Kong.
The Mess, is a huge place situated about 10 mins walk
or less from the town up a hill - we have delightful little gardens
in the mess & in the hospital which is a huge
rather ungrown collection of white buildings - 10 mins
from the mess - It was a Japanese hospital - and
the Japs are trying now (through the Peace Treaty)
to get it back for a training school - so I do
not know what will happen about it.
The Japanese are wonderful - with gardens and amazing
flowers - which are highly beautiful though very

expensive. There are all the spring flowers that you can buy at home (to buy.) the tulips - daffodils - snowdrops with stalks of 12 - 14 inches long! Also marigolds - and such flowers that we would have in the blossom - wallflowers - etc - and of course all different types of blossom - peach etc and the flowers come out before the leaves! Today is the special cherry blossom anniversary day for the Jap - I was too weary to change into battledress wear - I came off duty tonight - otherwise I would have gone into Kure to see what was happening (we have to wear uniform all the time except in the mess & the officers club, and for walks - in the hills.)

The gardens are sweet - mostly, rock gardens on a fairly large scale - usually with a pond - fountain little bridges and stone houses and a few trees - sort of willow pattern though they are not really - We have a very attractive lighting arrangement - large lamp in a little wooden house so! - and the gardens - in the front of the quarters & the mess.

Inside the mess is very attractive - here is every facility - a powder room for ladies - a room for gardener and then you walk into the largest room I have ever seen, it is delightfully furnished - blue carpets - lovely comfortable chairs & settees -

covered in a very attractive
red - little highly polished
coffee tables - a ceiling
of ☐☐☐ squares & ? bamboo

3 fans - lights and some Japanese pictures -
here are flowers everywhere - beautifully arranged -
huge shallow bowls with tulips - and a little miniature
Japanese vase in one of our etc - there is a
little room to the right - which is called 'The
Brother's Room' and if you have any 'other rank'
friends - you may invite them in there which is very
nice - Andrew was sick up and come to Japan
I think on the whole we live exceptionally well -
The Dining Room is large and airy and there are
about a dozen separate tables -
We have breakfast at 7am (on duty 7.30am) lunch
between 12 - 1.30 pm - (tea in our rooms if we are
off duty -) and dinner about 5.30 or 6.30 pm -
At 9 pm - tea & is served on Fridays -
and lots of delicious sandwiches and there first
cake every night - Its very friendly - because you
can have do many friends in in here every as
you like - and feed them on these trips (for
but we have any new idens they save all for us Knee)

5.

I was not angrily cross — because I didn't have a camera on the boat and missed many opportunities of wonderful views — I hope to send a few odd snaps later that were taken by different people when they are developed.

One feels in this hospital that one is working for something — its very name — British Commonwealth General Hospital — describes it. (We wear a superior flash on our battledress — at least I haven't bought mine yet and I believe that we get a 'gong' a service medal at the end of our tour of duty — here — I am dying for something to liven up my cape!) There is even nationalities here — Australian, New Zealander, Canadian, French Canadian — Turks — I believe etc. I am on the officers' ward and on the whole here are very few British officers — I like the New Zealanders but so few — though the Australians are very friendly — the Australian sisters have been far more pleasant to us than our own QAs.

There may be a slight chance — of some of us going to Korea — it is all very doubtful and vague but I suppose if there is a big 'Push' — somewhere

they can send one Q. As —
If I ever have the opportunity
of — that I doubt: because I
am a junior and not the one
trained — I shall jump at it and go like a shot.
I feel desperately sorry for these boys coming back —
they are filthy have no facilities for washing — the
awful dust gets everywhere and takes ages to get it out
of their hair etc — I not be seen sleeping in a
fox hole with the rats & things, poor little boys —
One of the very young 2nd Lts in my ward has lost
his leg — he is only a National Serviceman and it is an
awful shame — he was an excellent Rugger player —
another New Zealander — has been burnt, seventy both arms
up to the elbows and all over his face — he is
so patient — and much better than goodness.
They are all so cheery about it despite
the awful grimness of everything.

I shall never forget watching these boys disembarking
at Pusan — the eldest of them looked only about 18 —
all trying to look so grown up and brave —
and the time young officers that got off — one
had just been engaged and was awfully upset about

it all, there were Sappers to go in first
coping with mine fields.
come out last — I think that they are all quite wonderful
boys — both officers & men — & are all so very young
to go to such a loathsome place.

Must tell you about the climate — the weather is very hot at
the noons in the afternoons — bitterly cold at night & in the
morning when we get up. It poured with rain incessantly
all day on Monday — I had to buy a large Japanese
umbrella — | 3| 6!) (pure silk 35/-) It's awful rain
and apparently in July here is the rainy season &
it rains for two weeks nearly at a time — wasn't I glad I didn't bargain
for — the summer is remarkably hot & humid very
much like Singapore which I hated! The monsoon had to
in about six weeks — & it won't rain again

For our leave we can go to several different places
one a sacred island from here called Mia Jima — which
takes a 1½ hr launch to get there a 3 hrs by train —
we only have 5 days every 4 mths with two days
travelling allowed — it's very little really 15 days a
year — everybody looks tired — though the food —
food etc — I expect to the climate.
The Japanese women & girls are sweet and laugh &
giggle all the time. The men are rather dour — and have
look at you. (to like anyone coming like bear in!)
You call — old women Momma San — & young men
'Girl San,' Poppa-San — Boy San — & are called
'Sister-San' by the Japanese advertisers —
Hubba-Hubba means hurry up!

CHAPTER EIGHT
WINTER WINDS

IN KOREA ON 11 FEBRUARY 1953, GENERAL VAN FLEET RETIRES
AND GENERAL MAXWELL D. TAYLOR ASSUMES COMMAND OF
EIGHTH ARMY. GENERAL MARK CLARK PROPOSES AN EXCHANGE
OF SICK AND WOUNDED POWs.

Winter, and January in particular, were synonymous with dark leaden skies, flurries of snow and icy winds whipping through our uniforms as we struggled on and off duty. Huddled in heavy greatcoats we wore thick gloves, snow boots, illicit scarves and anything we had to protect us from the penetrating cold. Simultaneously we could only surmise over the conditions in Korea, where we knew that the temperature was sub-zero. Already I had heard that burns admissions had increased, mainly due to the malfunction of petrol heaters. Fortunately, in Kure our patients were as comfortable and warm as possible with the hospital heating on at full blast, unlike our own quarters where we were still rationed by day, and with no heating at all at night!

This meant that preparing for bed each night was quite a task, having to pile everything from greatcoat, travelling rug, jerseys into a huge mound on top of the bedding and then my ancient and overworked hot water bottle, Little Fatty, became a real lifesaver. Clutching this closely, I would climb into bed wearing a woolly cardigan over flannel pyjamas tucked into a pair of thick bed socks, which my kind Mama had recently sent to me, ostensibly for my Korean posting.

Saddest of all was the news from home of the tragic loss, on 31 January 1953, of the MV *Princess Victoria*, during a violent storm in the Irish Sea, followed shortly by devastating floods which hit the English coast from Norfolk to Canvey Island. This resulted in a further loss of 300 lives and much destruction. A few days later, the highest tide in recorded history breached eighty dykes on the Dutch coast, causing massive flooding and the drowning of 1,800 people.

❖

However, all was not gloom and doom in Kure. Soon after taking over Ward Eight – the isolation ward – I invested in a huge bunch of spring flowers to chase the winter blues away: crimson tulips, stately blue irises and masses of sweet-smelling yellow and white jonquils. These I arranged in a large, shallow Japanese cream china bowl, placing them on a small table just inside the ward entrance. As most of the patients were nursed in separate rooms, we left their doors open so they could smell the fragrance.

The isolation ward was a single building situated a short distance away from the main hospital; it was bright, spacious and designed to accommodate approximately twenty patients. Understandably, life on this ward was necessarily less hurried and conducted at a quieter pace. At the time I took charge there were only five patients, and for me this was an astronomical difference in numbers after the seventy-five or so I had had in my care over Christmas. This was an unbelievable bonus and meant that I was able to give each patient the individual attention needed, to help combat the tuberculosis from which they were all suffering.

For once I was blessed with sufficient staff, having some excellent Japanese orderlies and two exceptionally well-trained RAMC lads, and although from a previous spell on night duty I was already familiar with the ward, each time I popped in to see the sick men, observing their gaunt faces and thin, wasted bodies, I left feeling sad and somewhat dejected. They were such young boys – with one exception and he was only about five years older than the others. Putting things into perspective, I realised that I must do my damnedest to ensure that each one should gain as much weight as possible by augmenting their high protein diet with frequent egg flips, specially nourishing jellies and extra milk.

Apart from the significance of diet and their treatment – this was generally intramuscular injections of Streptomycin, in combination with either Isoniazid or PAS (Para-aminosalicylic acid) tablets administered orally – daily routine was of the utmost importance. This was to guarantee complete physical and mental rest avoiding any unnecessary exertion. The Red Cross ladies helped to keep them occupied with light occupational therapy, weaving scarves on tiny portable looms, and library books for those who felt like reading. Attached to the bedheads were earphones for listening to the local Forces radio, broadcast from somewhere outside Kure. To be confined to bed rest for so many weeks must have been tedious; however, the one bright spot that kept them going, was the thought of being repatriated to the UK, once they had gained the magic weight and were fit enough for the long voyage home.

Personally, I was grateful to Matron for assigning me to Ward Eight because apart from the challenge ahead the actual nursing care was far less heavy than previously, giving me some respite, whilst I myself was attending the Physiotherapy Department on almost a daily basis. After an hour of intensive exercises and treatment, it frequently felt as though my muscles had been dragged from their tendons, and as these sessions were usually in my off-duty time, there was little left for relaxation! The two physiotherapists were more than helpful, encouraging me along the way and after several weeks of unaccustomed aches and pains, I began to realise just how beneficial the treatment was.

Not for long did the unhurried calm prevail, as within only a few weeks the ward was full, due to an aggregation of the bitter weather and an acute shortage of medical beds. Every room was occupied, often with an extra bed and filled with an overflow of sick lads, suffering from the usual winter ailments of influenza, tonsillitis and bronchitis. Additionally, a number of the hospital staff were also afflicted. Consequently, we had to lend most of our orderlies to the depleted wards and were rushed off our feet, and there were several times when I was on duty with no staff at all.

Fortunately, despite this extra activity, most of my TB patients – who were well isolated from the medical ones – had all gained at least 4–5lb in weight, so the egg flips were really paying off, and hopefully they would be ready for repatriation quite soon; all but one poorly little lad who worried me, because despite all our well-intentioned efforts, Private Sampson had gained practically nothing and continued to look emaciated and suffer from irregular spikes in temperature, with night sweats.

Cynthia was also frantically busy, working on the huge casualty ward again. Finally, late one night, we managed to catch up with each other, in time to make some hot cocoa before crawling off to our respective beds. Whilst we were chattering away, all of a sudden the windows began to rattle, the furniture started to slide and the floor shook ominously. But before we could utter 'What next?' the uncanny vibrations subsided as quickly as they had begun – only to recommence moments later, for a second and last time. Following the two strong tremors, we both felt a sense of quiet eeriness, realising once again just how vulnerable we could be.

Neither the weather nor the pressure of work had abated by the middle of February, by which time the majority of sisters were beginning to look peaky.

Privately, I was finding my intensive physiotherapy course totally draining and Cynthia, too, was under the weather having recently had an awful cold. So after deciding to try for some much needed leave, we both applied to Matron to be granted a week's R&R leave from 8 March, with permission to spend it in Tokyo. Ma'am nodded her approval, at the same time admonishing us in sober terms, 'Depending on the exigencies of the Service!'

Luckily for me, one of the compensations of working on the isolation ward was the extra 3s per day I received as special pay. Admittedly, 8d of that was automatically deducted for income tax but the rest would be a real bonus for my holiday, as Tokyo was reputedly very expensive.

Sadly, my poorly twenty-year-old Private Sampson remained far from well, which was a continuous anxiety. He was such a stoical lad but despite all the tender loving care, egg flips and high protein diet, his weight remained at just over seven stone, when normally he was about eleven. Worst of all he looked so ill, with the typical fragile sallowness, luminous eyes and hollowed cheeks of a Tuberculosis patient. Talking to him, I discovered that he had only been married three weeks before sailing for Korea and I felt certain then – that like many of us coping with the bleak winter months – he was feeling desperately homesick.

There was also some depressing news via the grapevine: rumour had it that a Korean girl was to be publicly hanged for passing information to the enemy. The war seemed relentless in its tireless destruction of the young.

When walking through Kure during the recent icy weather, I noticed that a large number of the Japanese men who were out and about were wearing face masks. To me this appeared a quaint habit, especially as the masks closely resembled the white cotton ones worn for surgical procedures in hospital. However, I learned later that these were worn as a precautionary measure to avoid upper respiratory tract infections.

As the month of February passed the weather improved and the days began to lengthen, enabling the nice old Momma-*san* to push out her wooden hand-cart, which once again was laden with beautiful spring flowers and masses of early peach and plum blossom. Unexpectedly, one afternoon I came across a small orange tree positively laden with tiny, glittering fruit.

With the improvement in the weather, the number of winter associated illnesses decreased, greatly relieving the pressure of work on the wards. Already I had been looking after the isolation ward for eight weeks when latterly we had admitted and nursed various conditions ranging from scarletina, dysentry, tonsillitis and a lad very ill with meningitis. Marvellously, all the TB patients were responding well to their treatment and even Private Sampson appeared to have turned the corner at last, and was just beginning to gain some weight.

One of my kind patients presented me with the lovely Royal Stewart tartan scarf which he had woven; he had made two but told me that he had christened the other one the Commonwealth tartan, as it was full of mistakes! He was probably right as, at times, even our own Commonwealth Unit at the BCGH did not always jell…

On Shrove Tuesday (17 February), with few of us having paid much attention to the date, at lunchtime we were totally amazed to be given proper pancakes for pudding. This was unbelievable, especially after suffering the unappetising and tasteless Japanese apple-pears frequently plonked on our plates. This and other culinary improvements were a due to Captain Jess Milton QA, who had recently been lumbered with the unenviable task of Home Sister. Jess, ever resourceful, brilliantly undertook to train the Japanese cook-boys, so that sometimes we even had homemade rock buns for tea.

By then it was just a year since I sailed from Southampton and now, twelve months later, I appreciated the wise old saying that travel broadens the mind. This was reinforced with an invitation for Cynthia and me to attend the Japanese tea ceremony at a tea-house on the outskirts of Kure.

Cha-no-yu (Japanese for tea ceremony) is basically a religious cult, its origins stemming from the time when the Zen monks sipped tea together, and for the Japanese it is a mental discipline for pursuing a state of mind in which a person is calm and content. The ceremony usually takes place in a special tea-house reserved for the purpose, or alternatively in a private house, but wherever the venue, the ceremony is always performed with dignity and grace.

It was another grey and chilly Sunday, with a frigid wind tugging at our caps as we trudged down a narrow side road, small map in hand trying to identify the tea-house. This we eventually found, nestling in a cluster of similar little houses, and on arrival discovered there were another seven guests. These included a couple of servicemen and the rest were Japanese. As we gathered outside the tea-house, we were met by a Japanese gentleman who led us through the small garden to a rocky spring of running water, adjacent to the house. There he instructed us – in English – first to cleanse our hands, then to rinse out our mouths in the pure cold water, and this no less than three times each.

After the ritual cleansing we were told to remove our shoes and then, sliding open a small side door, he himself bent double before guiding us through an extremely low and narrow entrance, at the same time explaining this was traditionally designed to ensure that as guests entered the tea-room they were forced to bow, thereby humbling themselves sufficiently to lose any sense of importance they might have.

Entering the room, I was immediately impressed by its chaste simplicity, although neither room nor chamber was an adequate description of what seemed to be an oasis of oriental calm. Here we were welcomed most courteously by the smiling Momma-*san* in charge of the ceremony, and rewarded with a shy smile from her teenage daughter who was helping her. Both of them were splendidly attired in their national costume. Momma-*san* spoke quietly in English with a marked American accent, whilst she showed us to our individual *tatamis* (the large, woven rush floor mats). Obeying her instruction, we sank down onto them, squatting on our heels, for what ultimately seemed to be an unconscionably prolonged time.

As the two ladies busily prepared their utensils and the tea, I slowly glanced around, taking note of the surroundings whilst absorbing the atmosphere of unhurried calm. The room was about 15ft square with plain, whitewashed walls, sparsely furnished by Western standards with only a few brightly coloured cushions and *tatamis* arranged on the plain wooden floor. These were set in a large circle so that all the guests faced each other. The most striking area of the tearoom was the small alcove situated at the far end. In this recess hung an exquisite silk scroll, or *kakejiku*, painted in a typical oriental mix of misty greys. On the tiny dais below it, a miniature arrangement of delicate spring flowers furnished the little alcove with a shrine like appearance.

Our two hostesses were seated on mats in the middle of the floor and prepared the tea in a complicated fashion over an hibachi. This was a small circular charcoal stove used to heat both the water and, somewhat meagrely, the room. The senior hostess then explained how traditionally all utensils and bowls used in the process were handed down through the generations and that the tea we would drink was a special type of powdered green tea, originally introduced to Japan from China long ago. As the preparations continued, she explained (in some depth) the history of each utensil. I was much taken with one of them – which to me closely resembled a shaving brush – called a *chasen* and which she later used to stir the tea! She also told us the detailed meaning of every movement, finally instructing us on how to conduct ourselves throughout the impending ritual.

When all was ready, I was surprised to see that unlike in our own society where once the tea has been made, it is poured for everyone, in Japan only one person at a time is served, therefore lengthening the procedure by having to make a fresh bowl of tea for each guest. When at last my turn came, our exceedingly polite hostess ceremoniously handed me a lovely lacquered bowl of steaming frothy pea-green fluid. Remembering the etiquette as instructed, bowing low I accepted it, then turning to the person sitting on my right (who in fact had already been served), enquired, 'Will you have another bowl of tea?' He had previously been instructed to say 'No'. Then turning to the guest on my left I asked her politely, 'May I have this bowl of tea please?' After she had gracefully inclined her head, the crunch came when I had to drink it, which according to custom must be done in exactly three gulps, and after the final swallow, to show my sincere appreciation, I was supposed to add an elongated squelchy sucking sound. But having had something of a struggle to drink the strangely bitter brew, instead I woefully smiled my thanks, before completing the ritual of admiring the cherished bowl and returning it to my long-suffering hostess, with yet another bow.

After the ninth and final guest had partaken of their fill, to my dismay, I realised that it was going to be seconds all round, as we started the painfully slow process all over again. This time, however, the tea tasted less bitter and was quite refreshing, and I had by then become accustomed to the long quiet pauses between the preparation and consumption of each bowl of tea. These, we understood, were to enable the guests to meditate, or was it to contemplate? If only my knees had not been so painfully cramped, my thoughts might well have glided to a higher plane!

To make matters worse, during these complicated procedures neither Cynthia nor I could really keep a straight face. Glancing at her occasionally, I detected that she was suffering just as intensely as I was – from excruciating cramp and an uncontrollable desire to giggle… Two hours later, after the ceremony concluded and we were some distance away from the tea-house, our joint suppressed giggling burst into a loud cacophony of laughter.

Sunday 1 March started both early and ignominiously. Walking back to breakfast after Early Service, I happened to pass the Major-Ma'am on her way over to the hospital. Stopping dead in her tracks, she looked witheringly at me before remarking, 'Hall, you really must do something about your hair, it's far too long and very untidy.' And having delivered her message, she stalked off. To begin with it was a drizzly sort of day, I had got up in a rush to get over to church by 0800hrs and by cramming on my khaki cap neither I nor my hair had had a chance! So by the time I had reached the Mess I was positively fuming, but comfortingly over breakfast I was able to have a good moan to my friends, several of whom, I discovered, had suffered similarly…

However, although the English mail had been delayed (yet again), by midday life had much improved, with an unexpected opportunity to meet the Countess of Limerick from the British Red Cross at a small sherry party in our Mess. She was staying there whilst engaged on a short tour of Kure, having just visited Korea. The Countess was keenly interested in all aspects of the hospital care and I was impressed by her kind face, charming manner and genuine concern.

Four days later, with only two left before Cynthia and I were due to take off on our great Tokyo adventure, we still had no idea of our mode of travel – whether it would be by plane on Sunday or rail on Monday morning. Thursday was also a red-letter day as, to my relief, I completed my physiotherapy course that afternoon. Thanks to all the hard work and encouragement from the two kind physiotherapists, my muscles were much stronger and it was wonderful to feel really fit again.

Saturday 7 March in many ways was somewhat sad for me as I handed over my ward, although not as sad as it might have been, because on the previous Wednesday morning all six of my TB patients had embarked safely on the *Empire Fowey*. I was overjoyed when, at the eleventh hour, the medical officer pronounced that Private Sampson was fit enough to stand the voyage home, having miraculously gained sufficient weight just in the nick of time. These young lads had expressed their thanks very sweetly, by dedicating a special request on the Forces Radio programme for the doctors and nursing staff of Ward Eight, who had done so much to help them.

Banging excitedly on her door, I yelled, 'Cynth, are you there? I've got them – we're goin'…' As she opened it, I waved two leave passes at her, as she swallowed a mouthful of toothpaste.

'Matron's just given me these and guess what? We are flying to Tokyo tomorrow.' Flopping onto her bed with a handful of papers, 'I can't believe our luck, can you?'

'That's wonderful, Jilly, but Help!' she exclaimed with apprehension, 'didn't I tell you that I've never flown before?'

'Don't worry, neither have I and I'm sure we shall be okay. Anyway, these are our travelling instructions and Ma'am told me that a Tilly will pick us up at 0900hrs to take us to the ferry terminal to catch the 1000hrs work boat to the RAAF station at Iwakuni. Once there we shall be informed about the actual flight time to Tokyo.'

'Nervous as I may be about flying, I do think it's generous of Qantas Airways to give us a free passage. Did you realise that as part of their war effort they keep any spare seats for servicemen on leave?'

'I did and totally agree, but to more practical matters, I guess now it's confirmed we'd better finish our packing. Shall I stow the biscuits and chocolate I got in the NAAFI for our emergency rations? And shall we sort out the holiday budget over a cup of cocoa tonight?'

'Good idea. Oh, I've just realised, now that we are flying to Tokyo, and not spending eighteen hours on the leave train, we shall also have the time to visit Nikko.'

By the time we met for cocoa, we were packed and ready to go. Cynthia suggested, 'Shall we use this old purse for the kitty ?'

'Let's. Here's my contribution of five quid and ten bob but do you really think that is sufficient?'

'Thanks Jilly, it should be heaps as it's only to cover our extras, local train fares, theatre tickets, special trips, etc.'

'How much actual pocket money are you taking, because I shall have another £5 10s on me – will that also be enough?'

'Mmm, I should think that's fine. Quite honestly I can't afford any more because, as we're only allowed to draw out £15 from our salaries here, I'll have to manage on what's left of it until the end of the month,' she sighed.

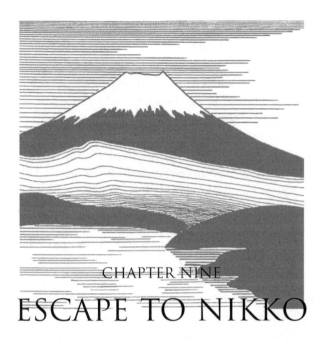

CHAPTER NINE

ESCAPE TO NIKKO

8 March 1953

'Good morning, Ma'am – or should I say Ma'ams?' smiled the nice staff-sergeant as he examined our papers. 'Going off on a spot of leave are you? Well you've got a bright sunny start to the day. Leave your luggage here and go forward please.' Saluting smartly, he turned to check in the next passengers, whilst we dumped our suitcases and picking up our black shoulder bags and mackintoshes we climbed on board the work boat.

Seeing there was still a choice of seats we bagged two up in the bow of the small launch to skim again across the lovely Inland Sea, but this time heading for Iwakuni on the mainland, which was some distance beyond Miyajima.

'We're off.' I whispered, as the engine started up and the mooring ropes were flung onto the quayside. Minutes later we headed out from the calm waters of the harbour and into the choppy waves. The weather was brilliant and the sea a peacock blue, although a stiff breeze caused the boat to bob about.

Disembarking two and a half hours later, we were driven to the RAAF Mess at Iwakuni, where we were informed by the Australian Transit Officer that our plane was not due to take off for at least another four hours.

After a snack, the time soon passed as there was much activity to engage us, with various military planes landing and taking off. Of these, the flying boats were particularly fascinating and we held our breath as they lumbered across the water in a seemingly laboured and noisy ascent, finally to disappear into the clouds.

'Was that really us this time, Jilly?'

'Yes, it really is the Qantas flight to Tokyo, calling all passengers to embark NOW!'

'Oh Lord! This is it then,' said Cynthia with feeling, as we grabbed our belongings to board the shabby old khaki transit bus which had just ground to a halt at the entrance. Then, with the other thirty or so passengers, we clattered and bounced across an uneven concrete track, to the runway ahead.

'Gosh, look at that, it's so elegant – do you think it's...'

'Our plane – yes – it must be, everyone's getting off – come on!' I urged as, looming over us, we saw the graceful, silver-grey Skymaster, waiting to transport us to Tokyo.

Stationed at the top of the short stairway were two smartly uniformed air stewardesses welcoming the passengers. One of them ushered Cynthia and me through the cabin to two forward seats on the left-hand side of the aircraft.

'You sit next to the window please, Jilly, as I'd be much happier sitting beside the aisle.'

'Thanks, I'd love to,' and with a frisson of excitement I sank into the comfort of the well-upholstered seat. Pampering us with pillows, cushions and even a rug to ward off the cold, the stewardess also showed us how to adjust our seat belts, and where to find the sick-bags...

On board the flight we reckoned there were at least thirty-six passengers, the majority of whom were servicemen, and from their lively chatter imagined that most of them like us were going on leave.

Moments later the overhead screen flashed 'Fasten seat belts' and simultaneously the slight vibration in the cabin increased in intensity, rapidly breaking into a crescendo as we began to taxi along the airstrip, when finally, after a sudden powerful burst and something of a shudder, we took to the air.

'Phew! That wasn't too bad, was it?'

'No, I hate to admit it and – I did have my fingers crossed all the time – but it was fine,' Cynthia said with relief.

Gazing intently through the tiny window, I was captivated by the detailed view emerging below us and, nudging Cynthia's arm, exclaimed, 'Look down there – I can't believe this – that must be Kure. There's the harbour with the sea just beyond it.' Checking my watch I added incredulously: 'But that's amazing because it's only about five minutes since we took off and to think that it actually took us over two and a half hours to get from Kure to Iwakuni by boat!'

Like Cynthia I, too, had expected to feel somewhat nervous during my first flight but instead, to our mutual surprise, we quickly settled down to enjoy the next few hours in unaccustomed luxury.

Although like most people in the twenty-first century, I have since flown quite extensively and much further afield, never have I forgotten the first sheer thrill of flying, nor the glow of that golden afternoon where myriads of tiny islands glittered like opalescent pearls on a grey silk sea. And later, I watched the changing brilliance of the setting sun, as it caressed the snow-capped mountains intensifying from diffuse pink to deep crimson. Finally it bathed the majestic bulk of sacred Fuji-*san*, immortalising the volcanic rim in burnished copper.

This was truly beginner's luck and later proved to be the one and only occasion when I actually saw Mount Fuji, despite attempts at other times.

The flight itself was smooth until we were past Nagoya and approaching the mountains, when suddenly we began to bump about. To the uninitiated this was a bit unnerving, especially as the interior of the cabin gradually darkened as we flew towards ominously black clouds. 'Fasten seat belts' flashed urgently, as the bumping and bouncing increased. For a while we felt confidently unaffected, until from my window seat I saw an evil-looking cloud of epic proportions looming ahead, just in time to warn Cynthia to 'Hang on, we'll be okay'. Crashing on through it, the plane shuddered violently, as simultaneously – but fortunately for only a brief interval – we experienced a terrifying sensation of falling, before the plane regained its stability and passed through the buffeting clouds.

'My God, that was a near one!' exclaimed a pale-faced Cynthia. 'But I'm damned if I'm going to be sick!' Soon afterwards, the captain announced the turbulence had been caused by a combination of strong winds and heavy cloud formation and that despite what had appeared to be a rapid descent, the plane had only dropped about a hundred feet. He also assured us that the remainder of the flight would be calm.

True to his word it was, with no more excitement until Cynthia leant across to point out of the window saying, 'Jilly, that must be Tokyo – just look at all those millions of lights down there,' and within moments we dipped gracefully to land at Tokyo's Haneda Airport. A cool breeze greeted us as we descended from the warmth of the Skymaster into the twilight, where a wealth of brilliantly lit, neon signs dominated the airport. As we walked across the tarmac to another somewhat shabby Forces leave bus, which was to take us on the final stage of our journey, we passed several huge international airliners, realising we had indeed arrived at one of the world's major capital cities.

An hour later, after jolting through the neat suburban districts and on to the outskirts of the city, we arrived at the Ebisu Leave Centre and Hotel. This was a vast complex of leave facilities specifically catering for all ranks of the Commonwealth Forces.

Checking into the hotel, Cynthia and I could hardly believe our luck when we were allocated a large and pleasantly furnished twin-bedded room, with the added attraction of a private bathroom.

Arriving late as we had, there was not time to indulge in the luxury of a bath before dinner, having only a few minutes to wash and change, before dashing downstairs to find the dining room, just in time for the last sitting and where we gorged ourselves on all five courses.

❖

Monday 9 March was our first real day of leave and after sleeping soundly for over nine hours Cynthia, waking up just after me, muttered, 'Breakfast?'

'Try ringing the bell and see what happens.'

As if by magic, a smiling little Japanese girl-*san* appeared, proffering a menu and enquiring, 'You likee breakfast now? Pleese to choose from card.'

This was unbelievable, especially the four courses which followed, and when later that morning we discovered that the actual cost of staying at the leave hotel was even more unbelievable – at a mere 3*s* each, per day. Cynthia sagely remarked, 'For all this and heaven too!'

Sensibly we rested up that morning which gave us an opportunity to catch up with our correspondence – Cynthia writing lengthily to James and me to my long suffering parents – thus leaving us free to explore Tokyo and its environs during the next few days. We also took time to explore the luxurious bathroom with its gleaming black and white tiles, spacious bath and sparkling chromium taps, taking it in turn to wallow in gallons of hot water, thankfully shedding the last vestige of fatigue.

After lunch, we set out to explore a little of Tokyo, conveniently travelling into the city by electric train on the nearby suburban line. On arrival, we were amazed at its immensity as we walked for seemingly miles along the neat pavements, passing numerous large and impressive buildings. Tokyo was considerably cleaner and more pleasant than Kure and it was a joy to walk through well-maintained streets, occasionally stopping to admire the many and varied shop windows. Studying our little map, we soon found the famous Ginza, reputedly the most exclusive shopping area and equivalent of Bond Street but, however much it was cracked up to be, neither of us was really much impressed. Our guide book referred to the up-to-date fashions to be admired in the Ginza. Rather sadly though, these appeared to be an unhappy mixture of East and West, resulting in a combination of styles that rarely suited, and as we jostled our way through the busy streets we observed this strange mix again and again. Groups of businessmen immaculately dressed in dark silk kimonos, shod in the traditional *geta*, but in quaint contrast wearing smart black trilbys and carrying expensive leather briefcases. There, too, we saw many beautiful Japanese ladies, most of whom were attired in a similar blend of part East and part West and these I felt sorry for, realising then how difficult it must be to adjust to such a rapidly changing culture.

The high spot of the day was our visit to the illustrious Kabuki-Za Theatre, arriving there in the nick of time to buy tickets for the evening performance scheduled at the early hour of 1630hrs. The seats, which were in the Gods, cost the equivalent of 3*s* each and were located on the high balcony of this large and quite modern theatre. The Kabuki was equally renowned for its dazzling productions of the old classical plays of Japan and for its cast of all-male actors, the majority of whom were trained to take the feminine roles – the antithesis of the Takarazuka Theatre in Kyoto.

We had been lucky to get the seats, as the house was packed for the full six-hour programme billing of three plays. The first two of these were brilliantly acted and much complimented by the splendid costumes, magnificent wigs, traditional masks worn by the accomplished cast, imaginative stage effects and fantastic scenery, with the entire performances bound together by the continuous and spellbinding strains of the *shamisen*. Despite the language barrier and with the help of a translated summary, we managed to follow most of the dialogue, much preferring the second play, *Kocho*. Based on a 700-year-old legend, we were soon transported into the realms of ancient Japan, as the story was narrated in great detail of how the infant Emperor Tenno was shipwrecked, and in the arms of his good nurse, the Lady Ni, slowly sank to the bottom of the sea... This was strong emotional stuff and incredibly produced with the ship sinking as the stage discreetly revolved, and the passengers realistically drowning as they disappeared one by one through a camouflaged trap door.

Bumping back into reality within a few minutes of the commencement of the final play, Cynthia and I experienced a sudden and somewhat chilling change in the atmosphere of the auditorium which rapidly transformed from one of calm intensity and national pride, to a noisy bawdiness. We noticed too a marked restiveness affecting the majority of the male audience, who were becoming increasingly boisterous; some shouting out what seemed to us to be ribald remarks – albeit in Japanese! Hastily realising that we two were probably the only foreigners in the audience whilst concurrently getting some odd looks from a nearby group of Japanese men, we decided that we had seen enough, baled out smartly, and then ran most of the way back to the station where, thankfully, we plopped onto the first available train!

The staff manning the information desk at Ebisu were helpful and friendly and the following morning extended their expertise in planning out an interesting itinerary for our remaining precious four and a half days, arranging for us that very morning to visit the studio of a highly respected wood-block artist. Cynthia and I drove to his address by taxi – actually a comfortable car and unlike the amusing but battered three-wheel motorbike cabs that we had to rely on in Kure. This was an interesting drive and some distance from Ebisu, passing through a residential area of Tokyo.

On arrival at the house, I noticed to my surprise that it was built in a Western style and not dissimilar to my home in Sussex. Standing on the doorstep, after ringing the bell, we both felt a little apprehensive as neither of us had had any real contact before with professional Japanese in their own homes. But our fears were quickly dispelled when greeted by the smiling young lady who opened the front door. Welcoming us and at the same time explaining that she was Mr Yoshida's son's wife, she asked, 'Please to come in.' We entered the small entrance hall where we immediately removed our shoes. These were substituted by a pair of soft slippers, before young Mrs Yoshida escorted us up a lovely wooden staircase and into a pretty sitting room, where she kindly invited us to sit down.

A few minutes later, as the door opened quietly, we heard a cheerful voice announce (in perfect English), 'Good morning ladies, I am Mrs Yoshida senior, and this is my son.' Rising to meet them, we saw smiling sweetly at us a tiny, elderly but sophisticated lady, and standing right behind her, the tallest Japanese gentleman either of us had ever seen, being well over six feet – which at that time in Japan was unusual.

Both Mrs Yoshida and her son were very welcoming and she also mentioned that unfortunately her husband was unwell and therefore unable to meet us, but they themselves would do their utmost to explain all they could about his art.

Sitting down with us, young Mr Yoshida gave us a detailed account of the art of wood-block painting and told us something of its history. This was most interesting and we felt quite honoured to be entertained by such kind and well-known people, and whilst we sipped tiny cups of delicate green tea and nibbled minute rice cakes, the conversation flowed.

After this we spent some time admiring Mr Yoshida's studio, which was a small circular room at the top of the house, and where his son – who told us that he, too, was an artist – showed us a wealth of his father's paintings. Subsequently, we both made purchases.

Cynthia bought a set of four parchments depicting typical Japanese street scenes, of which I much liked the rainy day one with its plethora of brightly coloured umbrellas glistening in watery sunshine. I finally selected two seascapes of fishing boats at dawn and dusk on the Inland Sea, happily reminding me of Miyajima. When it was time for us to leave, we felt that Mrs Yoshida was genuinely sorry to see us go. We too felt sad, having much appreciated the opportunity to spend an hour or so with this cultured family, far from the pressures of Kure.

Returning to Ebisu for a quick lunch, we soon set off again, this time by electric train, having discovered that Tokyo had an excellent service similar to our London underground, although this appeared to be all above ground. Having to change stations several times was confusing as, understandably, the majority of signs were in Japanese. Despite this we arrived at our destination after a little over an hour.

Kamakura was a small seaside resort which, centuries ago, had once been the capital of Japan but following the loss of its special status in 1603 had since become something of a backwater.

We had gone there to view the famous *Daibutsu*, the gigantic bronze figure of Buddha. This truly was a gigantic figure, seated on the top of a large stone pedestal in the open air, gazing down inscrutably through half-closed eyes. Dipping into the guide book, we read that the Buddha had been cast in 1252, was about 35ft in height and weighed many tons. Originally it was protected by a temple, but in 1495 this was swept away by a monumental tidal wave and since then the figure has been in the open.

Although admiring the immense serenity of the enormous statue, we were unimpressed by the amount of verdi-gris that was blanketing it, feeling that it could possibly do with a good polish with Brasso!

For me there was another reason for visiting Kamakura. Twenty years ago my father had bought an old Victorian house in Berkshire which belonged to an elderly recluse who had once been a missionary. Although only five at the time, I clearly remembered the house was then curiously named 'Kamakura' and now, by sheer coincidence, I was unexpectedly in Kamakura where, presumably, this brave old missionary gentleman had once lived.

Sadly the place left me somewhat disappointed by its tawdry, touristy atmosphere and I imagined much had changed from bygone days. However, after a prolonged search we found a little china shop where I bought an attractive miniature Satsuma teapot, its tiny handle fashioned from traditional bamboo. I posted it later to my mother as a small memento.

On Wednesday we travelled over a hundred miles and despite the extra mileage our budget seemed to be holding out well, probably because the train and subsequent bus fares were so reasonable, costing us a total of only 12s 6d each.

Leaving Ebisu quite early on a rather overcast and grey morning, we caught a mainline train to the coast. Once there we continued on by bus over some steep hills to the beautiful Hakone region of lakes and mountains, until arriving at the vantage point where we should have a magnificent view of Mount Fuji. However, the fates were against us; disappointingly, she was swathed in heavy mist which would obviously take several hours – if not days – to clear. So, making a snap decision, we elected to carry on in the same bus to the small coastal town of Atami.

This was a sweet little place and, unlike Kamkura, totally unspoilt. Despite the dismal greyness of the day, Atami looked immensely attractive with unusually dark volcanic sand and black jagged rocks. From the narrow shoreline we had our first view of the Pacific Ocean with big breakers tumbling over the rocks, differing much from the accustomed ripples of the Inland Sea. In contrast to the blackened rocks, the soil of the nearby hillside was a deep shade of red, with an amazing variety of vegetation, from lovely orange groves, stately pines and dense thickets of bamboo to a prolific white mass of plum blossom in the valley below.

Walking through the cramped streets of the little town, we passed a number of portly Japanese gentlemen dressed identically in blue and white kimonos and wearing *geta*, clattering along on the cobblestones on their way to the hot springs. Both of us wished that we too could escape from the intermittent rain and into the soothing heat of the sulphurous steam.

Relieving the dullness of the day during our bus journeys, we had seen many beautiful, tall camellia trees ablaze with crimson blossoms. Then, driving through various agricultural areas, we saw to our delight the first green fuzz of newly planted rice paddies and, amazingly, in one place the first hay harvest of the season was in progress dotting the terraced fields with tiny haystacks. So in spite of the inclement weather, it had been an interesting day, culminating in a memorable incident on our return journey by train to Ebisu.

Towards the end of the trip, neither of us was certain if we had to change trains at the next station and then, to add to our confusion, the train slid to a stop beyond the last signboard. Resourceful as ever, out hopped Cynthia to check where we were, when horror struck as the doors slammed shut and the train shot off, leaving her gasping on the platform and me in something of a panic!

Immediately all around me I heard the sympathetic sound of sighing, accompanied by voluble 'Ah so... So' and much sucking of teeth. Looking up I saw that the four or five Japanese ladies sharing our carriage realised that I had lost Cynthia and were genuinely concerned about my welfare. So, lacking the ability to communicate but with many kind gesticulations and the smiling of much encouragement, when arriving at the next station they bundled me out of the carriage, pointed furiously to the nearby station bridge, signalling me to cross over it and to catch the next train back to find Cynthia. This I did, finding to my relief that wisely she had waited there on the platform, hoping that I would do just that! However, but for the thoughtful kindness of the occupants of that small railway car, we might well have been seriously lost.

'What a lovely, lovely day and who would believe that only yesterday we were so damp and soggy?' Cynthia remarked happily. The bright sunshine flooding through the roof of the observation car embraced us in its comforting warmth, as we travelled at speed across the large and unusually flat plain north of Tokyo. After a cold and frosty beginning, it had blossomed into a beautiful day and although still decidedly chilly, there was an invigorating freshness in the air.

Already we had changed trains several times during the 140-mile journey to Nikko, reputedly the ancient land of shrines, Cryptomeria trees and magnificent mountain scenery.

'Have some more chocky, Cynth – what did you think of the last little station master? – Wasn't he so kind to us?'

'Thanks. Yes, I'm really flabbergasted at the courteous way that at every change-over we've made, each one has invited us into his office to keep warm by the stove, instead of having to hang around on a freezing platform waiting for the next train.'

Indeed, since arriving in Tokyo, we had been touched by the genuine helpfulness of all the Japanese whom we had met, and especially now, as we trekked further into the rural areas. And from the train it was heart warming to see so many chubby, rosy cheeked children running around in the fields.

Numerous small farms were dotted about, where every available inch of soil was under cultivation including paddy fields of newly planted rice and although we saw no cattle, there were plenty of sheep grazing. Japan was so thickly populated that hardly a blade of grass seemed to be wasted, to the extent, we noticed, of utilising the base of every poplar tree with a unique miniature haystack encircling the trunk.

In the distance, just before we left the huge plain, we had an exciting glimpse of the forests and foothills of the Japanese Alps. Twenty minutes later we alighted at Imaichi where we swapped the train for a local bus to drive on by road, in order to pass through the famous Cryptomeria Avenue. These were the innumerable and immensely tall, straight, Japanese red cedar trees, lining the road for most of the way into Nikko. Legend had it that these were once planted by a feudal lord who, at the time, lacked the ready cash to contribute to a new and lavish shrine. There were certainly hundreds of these magnificent trees dwarfing the road, in what surely must be his everlasting memorial.

The princely backdrop of mountains gave Nikko – the sacred seat of shrines – an air of unsurpassed beauty, and as we walked through the first of many *Torrii*, magically, it began to snow. Apart from a handful of reverent Japanese and several priests attending various shrines, there were few other visitors as we padded softly through the thick snow. It was very cold and strangely quiet standing there amongst the ancient temples of another faith, many enhanced by the pristine whiteness of freshly fallen snow. There were an abundance of shrines to see and in the limited time available, we managed to visit several; nearly all of these were elaborately decorated, some dating back to about 1600. The most illustrious was the Toshogo shrine dedicated to Ieyasu, who founded the Tokugawa Shogunate. Later, we learned that there amongst the overhead wooden carving was the famous panel featuring the three wise monkeys – 'see, speak and hear no evil'. Unfortunately for us at the time, the majority of these were obliterated by snow.

On leaving the shrines we just had time, before the wintry light faded, to walk along the road to see a pretty waterfall and then to find the hotel which had been recommended to us. This was an enchanting and palatial building, situated in an elevated position amongst ancient pines. Here we were extremely well looked after and having previously decided to share a room – for reasons of safety and economy – we had also decided, whilst we had the opportunity, to live Japanese style. All the rooms in the hotel were named after fruit or flowers. We were given the Plum Room, which on entering we found was spacious, minimally furnished and definitely chilly – with only wisps of warmth emitting from a tiny *hibachi* in one corner.

Dinner was served in the large and ornate Western-style dining room, with few other guests present. The food was delicious, particularly the freshly caught trout, which to us was a great luxury and one of the only two courses we could afford! Our waiter spoke a little English and from him we learned that the hotel was originally the Emperor's summer residence, and that one of its more illustrious guests had been the Duke of Windsor.

Returning to our room, we found a little house-girl waiting outside, and she followed us in to make up our futons. These were a type of a light mattress which she placed on the two *tatamis*, covering each one with a light cotton quilt and on the top of each she laid a thickly padded kimono. Then, in halting English, she suggested, should we perhaps like to have bath? Discreetly disappearing outside the door whilst we changed into the kimonos, she reappeared to escort us to the bath-house. In my haste I had forgotten to exchange my shoes for the slippers provided, so on my arrival at the surprisingly gloomy and unattractive bath-house, I was soundly ticked off by the bath attendant; not exactly a relaxing start to the ritual of a Japanese bath! As ever, the water was boiling hot so it took time and courage to immerse myself, eventually to emerge refreshingly clean, but smelling strongly of sulphur.

Next morning we left the hotel in good time to catch the local bus up into the mountains to go to Lake Chuzenji. According to the guide book, this was roughly a twelve-mile scenic route out from Nikko, culminating in a terrifically steep climb over a mountain pass of more than 4,000ft. Eventually our patience was rewarded, as the old bus clattered to a halt beside us, spewing out a large number of passengers. The vehicle was ramshackle and badly dented and in our judgement looked unworthy of attempting the slightest of inclines, let alone one of the steepest passes.

'At least it's got chains on the tyres which should stop us from skidding around.' Cynthia said encouragingly, as we embarked on what later proved to be a tortuous drive over icy mountain tracks.

The bus was nearly full, mostly of local Japanese but with a sprinkling of US servicemen and of course the two of us. Starting off was not too bad, as the snow was light and the road surface reasonable, but the further on the old bus progressed, the condition of the road worsened, until it eventually became dangerously narrow and treacherously icy. As we gingerly ascended the twisting track with its numerous chasms and hairpin bends, I found that I was always seemed to be the one on the outside seat with full view of every precipice!

At times the frequent bouncing and bumping was terrifying and about halfway up the pass this was exaggerated when a commotion, which had been gently erupting in the front of the bus, suddenly exploded, just as the driver was negotiating a frighteningly dangerous bend. For a while we had been observing the two

US soldiers, who even at that early hour were obviously the worse for wear and intent on ogling the pretty Japanese bus conductress in a loud and coarse manner. She, poor girl, had studiously but politely avoided them, but as the bus wheezed its way to a near asthmatic halt on this hazardous turn, the GIs took full advantage and lurched forward to drag her onto their laps. Miraculously, the bus swerved, the two men slid sideways, releasing the girl, who catapulted into the seat next to the driver – where she remained for the rest of the journey.

'Phew! That was a nasty incident…'

'Thank God the bus swerved when it did, because heaven only knows what might have happened,' countered Cynthia. 'And have you also noticed how very angry the other passengers are?'

'I have, and justly so. How could those two disreputable boys behave so disgustingly and I'm pretty sure they are drunk. You realise too, Cynth, that neither of us could have just sat here and let the poor girl be molested by them. Anyway thank goodness that it's okay now.'

During the final stages we counted no less than forty ghastly hairpin bends, and were more than thankful to clamber down from the rickety bus which had – to our mutual surprise – brought us safely to our destination. The pure mountain air was icily invigorating and the temperature too cold for snow, as we walked through the drab little town situated close to the shores of Lake Chuzenji. Although the day was miserably grey, the distant snow-covered mountains and expanse of frozen lake-side was impressive, particularly when on the horizon we glimpsed a dash of bright colours as a handful of skiers sped down a far-off slope.

After walking along the frozen shore for some distance, we pottered back to explore the cluster of little shops. There we found an interesting wood carver, and I sacrificed my lunch money in exchange for an attractive leaf-shaped fruit dish, which at the time seemed an expensive 7s 6d, but years later was still in daily use.

Our return to Nikko was uneventful, with the bonus of a modern bus, far less snow and a much clearer road. This left us time to catch the direct train to Tokyo subsequently to arrive at Ebisu that night.

Sorting out our financial state the following day, we discovered that despite having travelled hundreds of miles, eaten out on several occasions, plus one night's hotel accommodation, our joint expenses came to a total of £10 10s, meaning we still had 10s left in the kitty, plus the remains of our pocket money – we were rich!

The main railway station in Tokyo was packed with servicemen that evening when we boarded the sleeper leaving for Kure at 1800hrs. The return journey (eighteen hours' long) was tedious as the train chugged along at a snail's pace, stopping at every halt. We were both relieved when we finally rumbled into Kure Station at 1400hrs on Sunday 15 March.

'Back in the fold again and it doesn't look as though much has changed either!' remarked Cynthia as we made our way into the ante-room.

'We'd better look to see which wards we've been assigned, as I'm quite sure I am due to go on night duty again.'

'Here's the changeover list, Jilly – wait for it – you are down as a relief sister, when availa…'

Interrupting her, I sighed, 'Oh No! that's even worse…' Cynthia chuckled before continuing, 'Having charge of the ambulance train until further notice, report to Matron's office at 0900hrs.'

'I'm NOT – Oh Cynth you must be pulling my leg! Not ME on convoy duty? That's the most coveted job of the lot, and only comes round to the British every few months. Weren't the Aussies doing it last time?'

'Well done, Jilly, I'm really thrilled for you. And I'm very pleased too, as I'm going to Ward Eight, your old ward.'

'That's great – I know you'll love it.

CHAPTER TEN

CONVOY DUTY AND 'LITTLE SWITCH'

28 March, UN and Communist Forces agree to the
exchange of sick and wounded POWs.
20 April, Operation 'Little Switch' began

16 March 1953

Handing over a sizeable bunch of keys, Matron's orders were explicit: for the next month I was responsible for the ambulance train, with the assistance of one Australian (female) nursing orderly. The ambulance train was located in a siding at Kure Station and normally consisted of one hospital-type coach, which when in operation was attached to the main-line train running between Kure and Iwakuni. There was also a second fully equipped coach available if an unusually large convoy of sick and wounded was expected.

After giving me the authority to ring for transport whenever necessary, Matron warned that the working hours were long and that I and I alone was responsible for getting myself to the right place at the right time. Concluding with, 'Good luck Hall, I know that you will appreciate the privilege of being on convoy duty. Next month it will be the turn of the Canadians. Thank you, that is all.'

Having also advised me there was a convoy of convalescent patients due to leave the hospital the following morning, it was imperative that I should prepare the train as soon as possible. So, after ordering a supply of clean linen and the

Layout of the ambulance train.

necessary transport, I contacted my helper, arranging to meet her at the main entrance to the hospital at 1300hrs, where a jeep would pick us up.

Private O'Shea was a small neat woman with dark hair and whom I imagined to be in her late twenties. She had a marked Australian accent coupled with a somewhat bossy manner. En route to the station, I elicited that she had previously worked for a few days as relief nurse on the train and should be familiar with the routine. Five minutes later, it was with some trepidation that I caught sight of my new charge: one long railway coach – in appearance looking much like any other – sitting in a dark and gloomy siding at the far end of Kure Station.

Unlocking the wide double doors in the middle of the coach, we had a glimpse of our new workplace, as we stepped into a fair-sized, unfurnished, open reception area. This, we saw, was just large enough to allow any stretcher cases to be carried through into the small, white painted hospital ward to the right of us. There we counted a total of sixteen litters, or bunks, eight on each side with four up and four down. The beds appeared to be well constructed, with white iron frames, wire bases and comfortable-looking mattresses and pillows, and the added bonus of unobstructed views from the wide windows beside the bunks. Passing down the narrow aisle between them, we proceeded through a doorway giving access to the ablutions area, comprising two WCs and a small shower unit at the far end of the coach.

Returning to the entrance at the central division, we turned left into a short corridor with three small compartments to the right-hand side of it. Sliding open the first door, I found this was obviously the treatment room, spotlessly clean and, despite its diminutive size, generously equipped with cupboards. On closer inspection I noticed that these contained everything required to run a small surgical unit, from instruments to sterile dressing drums, plus a neat shelf to use as a dressing trolley top. Attached to one side of this was a stainless-steel container of antiseptic fluid, with a large pair of Cheatle forceps immersed and ready to use for removing instruments or syringes (after boiling) from the adjacent tiny, electrically heated steriliser. Close at hand was a small sink with hot and cold taps and above it, secured to the wall, a medicine and lotion cupboard. Finally, running full length against the opposite wall there was a comfortable couch where, if needed, I could change my patients' dressings during transit.

Sister's office was next to the treatment room, which although somewhat cramped was sufficient to seat about three on the upholstered carriage seat. Firmly attached to the opposite wall, there was a locked cupboard where I could safely secure my drug box, plus another smaller one to stow the patients' documents and finally a miniature desk top for writing reports. It was good to have such a cubbyhole for my nurse and me to dump our personal belongings, for whenever we travelled we should always be lumbered with caps, raincoats, shoulder bags and so on!

Of the three modest rooms, the third and last was the kitchen, most probably of the greatest importance. Again it was reasonably spacious, clean and basically equipped with thick white china mugs and plates, some odd cutlery, an enormous brown enamel teapot, a good-sized sink, draining board, two gas burners and a really big kettle.

'No doubt, we shall spend a lot of time here making tea and sandwiches for the lads, Nurse?'

'Too right, Sister, I reckon this is where most of the work is done. Did you know that the hospital kitchen provides the food rations on the day we transport? Though there should be enough tea, sugar and tinned milk left on board for emergencies.'

'I did, but thanks anyway. But one thing is puzzling me: that is, when we have walking wounded, where on earth do they sit? Obviously it must be in the entrance area – but what do they sit on?'

'Yep you're right to ask, there's a stack of folding chairs in the big cupboard, I'll show you it's through here.' Leading me from the kitchen to the end of the coach she showed me a large double-doored storage space and opening one side said, 'Here are the chairs; in the other side you'll find spare splints and crutches. Oh and this is a box of records for the portable gramophone which is in here. We usually hand this over to one of the fitter lads to play when the others feel like some music.'

'That's a good idea and there must be well over twenty records. What are they like? Have you got the current favourite?'

'What's that, Sister?'

'You must know it, the one the lads are always singing, *China Nights!*'

'Oh that one – but didn't you know that's banned by the powers that be?' Adding cheekily, 'I'd have thought being commissioned, you Sister, should have known that!'

'No! But what a pity as it's such a pretty tune.'

'Yep but it's the words that are the problem; maybe it's a good thing few of us here can understand Japanese!'

'Right, Nurse O'Shea, it's time we started. Let's dump our things in the office, find some hot water, antiseptic and clean dusters to damp dust the ward thoroughly before making up the bunks.'

Several hours later the ambulance coach was ready for the following day's convoy; all was sparklingly clean and highly polished, with sixteen litters made up with fresh linen. Making the lower bunks was no mean feat because in the confined space it was almost impossible to tuck in the bedding without scalping one's head on the wire base of the one above it. Switching on the ceiling lights to check their effect, the little ward gleamed expectantly, and even the overhead fan purred as it revolved.

One final check, from the kitchen right up to the ablutions, confirmed that our preparations were complete. All that was lacking were the patients, whom we should be collecting from the hospital early next morning.

Returning to my room that evening, I found that my kind house-girl had remembered to press my khaki slacks, laying them neatly on my bed. Wearing battledress and trousers was going to be essential on convoy duty, in the knowledge that we should be forever clambering in and out of a variety of high-sided military vehicles.

Despite the excitement of my first run on Tuesday 17 March, I slept soundly until the shrill ringing of my alarm clock at 0500hrs. It was a miserably cold, wet morning and I was somewhat damp by the time I arrived at the main entrance of the hospital at 0600hrs.

My instructions were to collect the Med-Air-Evac, a convoy of semi-convalescent patients from the BCGH Kure, and transport them to the RAAF Transit Hospital at Iwakuni by road and rail. The convoy consisted of twenty British patients due to be flown home to the UK (sixteen stretchers and four ambulant cases) and another nine Australian walking wounded bound for Australia.

Within the hour we had all twenty-nine patients comfortably transferred to the small fleet of waiting ambulances. Private O'Shea looked after the nine Aussies and I the others, having initially gathered up all the necessary documents – of which there was a mountain including twenty-nine cardboard folders of notes and numerous large brown envelopes full of X-rays, plus a basket of spare linen and the all-important drug box. In order to supervise the unloading of patients on to the train, I travelled down to Kure in the front of the first ambulance.

On arrival at the station, I was met by the Regimental Transport Officer (RTO), who to my utter dismay informed me that we had too many patients to travel in one coach and unfortunately the other ambulance coach was unavailable. However, he continued, the good news was the Japanese railways were supplying a spare sleeper for our excess patients, but the bad news was that in no way could this be ready to catch the 0755hrs train as booked! Therefore the second coach would be hitched onto the next train which would not leave Kure until 0830hrs.

'But that is very unsatisfactory, because it means that we shall be unable to travel together,' I pointed out as I argued my case with the middle-aged captain acting as RTO. 'And I have been given strict orders that whilst we are in transit, on no account am I to be parted from my patients.'

'Ma'am, Sister! There is NO other way – YOU will have to travel with the British contingent NOW, for the very good reason that your ambulance coach is already hitched up to the 0755hrs train to Hiroshima.' Which was indeed raring to go, noisily hissing steam and smuts beside us as we conferred. 'And I will personally undertake to see that your remaining nine walking wounded, with your nurse, arrive safely at Hiroshima Station, where their sleeper will be connected onto the rear of your coach. You will then continue the rest of the journey to Iwakuni together. I might add, this change will not upset the flight times for any of the boys, as none will be flying home for at least ten hours after arrival at the transit hospital.' And smiling at me, he said 'Don't look so worried – I promise, Sister, that all will be well. Now can you start loading the British lads please.'

Under the circumstances there was little I could do – apart from telephoning Matron which I immediately decided against – so using my initiative, I explained the situation to Private O'Shea and gave her my instructions.

'Nurse, you will now take charge of these nine patients and be responsible for transporting them in the second coach to Hiroshima, where hopefully we shall meet up in just over an hour. Fortunately your lads are convalescent and none's too poorly, so there shouldn't be any problem.'

'Don't worry Sister, we shall be fine, and if by chance there is a hitch, I'll get the RTO to let you know.'

After settling my lot down comfortably for the first leg of the journey, I remained anxious lest some mishap should occur to any of the patients I had left behind, before the re-hitching of the coaches occurred in Hiroshima, imagining the mortification of reporting back to Matron on my inaugural trip that not only had I lost nine patients but my nursing orderly as well! Yet another concern assailed me, of being the only medically trained person on the convoy, which was quite a responsibility, without the added problem of having to abandon a third of my patients – fit and well as they looked – to the charge of an unqualified orderly.

Hiroshima was about halfway between Kure and Iwakuni, a total distance of some forty miles by rail where, as I discovered, the track intermittently clung to the attractive coastline, passing amongst the steeply terraced hillsides, occasional trees of exquisite plum or cherry blossom and several pretty little coves. On board the majority of patients were effervescent with the sudden realisation that after weeks of hospitalisation, this short trip by train was really the beginning of their homecoming. Despite some being burdened by heavy plasters and others whose wounds had barely healed, most of them spent their time ribbing each other, cracking jokes or smoking and gambling for matches whilst playing cards.

Hiroshima Station appeared to be a busy railway junction, where later I discovered our ambulance coach would frequently stop to be shunted into a siding until the connection to Iwakuni arrived. Viewing the station from the train it seemed to be a large, dark, dreary place and subsequently I was always glad to escape from its sombre, sooty atmosphere.

Miraculously, on this first day, after only an hour's wait but with a great deal of smoke, steam, clattering and banging, we were finally hitched up with a resounding jolt. Shortly afterwards we were chugging happily on our way beside the lovely Inland Sea to Iwakuni whilst Nurse and I cut plates of sandwiches and filled the huge teapot for the ever-hungry lads, who by then were enjoying the old gramophone and its collection of records. The current favourite was Maurice Chevalier appropriately singing *La Mer*. And in spite of the initial delay, it only took us about two and a half hours to travel the rest of the way to Iwakuni Station.

There we were met by the efficient crew of a fleet of ambulances, plus a small baggage truck, where regardless of the incessant rain, both the patients and their luggage were skilfully transferred for the last stage of the journey. After checking to make certain that we still had sixteen stretcher cases and thirteen walkers, when the last one had been settled I collected up the drug box, documents and empty linen basket and climbed into the roomy but draughty cab of the last ambulance at the rear of the convoy.

The vehicles set off in slow procession from the station yard, their drab olive green camouflage enlivened by the large red crosses painted on each side. Driving on gingerly through the narrow glistening streets of the small, drab town, everything was bathed in a dismal shade of grey and there was little sign of habitation. I supposed that it was either lunchtime, or everyone around was sheltering from the persistent downpour.

Negotiating the last sharp corner on leaving the town, the road unexpectedly opened out into a broad and pleasant rural area, where immediately we increased our speed. Ten minutes later the convoy began to slow down, finally coming to a halt outside a vast but rather nondescript building. This I realised with a certain amount of relief must be the RAAF Transit Hospital at Iwakuni and checking my watch, I saw that the time was exactly twelve noon.

Disembarking the patients this time was an easier task and we soon had them comfortably installed in the transit ward, where we handed them over to the two Australian sisters who would look after them until the homeward-bound air evacuation flights were ready. All had survived the excursion well, and it was rewarding to note that even the palest of them glowed pink with excitement, as we wished them 'Bon Voyage'.

After a solitary snack lunch, we collected our one and only return patient for the hospital in Kure. This lad had flown in from Korea but was not badly injured and therefore classified as walking wounded, so the three of us were driven to Iwakuni Station. There we caught the 1500hrs civilian train to Kure, with Private O'Shea clutching on to the laundry basket and I the drug box. My orders were to leave the ambulance coach at Iwakuni, where it would remain until the next convoy of wounded were flown in from the front. This also meant that when we were recalled to Iwakuni, we should have the added benefit of returning by launch across the Inland Sea...

Unbelievably, by the time we were back in Kure the rain had stopped and through the dark grey clouds we glimpsed a pale watery sun. Handing our patient over to Sister on Ward Ten, Nurse disposed of the laundry basket whilst I checked in the drug box for safekeeping. It was exactly 1800hrs when we finally completed our duties for the day and I had to sprint over to the Mess where I was just in time to grab an evening meal.

Because of its sporadic nature, convoy duty was intermittent, depending on the numbers of casualties for evacuation from Korea, as well as convalescent patients requiring medical transfer to their home countries. However, after the first few days, a pattern of duties evolved, so that whenever I was on convoy duty I was up with the lark and away, whereas intervening days were spent as a relief sister, working on any ward which happened to be short staffed.

It was during one of the intervening days that I had a surprise invitation to an exhibition of classical dancing, performed by the young daughters of the local Japanese Christian Society in Kure. This society, I was told, was eager to promote friendship between East and West, mainly because its members were afraid that the Commonwealth troops stationed in Kure would only see the sordid side of life in Japan and little of its genuine culture. The display took place in some beautiful gardens, illuminated with an abundance of brightly coloured paper lanterns which reflected prettily in the still waters of several small pools. Beside these pools, the tiny dancers – some of whom seemed just four or five years old and despite their diminutive size were traditionally dressed – performed their intricate and very graceful steps. Such lovely little girls and such proud parents too. After meeting many of the kind Japanese there, for me that glimpse of normality was uplifting, whilst the conflict in Korea continued, with its daily toll of casualties.

However, there was a glimmer of hope in the potent rumour prevailing that some of our United Nations POWs captured by the Communists were soon to be repatriated. I truly hoped so; if only the peace negotiations could really get off the ground this time and stop the misery. To me it was still shattering to realise that few people at home in the UK had little idea of what was going on in Korea and it was no wonder that this was fast becoming the far forgotten war…

To my surprise, after the recent warm spell, I woke on Sunday morning to see that the surrounding hills were covered in snow and once again the weather was bitterly cold. It was 29 March and I remembered that it was exactly a year since Pat, Helen, Georgina and I had disembarked from the *Empire Trooper*, realising at the same time what a wealth of experience we had all had during the past twelve months in Kure. Having filled in our Reversion to Home Establishment forms yesterday, amazingly now there were only another six months left to serve in Kure.

Two days previously, whilst on convoy duty, one of the patients we collected from Iwakuni was the captain of a Sunderland flying boat which had crashed during a 50-knot gale, whilst attempting to land on the sea near Iwakuni. Tragically, the plane broke up on impact, rapidly sinking and trapping some of the crew. Thankfully, that particular afternoon we had only half the number of lads on board, so I was able to give this poor man my full attention. Lying on his small bunk, looking grey, drawn and totally washed up, he talked quietly but incessantly, as the train swayed and clattered noisily on over the rails.

His feelings were of unremitting guilt, because he had survived whereas several members of his crew had perished. Despite his prolonged bravery in searching for them in the darkness and struggling alone for two hours in the surging waves before rescue came, he continued to blame himself for having survived the catastrophe when some of his men had drowned. Happily, I was able to comfort him a little as, by chance, that morning I had already met the remaining survivors in another ward and was able to reassure him that they were all well on the way to recovery. I was very touched he had confided in me but at the same time upset to hear of such a terrible disaster.

Another sad event which occurred during that week was the death of HM Queen Mary, our much respected Commandant and Colonel-in-Chief. So, once again, we were in mourning, wearing black armbands on our battledress.

With the beginning of April the weather improved and it was far more pleasant to get up in the early morning when the sun was shining and listen to the birds chattering away. Also, it was significantly easier to transport the patients to and from the train in this lovely springtime. This just happened to be one of the busiest weeks I had had so far, with convoys several days running. On the Thursday, because my nurse was not available, I had to take the empty train single-handed to Iwakuni, where I was to collect a convoy of sick and wounded. Having to make up all the litters with clean sheets on my own – whilst the train was in motion – was quite a job. And worryingly, soon after leaving Kure, suddenly – without any warning – I had the most excruciating abdominal cramps and had to dive for the lavatory. Sitting there ignominiously, I spent a considerable time literally watching the rails go by!

During a much needed lull, I raided the medicine cupboard grabbing the nearest bottle of Mist Kaolin Sed. This I dosed myself with at frequent intervals, being determined to bung up whatever was irritating my poor old insides. Fortunately for me, throughout that long day my guardian angel must have been working overtime, because by the time I arrived at Iwakuni things had considerably improved. Several hours later, when I had delivered my nineteen patients safely to the hospital in Kure, whatever had been the cause of my embarrassment had by then thankfully subsided.

On the following Saturday afternoon, I and two other QAs decorated the garrison church with a lovely variety of spring flowers. When all was arranged we were delighted to see St Peter's sparkling with colour for the Easter Sunday service, which we were told would be broadcast by the BBC. The Easter weekend for me was much like any other, with convoy duty on both Good Friday and Easter Monday, and relief sister in between.

Although, to my surprise, by the middle of my fourth week on convoy duty I had not received any threat of an imminent handover, I realised sadly that it was bound to come soon. Latterly life had become exceptionally hectic, both on and off duty. This was because the Dramatic Society had put on a play at short notice, producing it – in just two and a half weeks – on Friday 10 April. I was given the only female part, with a multitude of lines to learn. The play, *Someone at the Door*, was a thriller by Agatha Christie and had lots of toy guns popping off. However, it went down surprisingly well with the audience, amongst whom was the Chief of Staff, and after the performance I was introduced to him at the small party where he was quite enthusiastic about our hastily cobbled together drama.

Following that late night, I was up again at 0500hrs and soon en route to Iwakuni with a full house of British boys for medical air evacuation. After handing these patients over to the transit staff and gobbling down a hasty lunch, Private O'Shea and I waited for the expected flight of sick and wounded, which was due in from Korea but considerably delayed, eventually touching down over two hours later.

This was a convoy of especially sick lads, with twenty stretcher cases and four walking wounded, most of whom were far from well. The two of us worked flat out trying to make them all as comfortable as possible whilst the extended coaches jolted on and on along the bumpy tracks. We spent most of the time dishing out mugs of hot, sweet tea and lighting fags for any of the poor lads whose injuries made it impossible for them to do so, and also keeping a wary eye on one of the walkers sitting rather too close to the open window in the reception area, as he seemed somewhat shaky and could have been suffering from shell shock.

Thankfully we had them all safely in Kure and the relative comfort of the hospital by 2000hrs. This had been the longest day yet and after handing over the essentials, I felt too weary to eat, and just managed to crawl across to my room, collapse on the bed and fall asleep…

One recent excitement was that most of the British mail was now flown out by Comet – the first commercial jet airliner – taking only a few days to arrive, and I was amazed to receive a small (airmail) package of homemade shortbread from my mother, within only thirty-six hours of posting. Unfortunately, when thanking her – as ever – I had to include an urgent request for some suspenders, new pants and an ST belt! None of these necessities of life were available at that time in the NAAFI.

By mid-April heavy rain was plaguing us again, everywhere was squelching underfoot and we felt particularly sorry for the Marchioness of Reading, head of the WVS, when she visited the hospital on the 15th, as it was bucketing down all day. And just to keep us on our toes during that week, there were a number of unpleasantly strong earth tremors. The Marchioness was kind and charming, and keenly interested in the patients and their welfare.

Some weeks before I had been told that Betty had been unwell and that she was returning from Korea for transfer home to Australia on the next troopship. So, hearing on the grapevine that she was now safely on board, I managed to dash down to the docks during an afternoon off to visit her briefly before she sailed. I imagined that the strain of serving in Korea through the bitter winter months must have taken its toll, and hoped that once she was home again with her lovely family she would soon recover.

Expecting at any moment to be told that I was to hand over my train, my summons to Matron's office a few days later was not too much of a surprise.

'Ah, come in, Hall, I wanted to see you about the handover of the ambulance train.' My heart sank but, knowing it was inevitable, I began to fumble for the keys in my pocket, when Matron unexpectedly smiled, adding, 'But not quite yet!' Leaning forward across her desk, she continued, 'You see, we have just received some excellent news, which is that shortly in Panmunjom, we are hoping there will be an exchange of a small number of our sick and wounded prisoners of war. And it is essential, whilst the repatriation is taking place, that we should have an experienced sister in charge of the ambulance train. Therefore we have decided that you will remain on convoy duty, until all the POWs have been released.'

'That's wonderful news, Ma'am, and I'll do my utmost to make certain that everything runs smoothly during the repatriation and thank you for the privilege.'

Matron then instructed me, as far as possible to prepare the train in advance, because as yet, neither the numbers of POWs nor the imminent date of their release was definite. She then explained at some length, though she appreciated that under normal circumstances I managed to run the train with only a single helper, since this would be an event of international importance – with the eyes of the world resting briefly upon us – understandably on this occasion many others would wish to help. Therefore from the first day of repatriation, my staff would be increased to include a doctor, two Red Cross ladies and, more significantly, a Japanese cook-boy, which would absolve me from the washing up!

Her last request was to say nothing about this incredible news until it was official, also cautioning me, that once the wheels were in motion and we were literally on our way, to beware of the Press.

Practically the whole of the next weekend was spent in preparing both ambulance coaches, having been allocated the extra one until the evacuation was completed. By Sunday afternoon the little train was positively gleaming, and its cupboards bulging with every conceivable form of equipment and comfort we could possibly need.

On Monday, the day before we hoped 'Little Switch' – the code name given to the exchange of POWs – would commence, my nurse and I did our usual run with the single coach to Iwakuni to collect a convoy of wounded flown in from Korea. Everywhere there was an air of expectation and even these poorly lads asked if we had heard anything definite yet about the release of their comrades. We told them, 'Hopefully very soon, we're just waiting for confirmation now.'

Waking early on Tuesday 21 April 1953, a wave of excitement engulfed me as I dressed with care, preparing myself for the momentous day ahead. The sun was shining brightly and birds were singing cheerfully, as I made my way over to the hospital to join our team before boarding the train at Kure Station.

As we rattled our way over the rails to Iwakuni, I spent the time re-checking every inch of the train. The two wards were spotlessly clean, where the smooth white linen on the litters looked invitingly comfortable, and in the reception area there was a neat pile of records stacked beside the gramophone, just in case some music was required. The two Red Cross ladies were busily sorting out their last minute arrangements. Checking out the Japanese cook-boy in the tiny kitchen, I found that he was excelling himself by preparing plates of daintily cut sandwiches – best of all, he understood a little English. The young RAMC doctor was diligently checking through the drug boxes ensuring he could cover any emergencies, because that morning none of us had any idea of what to expect in the way of either illness or injuries affecting the repatriated POWs.

On arrival at Iwakuni, we were driven to the Transit Hospital where security was much tighter than usual. Once there, it was obvious to see from the large number of Press men in evidence that there was something of a commotion going on. Luckily for us, we were escorted right through the building to the wards, avoiding any contact with them.

My first duty was to collect the walking wounded who were patiently waiting in the ante-room of the ward. Momentarily overwhelmed by the magnitude of the occasion, I breathed in deeply before entering the room. Then, smiling broadly at the cluster of weary looking, khaki-clad youngsters, said in a clear voice, 'It's so good to see you, because we have all been waiting for this moment for such a long time.' Their happy faces reciprocated and very soon we had them and the stretcher cases transported safely to the waiting ambulances.

Possibly because none of them was seriously ill, these were truly the best crowd of patients that I had so far been privileged to look after on the train. Most of them were excitedly cracking jokes, perhaps realising that now they really had left behind the terrible days of captivity and despair they must have endured, and at the same time beginning to relax as the pretty scenery of high hills, bright green rice paddies, snow white plum blossom and glimpses of the beautiful Japanese coastline rolled by. The Red Cross ladies were a tremendous help, reassuring each patient about sending messages home and making certain that they had all that was needed. Nurse and I were busily occupied, checking that their dressings were still intact, the lads with plaster casts were comfortable and dishing out mugs of hot sweet tea with the cook-boy's delicious sandwiches, which were particularly appreciated. Fortunately, it was the doctor who seemed to be the only one who was virtually unemployed as, on the whole, most of this first convoy of POWs were in relatively good shape.

We finally arrived in Kure at a little after 1800hrs, where all the lads were admitted to the Australian section of the hospital.

In spite of the excitement of the day, after dinner I dashed down to Kure for a meeting at the Green Room Club, at which we were all very surprised to hear that we had just been invited by the American Cultural Society to perform our 'best play' to an invited audience of Japanese intellectuals – in three weeks' time! The venue was to be a hall in Hiroshima…

As this was rather short notice, plus with the knowledge that I was bound to go on night duty soon, we unanimously decided to put on our current production of *Someone at the Door*, at the same time desperately hoping that the audience would not be too highbrow.

The following day, Wednesday, was again hectically busy, as we set off with the same team for Iwakuni, only this time whilst in transit Nurse and I were frantically remaking the litters in preparation for the incoming convoy. By now the news of the released POWs was widespread and before leaving Kure Station we were beset upon by the Press, most of whom were fended off. Unfortunately, as we were about to leave, whilst standing in the doorway of the coach I was unexpectedly grabbed by a persistent journalist from the *Daily Mail* who, recognising me as a nurse, misguidedly imagined that I was fair game for a good story. Pushing hard he tried to clamber onto the train as it was just about to pull away from the platform; luckily the Medical Officer heard the disturbance and he, with a couple of other onlookers, managed to eject him!

This next group of British repatriated sick and wounded whom we collected that afternoon, although thrilled and delighted to be on their way home at last, were subdued and far more poorly than the previous day's patients and needed all our attention. At the same time they impressed me immensely by being such a courageous bunch of lads, without a grumble or complaint throughout their journey, despite the constant clattering and uncomfortable jolting of the train. I was relieved, however, when soon after 1800hrs we were able to transfer them to their hospital wards in Kure, where they could begin their road to recovery.

By this time the buzz about the released POWs had really got around and when I walked into the ante-room later that evening, to my embarrassment, quite a cheer greeted me and I was peppered with questions. Although I could say little that was not confidential, just for a moment my kind colleagues made me feel that I was almost a VIP! It was only some time later I realised that I had had the privileged position of being the only British QA to look after the released POWs during their short stay in Kure.

Once again, as it so often happened after a busy day, my evening was much occupied. This was because Cynthia, with a number of British servicemen, was confirmed that evening by The Right Reverend Cuthbert Bardsley, Bishop of Croydon, in the Garrison church of St Peter's. It was a moving service and a happy one too, with all the candidates smartly turned out in their No.1 dress uniform. After the ceremony, we were all invited to the parish party given by our senior chaplain. He was lucky enough to live in a genuine Japanese bungalow, with its own private, pretty garden, which the Padre had illuminated with a myriad of Japanese lanterns. The Bishop circulated amongst us and we were all much impressed by his warm sincerity. He was due to fly on to Korea very shortly to visit the front line where, we were certain, with his keen sense of humour and genuine understanding, he would be a tremendous hit with the troops.

On Friday we collected the last of the released POWs in a small convoy from Iwakuni – four British lads and one Canadian – but as ever these sick boys were as outstanding as those who we had previously transferred; they were all such wonderful lads from whom we had glimpsed the pervading spirit of comradeship and great courage. During Little Switch we had evacuated approximately thirty, mainly British, ex-POW patients.

Friday 25 April was my ultimate day on the train. This was a normal run with just my nurse and me to look after twenty-two British ex-POWs who were returning to the UK by Med-Air-Evac. These lads had recovered well, looked much fitter and were very excited. When we said goodbye to them in the transit ward at Iwakuni, they were sweetly profuse in their thanks, shaking hands and treating us quite regally. We wished them Godspeed, a safe journey and a wonderful homecoming, then leaving the ward a trifle sadly, we collected our belongings for the return trip to Kure and our final duties on the ambulance train.

Saturday was my first off duty, since working almost continuously for the last twelve days and during the past week alone I had travelled approximately 600 miles. It was then sheer bliss to have breakfast in bed that morning with the luxury of a free day ahead – even though it was only until the evening, when I was on duty as Orderly Officer, with two weeks of night duty commencing the very next day.

In mid-May the weather had changed quite dramatically and once again we were feeling the heat and humidity of summer, so we were relieved when the order to change into khaki drill was published for the 18th. A week or so before this, we heard the devastating news that the Comet had crashed whilst flying out – from possible metal fatigue – a terrible accident and how awful for the victims and the bereaved.

I was much relieved to get my two weeks' night duty over with, as I had had charge of three wards, one of which was the detention ward. There quite frequently my orderly and I would have to cope with some young servicemen who had committed a misdemeanour – usually just another laddie whose consumption of the local Asahi beer had got the better of him. On the whole these boys were reasonable, particularly when realising that a QA sister was looking after their ward, but as always there could be the odd exception.

One night the Military Police brought in a real tough guy who was abysmally drunk and incapable of coherent behaviour. This was rather an unpleasant experience, as the big burly man towered over me stinking of stale beer, and swaying precariously as he shouted obscenely at us. But the real problem was to get him into a bed which, in his inebriated condition, he flatly refused to do. Eventually, in sheer desperation, I gave up the argument and told him very firmly that if all he wanted to do was to sleep on the floor, he could do so. He did too, and having partially recovered from a monumental hangover appeared somewhat sheepish when confronted by me during my morning rounds!

Ward Eight, isolation, and Ward Thirteen, medical, were also in my care, but at the time neither was full nor particularly busy. Most of the medical patients were recovering from infective hepatitis, requiring plenty of rest and a fat-free and very dull diet. Two nights before I finished, I was feeling a bit under the weather, almost as though I had a chill, but hoped I could shake it off and knowing the hospital was short staffed, I really didn't want to worry the Night Superintendent. So, after checking that all my patients were sleeping peacefully, I told the ward orderly that I was going to have an hour's rest and that if, by chance, I did doze off, would he be certain to wake me at 0400hrs with some tea please.

Retreating to my office with a blanket and a hot water bottle, I settled down in the only comfortable chair to read a book, which I continued to do until 0400hrs when all was ominously quiet. Giving Private Smith the benefit of an extra five minutes, I cleared away my comforts and checked the ward before going to the kitchen, only to find that he like the rest of the patients was sound asleep! I could have cheerfully throttled him, but the poor lad was very apologetic and thereafter rushed around like a scalded cat.

The final benefit of finishing night duty was the thought of having some decent food again, as our main meal was served at midnight whilst on duty on the ward. Each night the food had been disgusting and for the last night's supper I was served three small, under-cooked potatoes, a dollop of soggy, stewed cabbage and one burnt sausage, plus a slender portion of cake and custard.

*

My five nights 'off' from 11 May were more or less wrecked by a streaming cold which, with the hot weather and sticky atmosphere, took me longer than usual to shake off. An added problem, and a major one, came to light at the Monday meeting of the Green Room Club when finalising the details of our Hiroshima play, we discovered that one of the cast had unexpectedly been posted. Just three days before taking part in this international event was too short a time for anyone else to learn the part. After a long discussion, we decided that with the limited time available, our best – and only – plan was to abandon the play and instead present some well-known readings from Shakespeare.

Three evenings later, on Thursday 15 May (and after only one rehearsal), five of us – a sergeant, a corporal, a private, myself – the only female member of the cast – with a captain in charge, set off in a staff car for Hiroshima. It was a lovely, fresh, sunny evening and I was feeling much better, having had my hair shampooed and set that afternoon. Arriving at the large hall in Hiroshima, we saw that it was packed solid with Japanese (many of whom were school-children) invited by the American Cultural Society to enjoy this special event and celebrate in a week of International Culture. Backstage, whilst waiting for our call, the four men were feeling somewhat apprehensive, whereas I felt positively nervous.

At last it was our turn and we began by reading the cross-gartered and yellow stockinged scene from *Twelfth Night* and concluded with the trial scene from the *Merchant of Venice*. I read Portia and to my surprise enjoyed every moment of it, except, when in full flight during the quality of mercy speech, I was suddenly thrown by a loud interruption from a fat flatulent Japanese gent, burping boisterously in the front row, almost reducing me into hysterical giggles. Later I wondered whether the eruption was due to flatulence, or had it been in audible appreciation?

At the conclusion, the audience was most enthusiastic and applauded us generously, although exactly how much they had actually understood would forever remain a mystery. The lady from the Cultural Society gave us a lovely thank you speech and hoped that we should return again soon, only next time with a full production.

To celebrate, we decided to have dinner at a modern but modest hotel which Captain White knew. Even there the food was expensive and not particularly delectable. Despite the cost it was sheer escapism to have a meal away from the Mess and although at the time I quite enjoyed it, I did have some misgivings. This was mainly because I was the only lady present and by then out of uniform, and I was also aware that for some reason or other we were not allowed to eat in unapproved restaurants; whether this one came into that category I didn't know but hoped that the captain did. Finally adding to my unease I realised too, that we were in a party of all ranks, putting me into something of a quandary, as since joining the QAs, I like the rest, had had it drummed in that we were not allowed to mix socially, other than on official occasions…

So, by the end of the evening, I was fervently hoping that the buzz that I had eaten out with three National Servicemen (albeit in the company of another officer) in what may well have been an unapproved restaurant in Hiroshima, would not reach Matron's ears! However, since that evening and to this very day, I have never been quite certain whether the bush telegraph activated Matron's office, as only the following Monday evening, I received the biggest bombshell, which in itself could not have been a more wonderful surprise.

Walking across to the hospital for the evening shift, my heart sank when I saw the Major-Ma'am approaching me from the opposite direction, and I automatically came to a halt as she steamed towards me.

'Oh Hall, I'm glad to have caught you, because your posting to Korea has just come through, and you will be flying over to Seoul within the next few days. Report to Matron's office at 0900hrs tomorrow when you will be given details of your posting order.' And nodding dismissively, she sailed off in the direction of the Mess, leaving me utterly flabbergasted and rooted to the spot … until disbelief was replaced by realisation, followed rapidly by a surge of excitement.

My first sensible thought was that I should have to cancel my new appointment to the Board of Examiners for the forthcoming Surgical Nursing examinations, of which I had recently received notification. Then I must tell Cynthia, thinking too what a coincidence it was that we should both be leaving Kure within a few weeks of each other, when she returned to the UK in early July.

Fortunately, as it happened, due to a shortage of flights, my departure was delayed by several days and the extra time was a real bonus as I dashed around in my off duty in a haze of rushed packing. The actual packing was a major event as I literally had to pack up all my belongings and vacate my room (in case the accommodation was needed). It was a blessing that we had changed into khaki drill, as I was able to stow my winter uniform in my trunk and deposit this with the rest of my heavy gear in the storeroom. My other personal bits and pieces I gratefully left with my many friends for safekeeping.

Among my instructions for advancing to the war zone, there were two which particularly impressed me. The first was that under the circumstances it was advisable to make a will and to deposit it with my family; glancing through my few possessions in the chaos of my room, I considered this to be a rather unnecessary exercise. Having little idea of the construction of a last will and testament, I hastily picked the brains of one of the more experienced QAs; Freda was really helpful and between us we concocted something suitable, which I then mailed off to my parents.

With that out of the way I could concentrate on the other major problem, which was to minimise the number of personal effects and essential uniform I had to take to Korea for my two months' service in Seoul. Already Matron had given much advice on the subject, repeating adamantly, 'On no account, Hall, are you to take any excess baggage. Each item must be weighed, including yourself and please make quite certain that you are correct in your calculations.' Adding with emphasis, 'We do not want to cause an international incident with the Commonwealth Airport Authorities, by having one of our nursing officers carrying excess weight. (Little did I know then that however conscientiously I tried to weigh everything, in the end I should inadvertently slip up!)

'Yes Ma'am,' I meekly agreed, having already heard via the grapevine that some of the old Dakotas used to transport the troops were quite liable to crash; in the past there had been several mishaps and I did wish to become an additional hazard.

Without Cynthia's help and encouragement, I should never have survived the next few days. Between us we sorted out my kit and lugged my suitcase over to the hospital to weigh it (and myself) on the only pair of scales available, situated in the bathroom of one of the medical wards.

Paludrine, the anti-malarial tablets, were another must. These I started taking immediately, because on arriving in Korea I should be in a malarial zone.

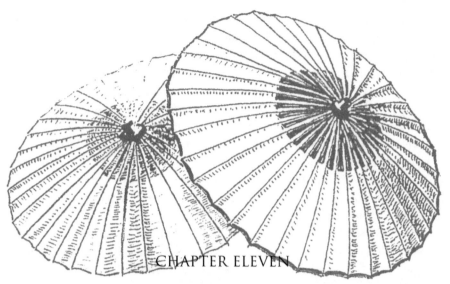

THUNDERBOX AND BLUE RUBBER SHOES

28–29 May, Battle of the Hook – Duke of Wellington's
Regiment. 8 June, the President of South Korea rejected
the ceasefire terms.

Tuesday 26 May 1953

Despite the late afternoon sunshine, a stiff breeze blew across the water whilst Cynthia and I waited on the quayside, idly watching a small draft of troops embarking in the work boat for Iwakuni.

'Jilly, are you okay, have you got everything? Oh and here's some chocky to keep you going!'

'Thanks a million, Cynth, I should never have made it without your help. But I'd better grab a seat now as it's filling up, and anyway you must be getting back to the Mess. I can't thank you enough for coming to see me off. Oh hell's bells, I hate goodbyes – I shall miss you so much when I get back from Korea – just think, in less than two months, you'll be well on your way home to a fantastic reunion with James.'

'I'll miss you too, take care and good luck!' Cynthia smiled, waving to me quickly as she climbed back into the Tilly.

Boarding the small open vessel, I sat on one of the wooden benches and dumped my baggage on the floor. Glancing at the troops seated around me I reckoned there were about eighteen or so on board. All were young soldiers wearing khaki battledress like me, but unlike me they were burdened with tin hats, heavy boots and armed to the teeth with an assortment of guns, bulging kit-bags lying across their feet. To our mutual embarrassment, I realised that I was the only female passenger sitting amongst these tough-looking lads, with instead of a weapon or kit-bag beside me just an ordinary brown suitcase. Clutching a pink Japanese paper umbrella in one hand and steadying a tennis racquet across my lap with the other, I looked as though I was going off on leave, thinking at the same time that maybe this was not the most appropriate way of going off to war…

Unlike on previous occasions when travelling by launch to either Miyajima or Iwakuni, the atmosphere on board was totally different. Instead of the usual light-hearted sense of humour and general camaraderie of the lads, this time an uncanny quietness and gloominess prevailed.

We set off promptly at 1700hrs and although the afternoon remained bright, there was a strong sea running, causing the small launch to bucket around on the choppy water. Not long after leaving the harbour I noticed that several of the lads were looking somewhat green about the gills. For me, however, already suffering from the acute embarrassment of being the lone female on board, I was damned if I would let the side down by being sick as well!

Arriving at Iwakuni two and a half hours later, we were weighed in, allocated our accommodation and given a hot meal. Knowing that we were to have an exceedingly early call, I went to bed at about 2100hrs, but with the general excitement, combined with a painfully hard mattress, sleep was elusive until I eventually dozed off for an hour or so, before being called at 0315hrs.

Breakfast – an enormous sort of Last Supper – was served at 0400hrs and twenty-five minutes later, whilst still digesting it, we were driven out to the airstrip and the waiting plane. This was an old RAF Dakota workhorse, looking surprisingly small, rather tinny and after my sole experience of flying with the luxury of Quantas, boarding it was something of a shock. There were no neat rows of upholstered seats in its spartan interior, just a bare fuselage with long canvas litters stretching from end to end on each side of the plane. Attached to these were canvas back rests and safety belts. To add to my chagrin, when attempting to buckle mine I found that it was both complicated and stiff and consequently one hell of a job to fasten. But, as once again I was the only female amongst the troops, I was equally determined not to ask for help from the soldier sitting next to me…

Taking off at 0500hrs we flew with the colourful splendour of the rising sun, its dazzling rays penetrating the small square windows of the Dakota, temporarily softening the utilitarian interior. With my back firmly fixed to the fuselage, I could see little without craning my neck and only then a few snatched glimpses of Japan, before flying over the sea. Later on I caught sight of a barren land below us which, I thought excitedly, must be Korea.

Shortly afterwards, above the noisy vibrations I felt the plane begin to turn, then circle twice, before landing at a small airstrip somewhere in South Korea.

There we were given half an hour's break to stretch our legs on the muddy grass, whilst a few more passengers and stores were taken on board.

What little I saw of Korea from the plane appeared to be a composition of numerous barren, craggy, towering hills surrounded by jigsaws of paddy fields. We touched down safely at our destination, Kimpo Airport – or what remained of it – at 0900hrs on Wednesday 27 May 1953. After disembarking and checking through the formalities, I was shown into a reception tent and given a welcome cup of steaming hot coffee.

A few minutes later a jeep drove up and out stepped a slim, attractive lady wearing the khaki uniform of a captain in the Royal Australian Army Nursing Corps. Walking purposefully towards me through the open flaps of the tent, she proffered her hand and said with a kindly smile, 'Hello, you must be Lieutenant Hall, our new Sister. I'm Belinda Smith, Matron of the British Commonwealth Zone Medical Unit. Welcome to Seoul.' Captain Smith, then in her early thirties, was many years younger than any other Matron I had met.

From the airport it was about an hour's drive to the hospital and by the time we left, the sun was up and even without its plastic window panes, it was hot sitting in the front of the jeep. We drove towards and eventually on through the city, where I saw some of the devastation which had occurred during the long years of war. There were numerous wrecked buildings, piles of rubble and crumbling roads full of colossal potholes. However, as we drove along, Captain Smith told me that before the war Seoul had been one of the most modern cities in Asia, with broad tree-lined boulevards, flanked by large and substantial buildings. Some twenty minutes or so later, we clattered across the extensive iron spans of the one remaining bridge, from where I caught a glimpse of the local women pummelling their washing on the banks of the famous river Han.

It must have been about 1030hrs when the jeep finally slowed up somewhere on the outskirts of the sprawling city, pausing beside the whitewashed walls of the entrance to the hospital compound. There, after a brief glance at Matron, the armed guard saluted smartly, raised the barrier and we drove through to stop outside a substantial, tall three-storey, old Western-style building, which I noticed had two adjacent but separate front entrances.

'I'll take you up to your quarters first and you'll be able to see the hospital later on, Hall. This way – the driver will see to your baggage.' I followed Captain Smith up the narrow flight of stone steps, into a dark and gloomy hall. 'Our quarters are at the top of the building – this you see is a mixed Mess – so perhaps we are safer up there!' She chuckled as we climbed on up an old wooden staircase until ultimately arriving on the top floor. As we progressed, she also told me she thought that this had once been a school – hence the reason for the two front doors, presumably one for girls and the other for boys. At the same time she mentioned the hospital was of a more modern construction and just a short distance from the Combined Officers' Mess.

'Right, this is where we live and now your home for the next two months, Hall. The sisters were only allocated these two large rooms but since they have been adapted they are more than adequate.' By this time we were standing in the middle of a spacious and airy, but sparsely furnished, room, with white net curtains fluttering across the dormer windows. 'This is our sitting room; you know Jess Milton don't you? Well she has done a marvellous job distempering the walls in her free time and now we have managed to scrounge a few old armchairs, plus this little table; it's really quite comfortable.'

Leading me on through a tiny passageway, she continued, 'Our cubicles are through here, all thanks to the Quartermaster, who had the brilliant idea of sub-dividing this second room into six small cubby holes. We have one each, with a spare for any visiting female who requires a bed in Seoul. This is yours – it's basic but sufficient and sheer luxury compared to what the lads at the front have to live in.'

'I had no idea that we should have so much space here and thanks very much…' my voice trailing off with some embarrassment, as I was not quite sure of the protocol required, whether to address her as Ma'am because as a junior officer it was not necessary, although for one who was also my Matron it might well be.

'By the way, you will meet the others when they come over for lunch. As you know, there are only five nursing sisters here in Seoul, since the two Canadian nurses pulled out to form a small tented unit some miles away. Captain Jess Milton is the senior QA; there are also Lieutenants Irene Chesters and Cynthia Mills whom you are relieving. She will be returning to Kure shortly. Annie Green and myself are the only two Australian sisters. Incidentally, she is on night duty, so we had better not disturb her now. I'll leave you to unpack and to sort yourself out.'

Smiling again, she continued, 'Take the rest of the day off too, as I know what a tedious journey you've had. I hope you will be happy here at the Britcom Z Medical Unit.' She added with a smile, 'By the way our nickname is The Bastard Unit, because on paper we are not supposed to exist! In fact we are very much a temporary hospital of just 100 beds but also one successfully relieving the Field Ambulances and other busy units of their medical overflows, so don't worry – there is absolutely no fear of being disbanded.' Before leaving, she told me lunch was served in the dining-room on the ground floor at 1300hrs, and that she would see me again then.

Peeling off my cap with relief, I threw it onto the bed and flopped down to take stock of my new surroundings. My little cubby hole was roughly 5ft x 7ft in size, partitioned by light plywood screens and with a brightly coloured curtain across the doorway for privacy. The furnishings may not have been quite up to the Ritz, but were more than adequate, consisting of a small chest of drawers, a low bench, a low collapsible bedstead, one folding chair and three orange boxes balanced on top of each other. The bottom of this ingenious arrangement I visu-alised as a storage space for shoes, whilst the top obviously acted as a washstand, with an enamel bowl and tooth-mug provided. There was a pair of bent nails on the wooden screen for hanging my uniform on and on the wall proper, at the end of the cubicle, I was lucky enough to have a small window with curtains and a view overlooking some dusty trees in the compound below. Over my bed was an electric light bulb and on the floor beside it a narrow strip of old carpet. What more could I possibly want? Once I had unpacked my belongings it would look positively homely.

At lunchtime, Matron introduced me to everyone present, including our Commanding Officer who was British and a major in the RAMC, the adjutant who was a Canadian, and some of the other medical and administrative staff who came from various parts of the Commonwealth. Unlike in the huge all-female Mess in Kure, the atmosphere was informal and friendly and I immediately gained the impression this was a small and happy unit.

We ate at a large wooden refectory table: medical officers, sisters and admin staff all mixed up together, plus as far as I could gather anyone else remotely connected to the Medical Services and who was just passing through Seoul. An added bonus was the food, which was unexpectedly delicious – boiled ham and all the trimmings, followed by the sheer luxury of real ice cream with crushed pineapple. I was assured that dinner would be even better and that the secret of such successful catering was that our unit was supplied with American rations.

It was good to meet up with Jess again (who had preceded me to Seoul by several weeks) and after lunch she kindly took me under her wing to acquaint me with the ablutions. These necessities of life were situated just a short walk across the hospital compound, in what appeared to have been some old stables. Pushing open a creaking door marked 'Ladies Only', she guided me into a small room which smelt strongly of Jeyes Fluid (and other things) to meet the Thunderbox – the longest privy I had ever seen and officially listed as a four-seater! Keenly observing the perfectly scrubbed seats, I counted four apertures cosily arranged in one neat line.

The shower block was adjacent and there I was intrigued with the ingenious way the military had rigged up the showers. Spaced at intervals along the top of the crumbling brick wall at the back of the shed, there were five or six old 4-gallon petrol cans, thus giving each bather sufficient room to shower whilst at the same time manoeuvring the single string attached to the can. When pulled, this important bit of string, explained Jess, would sprinkle just enough warm water for a quick shower before it ran out, by which time I began to realise that the lack of privacy when using either the thunderbox or communal shower was not for the fainthearted.

Handing me a pair of blue rubber shoes she said, 'Here Jilly, Matron bought these for you to protect your feet when you shower, and if you look at the floor you'll see why!' Glancing down, I saw several of the bricks on the rough floor were broken and what remained of the cracked surface was something of a hazard for bare feet. Gratefully, I took the little blue shoes, noticing they were upturned with very pointed toes and similar to a pair of Turkish slippers. Seeing my interest, Jess said that the shoes were actually Korean slippers Matron had found in a market place in Seoul, which she had thoughtfully supplied us with to prevent any accidents. Jess went on to explain that, because this was the only bath house in the unit, it had to serve everyone. Therefore each section was allocated its own time and we sisters were only allowed to shower from 1600hrs to 1700hrs daily.

On the way back to the Mess, she added cheerfully, 'By the way Jilly, I'd better warn you that we always have something of an audience when it is what the boys call "Sister's Shower-time". You see all the up patients tend to congregate by the windows to whistle when we troop past clutching our sponge bags and towels!'

'Thanks for the warning, but it was a wise old Matron who once said: it's when the troops stop whistling at you that you really need to worry!'

The rest of the day passed quickly and it was nice to meet Irene, an attractive fair-haired girl, both a little older and more senior than me. She surprised me by mentioning that being on Active Service we were entitled to the same free weekly rations as the troops, consisting of fifty English cigarettes, some bars of American candy and one tablet of soap! That evening after supper she took me over to the small NAAFI canteen where, with some of the patients and staff, we watched an old black and white film.

Sleeping like the proverbial log, after what had been an elongated day, the next morning I was woken up by a little Korean girl with a jug of hot water for washing. Knowing no Korean, I could only smile and thank her in English. Sadly, for all the weeks that I lived in the Mess she never responded and like the majority of Korean people who we came across, few appeared to want to have much contact with us.

Breakfast was at 0730hrs and we reported for day duty at 0800hrs, a pleasant change from the slightly earlier time in Kure. Irene explained – as in Kure we had three hours off duty each day – that the extra half hour gained each morning was to compensate for the loss of a weekly day off and instead at weekends we had alternate half days, with either the morning off until 1300hrs, or free 'after handing over' for the rest of that day. This was a sensible arrangement, as I had already gathered there were few places to visit. Matron's strict instructions were that, to ensure our safety, if we did venture into the city, the following rules must be observed:

1   We were only allowed to go out in pairs.
2   Before leaving the Unit, we must either sign the out-book or inform Matron of our exact destination.

I realised then that with just five sisters to cover the hospital, it would be difficult to escape from the confines of the BC Z MU more than very occasionally.

❖

Irene took me over to the hospital, which appeared to be a shabby and somewhat battered collection of buildings in the compound of the old school. The hospital itself was housed in the largest building constructed in the modern style of the 1930s with a rather bleak and box-like exterior, protected by a long flat roof. The main entrance, with its double doors, was situated in the three-storey central square tower, which provided a division between the smaller two-storey section to the left of it and the larger one, with a continuation of the three floors on the right. All the windows – and there were many – were made up of small panes of glass, similar to Crittal windows. Several panes were missing, presumably due to bomb damage as I had noticed a small crater on my way to the bath-house. Outside the building were a couple of tall, dusty-looking trees, and a few tired bushes in a deserted flower bed in the middle of the driveway.

Walking through the double doors into the gloomy entrance hall of the building, the wide central stone staircase conveniently divided the interior into the smaller administration block – including the ambulance services – on the left-hand side, with the larger and lighter ward areas situated on three floors on the opposite side, accommodating approximately 100 patients.

It was quite a climb up to the top ward where about thirty (collapsible) beds and a number of folding chairs were closely, but neatly, arranged on either side of the whitewashed walls. Beyond the ward there was a basic and small kitchen area, ablutions and a tiny office.

This seemed small after working in a hospital ten times the size, until the reason was spelled out to me: the lack of water available to the unit. The city of Seoul had been so devastated that our supply was non-existent and consequently all the water was delivered by bowsers, so that every drop required to run the hospital had to be carried in large cans. This explained why we were purely a medical unit, because under the circumstances surgery was impossible.

My first day on duty I spent working on the upper floor, in a ward full of sick soldiers from most parts of the Commonwealth. It was fascinating to listen to their different accents and in particular to a couple of French-Canadians, who frequently lapsed into French. Working on the wards and aiding us in the care of the patients, we had a small, mixed quota of British, Australian and Canadian nursing orderlies. On duty as it was the hot season and we wore our grey dresses but, because of the difficulty in laundering them, without the traditional QA veils.

During the late afternoon, when admitting a new patient, I was amused to note his reactions because, as I went forward to help him off the stretcher, 'Gee!' he said with surprise, 'A real Sister, in a real dress, here in Seoul – I don't believe it!' And as we lifted him into bed, added, 'Not real clean sheets as well?' Repeating with pleasure, 'I don't believe it – it's just too good to be true.' The poorly, tired and scruffy lad must have had a tortuous trip down from the front like the many others I admitted later, and who, when they saw the QAs were also there in Seoul – plus the added bliss of flopping into a properly made-up bed – reacted with the same amazement.

Despite the unfamiliar surroundings of the BC Z MU, I quickly adapted to the different environment, nursing routine and tapless situation – where all the water was carried by hand to the three main ward areas of the hospital. These were on the ground, middle and upper floors of the old school. All were basically furnished with low-level, folding metal beds, a few standard chairs and one or two small tables, thus giving just enough sufficient comfort and space to the sick lads for their recovery, before they returned to the front.

The QAs worked on whichever floor we were required within the hospital. Apart from supervising and helping with the important basic routine nursing care of bedmaking, bathing, recording of TPRs, fluid and blood pressure charts and checking of special diets when necessary, plus four- to six-hourly medicine rounds and penicillin injections, by the end of the day I began to realise, somewhat disappointingly, that most of my time had been spent in documentation.

'Please come, Jilly,' pleaded Cynthia Mills later that same evening. 'You see when you've been here a bit longer, you'll find there are few opportunities to escape from the Mess and I'd really grab this one if I were you.' She had just asked me to go with her to a dinner party – to which we had unexpectedly been invited – and I wasn't too keen to go, but as she was returning to Japan quite soon, I felt that perhaps I should.

'But what on earth do we wear? Because my khaki drill fits so badly I hate going ashore in it.'

'Don't worry about that as we are all in the same boat. Anyway, Jess allows us to wear a silk cravat in the evenings and as you well know, it is etiquette to roll down your sleeves after sunset.'

'Honestly Cynthia! Is that really to conceal one's lower arms or to avoid being bitten by the blasted mosquitoes?'

'A bit of both; but will you come – please?'

Prevaricating further, 'No, I'm sorry I can't, as I haven't got a cravat, so that settles it!'

'No it doesn't, Bill the MO has several spares. He's in the Mess and I'll get one from him now,' she retorted and shot off before I could reply.

After a quick bird-bath in my enamel bowl, I changed into my khaki drill skirt and jacket, dutifully rolling down the sleeves and winding the maroon silk RAMC cravat around my neck, whilst thinking – I suppose it's a type of red, even if it's not exactly scarlet!

The evening was wet and chilly and a heavy drizzle blew through the open-sided jeep as we bounced our way along eight miles or so of excruciating pot-holes, so on arrival neither of us felt exactly dressed for dinner, with crumpled uniforms and damp, lank hair. We immediately cheered up, however, when Mathew (an officer in the US Army) welcomed us into his impressive tent. This was an extra special tent, the like of which neither of us had seen. To satisfy our curiosity, our kind host suggested a conducted tour, courteously indicating the bathroom should be our first port of call. There, perfectly screened behind olive-green canvas, we were dumbfounded to see an authentic bathroom with, of all things, a proper, full-sized bath, but of course – no taps!

After sprucing ourselves up, Mathew showed us into a small bar with prettily shaded lights where, to my immense surprise, we were served dry Martinis, before transferring to the dining area of the tent for dinner. There were six of us at table, two Americans, a Canadian, an Australian, Cynthia and me; quite representative of the United Nations. Unbelievably, we ate hors-d'oeuvres and soup, followed by a huge steak with freshly cooked vegetables, and finished the superb meal with some delicious coffee. The table was set with a crisp white linen cloth and everything was perfectly served, with only two tin plates amongst the china ones.

It was a pleasant evening, with the additional bonus of Mathew's cuddly Korean puppy, called 'Pooch', a fluffy, golden-coloured dog with sad droopy eyes, resembling something of a bloodhound. However, at the same time, it did seem incredible to be indulging in such luxury and rich food, when only forty miles or so away from the front line. Only that morning, when crossing the hospital compound, I had heard the rumble of distant gunfire.

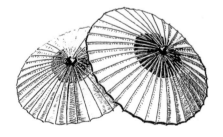

CHAPTER TWELVE
CORONATION DAY

30 May 1953

It took me a good forty-eight hours to settle into the routine in Seoul. Even the climate differed from Kure; unexpectedly cooler and at times definitely chilly and if Bill – the kind MO – hadn't insisted on lending me his spare khaki pullover, I would have been frozen. This I wore over my grey dress for a few days; fortunately Jess, our senior QA, did not mind the temporary breach of uniform, as it was just a matter of keeping warm.

So far the rare glimpses I had had of the Koreans had given me the impression that they were very unlike the Japanese, appearing less sophisticated and much more of a peasant stock. This was not surprising, considering their country was until quite recently occupied and subdued by the Japanese. The few with whom I had briefly had contact looked incredibly sad after surviving three long years of war. In the distance across the road from the hospital, large numbers of pathetic-looking shacks extended up along the slopes of the barren hillside, where it seemed the majority of the civilian population were huddled together in poverty and squalor.

Although the peace negotiations between the UN and Communists contin-ued, the war went on relentlessly with news filtering through the grapevine that within the past forty-eight hours there had been a terrible battle – later referred to as the Battle of the Hook (28/29 May). Then, tragically, the Duke of Wellington's Regiment suffered 149 casualties, including sixteen captured and twenty-nine killed when their trenches collapsed under a succession of direct hits. Apart from the occasional and distant gunfire, the night before I had heard at least one bomb exploding, but luckily some distance from the hospital.

As Cynthia Mills and I were both off duty until 1300hrs on Sunday 31 May, Matron asked us to represent the Unit that morning at the pre-Coronation Service in Seoul Anglican Cathedral which was situated some distance away. Sitting in the front of the jeep, I was able to appreciate the extent of devastation as we passed through the city. Practically every dusty street had its quota of wrecked buildings, as little had escaped the onslaught of the invading and retreating Communist armies, until Seoul had been recaptured two years earlier by the UN Forces on 15 March 1951.

Entering the large cathedral church of St Mary and St Nicholas, we found that it was absolutely packed with the military uniforms of almost every member of the sixteen countries of the United Nations serving in Korea. Cynthia and I were shown to our seats which were somewhere in the middle of the nave. Next to us was another lady, who told us that she was a missionary doctor and had been working in Korea for several years. Later, to our mutual surprise, we discovered that we three were the only women present in an exceedingly large congregation of men.

The service was impressive and the lesson was read by Lieutenant-Colonel Dinsdale, Welsh Guards. At the conclusion, as the congregation stood to attention to sing the national anthem; the effect was electrifying and I felt very proud to be British. By the time we returned to the Unit, our uniform and hair were impregnated with the gritty white dust, something to which I was already becoming accustomed.

That evening, after duty when I was talking to our Quartermaster, Major Black – a kindly middle-aged man with a long Army experience – I tried to explain to him how sad I felt at the amount of destruction I had seen during my few short days in Seoul. In particular, the desolation within sight of our own small, well-manicured unit: the pitiable squalor of the rabbit hutch-like hovels in which these impoverished people existed. To me, most pathetic of all were the numbers of little children I had seen in the streets, flimsily dressed in an assortment of patched and tattered rags, dirty, unwashed, with constantly running noses. These small kids appeared to spend their time hanging around on street corners, selling anything that they could get hold of – from American chewing gum to tiny Korean cakes. Their average age could not have been more than about six and I had the impression that the poor kids had been thrust onto the streets by desperate families.

Major Black listened to my indignation with interest. Then he explained that as a result of the war many hundreds of children had been orphaned, but I should also understand that although it was impossible to help them all, there were several orphanages in the area, all of which were assisted by the armed forces. In actual fact our own unit supported one of these, adding modestly that he himself was responsible for it. Quick as a flash I asked if I could visit it with him one day. With equal speed he replied sternly, 'No! It's much too sad for you to see.'

'But why so?' I enquired – feeling slightly put out.

'Believe me, Sister, it truly is a desperately sad situation and worse still, one that is practically impossible to resolve. The orphanage is full; admittedly the children have the bare living essentials but with so few helpers, there are far too many for them to love, resulting in something of a harsh regime. Poor little devils…' Then, smiling kindly, he added, 'Perhaps if things improve a bit, I'll take you there – but not yet!'

Later that night, I wrote a long and somewhat depressing letter to my parents, suddenly swamped by a combination of homesickness, frustration and sadness. My first five days in Seoul had made a vivid impression, in stark contrast to the knowledge that few people at home in the UK had any idea of the misery which so many were suffering in Korea, or even for whom everyone was fighting…

Coronation Day, Tuesday 2 June 1953, was an extraordinary day at the unit, where promptly at twelve noon all the patients and staff drank a loyal toast to Her Majesty Queen Elizabeth II, our new Queen. The whole atmosphere was reminiscent of Christmas, as magically the gloom lifted; everyone was in a holiday mood and better still none of us had too much work to cope with. As members of the 1st Commonwealth Division everyone was given a commemorative edition of the Forces Newspaper, *The Crown News*. This special publication – unlike the usual stereotyped black and white sheets – was bound in a thick, pale blue paper cover, with an inset on the front cover of a stunning colour photograph of the lovely young queen. The contents included a large map of the royal route, listing the various processions taking part in the Coronation Parade. There were also loyal messages from all over the Commonwealth, with an especial gem written by Sir Winston Churchill:

> It is the golden circle of the Crown which alone embraces the loyalties of so many states and races all over the world. It is the symbol which gathers together and expresses those deep emotions and stirrings of the human heart which make men travel far to fight and die together, and cheerfully abandon material possessions and enjoyments for the sake of abstract ideas.

In fact, the whole paper was aimed at making each one of us feel that we too, although thousands of miles away, would in some small way be able to participate in this momentous day.

After lunch Jess and I, with Gay – a Royal Australian Air Force sister recently attached to the unit on a temporary basis – drove to the City Stadium in a jeep decorated with two small Union Jacks, to watch the Coronation Sports, in which members of the 1st Commonwealth Division were competing. The afternoon was dry and warm and it was relaxing to soak up the sunshine, as we idly watched the various activities taking place in the arena.

Seoul City Stadium was situated not far from BC Z MU and was part of a huge complex built by the Japanese ostensibly for the Olympic Games in 1940, though this was cancelled due to the Second World War. Jess mentioned there were other facilities, including two Olympic swimming pools, adding surprisingly that these were to be found right behind our Mess, and that somewhere near them there were supposed to be some old tennis courts – so perhaps my racquet might yet be useful!

That evening in the Mess, we had a rare treat, roast turkey with delicious American sweetcorn for dinner, then it was time to change into our glad-rags, because all the Mess members who were free to go had been invited to a Coronation Day Party at Headquarters. Jess – being the senior – made the critical decision that instead of turning up in crumpled khaki drill, at this important event we should wear our distinguished scarlet and grey. Because I had only my tropical kit with me in Seoul, she kindly lent me one of her Tippets and for this special occasion we wore our flowing white veils.

It was a colossal party – with everybody who was anybody present. Consequently, it was heavily loaded with top brass and never before had I seen so many colonels in one go. During the evening Jess and I were introduced to the Commander-in-Chief, General Maxwell D. Taylor, the three star US General in command of the Eighth Army. This was exciting and also a bit awe-inspiring until, when shaking hands with me, he smiled and addressed me as Ma'am! I could not help thinking just how tough and handsome he looked. Champagne was running like water, with the majority of the guests drinking considerable amounts. In fact this was noticeable wherever one seemed to be, either in Kure or Seoul, and at the time made me wonder whether the habit of seemingly drowning one's sorrows was due not only to the continuous war but also partly to the artificiality of life whilst on Active Service.

Then, to everyone's delight, the rumour which had been circulating was confirmed – that during the day the patriotic Gunners at the front had fired red, white and blue smoke over the lines of the Gooks (the nickname given by the UN troops to the North Korean and Chinese Communists). Although by far the most sensational news to reach us late in the evening, and to bring a fitting climax to the day, was the conquering of Mount Everest by Sir Edmund Hillary and Tenzing Norgay, with the expedition organised by Brigadier Hunt, of whom we in the Army felt especially proud.

As we were leaving, I literally bumped into Anne, one of my friends in the British Red Cross and normally based in Kure. She explained that she had been temporarily attached to our unit for a few weeks. It was a lovely surprise, realising that she had only just flown into Seoul where she had been caught up in the celebrations.

❖

By early June the weather was drier and hotter and I had settled well into the drab surroundings of the hospital and its routine. My only real disappointment was that, as a ward sister, most of my time appeared to be spent in written work and documentation, due to the large and fairly rapid turnover of patients admitted and discharged. All three wards were staffed by experienced nursing orderlies to look after the patients, usually with one sister in charge. Though often sick, these lads were rarely seriously ill, as patients admitted to the hospital had previously been diagnosed with non-urgent medical conditions, which could vary from chest or urinary infections, skin complaints, gastric conditions, tonsillitis, headaches or abdominal pain. If a patient's condition worsened and required surgery, then he would be immediately transferred (most probably by helicopter) to the American hospital in Seoul. However, the unit was a very happy one, with each one of us part of the team relieving the field hospitals of the medically ill, with the majority of patients returning to the front as soon as they had recovered.

The lads admitted were always so pleased to see us, and usually they were a mixture of Commonwealth troops. Occasionally we had American GIs and recently we admitted two Republic of Korea soldiers. Unfortunately the language barrier helped none of us, but as neither of them was too poorly they were soon discharged.

The previous morning, when I was off duty from 1000hrs until 1300hrs and thinking that I should occupy myself with some embroidery, Anne, realising I was at a loose end, suggested I should accompany her to the American hospital in Seoul where she would be visiting the British Servicemen hospitalised there. She added, 'You see, Jilly, if they aren't too sick, you could have a chat with them. I know they would love that because they do get homesick and if you could just listen whilst they tell you about their families, it would be really therapeutic.'

Accepting her invitation with alacrity, I rushed off to change into khaki drill and seek permission to leave the compound. Joining Anne some minutes later in the hospital forecourt where her jeep and driver were waiting because, as a the Red Cross visitor, she was blessed with her own transport. For me it was sheer heaven to clamber into the jeep, knowing that I could escape from the hospital compound for a couple of hours.

The American hospital was some distance across the city, and on arrival I saw was extensive in comparison with our own small unit, although in appearance as equally drab and bare, being mainly a collection of large old buildings, tented areas and modern Nissen huts. Situated close to the hospital entrance there was a helicopter landing pad with a huge distinctive white 'H' painted on the tarmac.

I was much impressed with all I saw, as Anne showed me some sections of the vast hospital where the medical staff were doing a magnificent job under difficult conditions. Then she guided me through various corridors to an upstairs ward where there were several badly wounded British lads, all of whom had suffered gunshot wounds but fortunately were now recovering well from their recent surgery. I sat and quietly talked with them until their lunch appeared, when the Senior Nurse on duty gave me an unexpected lecture, on the importance of colour co-ordination in food! Judging by the brilliance of her nail varnish which matched exactly the puce of the beetroot dumped on the plates – and not wanting to cause an international situation – I mentally disagreed!

However, the other nurses I met that day were kindness itself and when Anne had to go off to sort out a problem elsewhere, two of them suggested that I should go across to their quarters with them. These were large utilitarian Nissen huts, with drab exteriors but basically comfortable within. Whilst chatting to one of the girls, I happened to mention that my hair was in a mess, and with that swift warmth of comradeship, which most American women possess, she immediately suggested that while I was there I should make use of their own hairdresser and whisked me off to the salon, which was close by in another Nissen hut.

The hairdresser was not unsurprisingly American but, surprisingly, had been trained at no less of an establishment than Helena Rubenstein. I could hardly believe my luck, which, however, was to be short lived. Visibly shuddering whilst assessing my Japanese trim and flinging an enormous grey nylon cape over me, he pushed me down into the big black barber's chair. Then, waving a large pair of scissors over my ragged fringe, he pronounced in an ear shattering voice, 'This sure must be another bundle from Britain…'

Despite my vivid blushes, acute embarrassment and his apparent rudeness, he cut my hair superbly well. Needless to say it was a costly business, as the five-minute trim swallowed up one precious dollar – the expensive equivalent of 7s 6d.

Despite the somewhat dull daily routine on duty, living in Seoul was a fascinating experience, particularly as one was never certain as to what might happen next. We heard on the news that the Peace Treaty talks were continuing, although these were not progressing too well. The South Koreans living in Seoul appeared to be more than a little upset about the terms of the proposed ceasefire, because during the last few days there had been huge demonstrations all over the city. Even from the hospital compound we frequently heard and saw long, thin lines of people, demonstrating volubly, as they shambled past.

These pathetic processions were mainly composed of elderly men and women, some of whom were frail, old and bent, as they shuffled wearily by and always accompanied by the children – lots of them – some chanting, some shouting. Many of the protesters carried large banners with 'Unification or Death', painted on them in English. Most of the adults were dressed in typical peasant fashion, the men wearing wide-brimmed, conically shaped straw hats, loose white shirts and baggy trousers and the women in their traditionally high-waisted dresses with long skirts and upturned shoes.

The tense situation in the city reverberated on us as we were confined to barracks until further notice, with an extra six armed men deployed to guard the hospital compound.

Although on the whole our ward duties in Seoul were surprisingly lighter than in Kure, at times I still experienced a certain amount of fatigue or general weariness. Trying to shake this off with an early night on Monday (8 June), I was rudely awoken around midnight by two loud explosions. Leaping out of bed, I threw on my khaki slacks, pullover and shoes and rushed over to the hospital but halfway down the stairs I remembered that according to the drill I should be wearing my dog-tags (metal identification discs) and dashed back up to grab them. By the time we had assembled at our emergency posts and when all was quiet, the air-raid sirens sounded…

Reviewing the situation some minutes later, the commanding officer decided against evacuating the patients from the upper floors, unless there was further activity. Fortunately there wasn't, and after an hour or so we all thankfully tripped back to bed. Doubly so for me, having endured the embarrassment of forgetting, in my haste, to put on a bra, consequently suffering the loss of an uplift, and with the added the irritation of an Army-issue pullover!

Well into June, the weather became increasingly hotter and at the unit the swift turnover of patients continued, with the majority only requiring a few days' hospitalisation. This was perhaps a bonus for them but left a certain amount of frustration for us, as we rarely had time to get to know them.

Since the initial blasts on 8 June from the bombs dropped by the Gooks on the outskirts of the city, things were quieter, although there had been a few minor air raids and several more demonstrations, so we were still confined to barracks. However, my own peace was well and truly shattered with the arrival of the mail one morning, which included one hell of a rocket for me from the Matron in Kure. Her letter stated in no uncertain terms that she had received a serious complaint, to the effect that during my recent flight to Seoul both myself and my luggage were overweight. And that was after all the soul searching and weighing which Cynthia Gould and I had put in to it in Kure. This was upsetting because, somehow or other, I should have to prepare a reasonable written defence, which I knew would take up any spare time I had.

The English mail had also arrived and with it my parents had sent me a huge bundle of newspapers describing the Coronation, as well as my mother's account of the television party which they had given for their friends on 2 June. This really cheered me up and that afternoon I spent my off duty concocting a statement to the authorities in Kure, counteracting their claim and stating firmly that, as requested, I had religiously weighed every item. At the same time I wrote a letter of explanation and apology to the Matron, fervently hoping that, with luck, this might conclude the embarrassing saga.

Recently, the skies above us had seemed busier than ever with more and more helicopters flying overhead. Since living in Seoul, this was something to which we were all accustomed: it was commonplace to hear the whirring blades and chopping sounds of the engines, as the pilots of these friendly little planes navigated by following the roads ferrying both men and materials. Two days previously, during a lull in activities, I was able to get permission to visit the American hospital again with Anne. This time we were provided with an armed guard for protection – a charming Canadian soldier with a cheerful grin and an impressive moustache. Driving along over the potholes, Anne glanced up, remarking, 'Heavens! Just look at the numbers of choppers up there today. Don't you sometimes feel that we are living in a sort of enormous goldfish bowl? Wow! Look at that…' As she spoke, passing noisily over us we identified an ambulance chopper, heading in the same direction as we were, carrying an extra outside stretcher and a patient well wrapped in blankets on it. This was not the first time I had seen patients being transported on the exterior of these amazing little aircraft.

Getting out occasionally with Anne, instead of being incarcerated in the Mess, was a tremendous bonus and as we drove through the city streets we often saw Korean women in traditional dress. Wearing either white or black short attractive boleros over their high-waisted and full-skirted long dresses and with rubber bath shoes on their tiny feet, they wore their jet black hair long and straight or scraped into a severe bun at the back of the head. The older men wore baggy trousers and were frequently seen staggering under the weight of a heavy A-frame, bearing fodder or firewood. When I had managed to get into the city with Irene we happened to see several Republic of Korea (ROK) soldiers as well as a handful of Korean Naval personnel. The ROK soldiers whistled at us in an uncomplimentary way, presumably because they were unaccustomed to European women on the streets of Seoul. It was evident too from their demeanour that they did not much like the US or UN troops, and on another occasion we were actually spat at – but as they missed, no harm was done!

A week or so later, due to increased usage, my old fountain pen gave up the ghost so I had to take some drastic action to purchase a new one. This was when I was lucky enough to visit the bulk NAAFI in Seoul with Matron and Irene. At the same time we were hoping to stock up with some of the necessities of life. Fortunately I was able to buy a beautiful Parker 51 there which, although expensive, was ideal for the daily form filling. While we were trying to shop in the large, basic, hutted building, we noticed in the busy crowd of servicemen who were milling around that a considerable number of the GIs were buying up as many bottles of Scotch as they could – which presumably they were unable to obtain in their own PX (Postal Exchange, the US equivalent of the NAAFI). Frustratingly for us, it appeared to be much less of a hassle to purchase an expensive fountain pen, than to find, let alone buy, the smallest bottle of deodorant or a packet of Bunnies (as sanitary towels were nicknamed)!

CHAPTER THIRTEEN

BEDCHECK CHARLIE

10 June, Communist Forces launched an offensive against South Korean positions; by 16 June ROK11 Corps pushed back to new Main Line of Resistance. 17 June, revised demarcation line settled and President Syngman Rhee orders South Korean guards to release North Korean prisoners who do not wish to be repatriated. 23 June, the South Korean Government repeated its objections to the ceasefire terms.

From the middle of June onwards the Gooks stepped up their air raids, and it became a nightly occurrence to wait up for 'Bedcheck Charlie', as we had named the Communist bombers. We knew from the grapevine that the ceasefire negotiations were stalling and thought the extra aerial activity could be a psychological attempt to blackmail us – instead it had the opposite effect.

Immediately the siren sounded, we slipped into our emergency routine, dashing across to the hospital and evacuating the patients from the upper floors to the shelter of the ground floor corridors where everyone remained until the all-clear. Prior to the previous night, when we heard some explosions in the distance, there had been little real activity and it was rumoured that the Gooks had only a small arsenal of bombs, mostly second-hand stuff left over from the Second World War. For me the worst annoyance was that, having gone to bed early the night before I was due to start night duty, we had to get up for two false alarms.

My seven nights on duty from 16 to 23 June, when I was in charge of the hospital were very busy and a time when it was a real advantage to sleep undisturbed by day, unlike the poor day staff who, because of the increased activity by enemy aircraft, were having to get up several times each night. On 17 June, there were no less than six warnings within twenty-four hours, so that even I lost out.

As night sister, when an air raid was imminent, I received a special early warning signal, designed to give my staff and me time to light a few candles before the Unit blacked out and the siren blasted off and the lights were automatically extinguished. During my fourth night, Bedcheck Charlie postponed his visit until about 0300hrs, much later than usual. This turned out to be a real nuisance raid which lasted for at least a couple of hours. My main task was to resuscitate both the poor patients having yet another disturbed night and the weary day staff who were once again on their feet.

During these disturbances tea in vast quantities was of the utmost importance and I quickly became adept at organising lashings of it, remembering another emergency in Aldershot when, as a new and very inexperienced QA, I was much helped by my then Deputy Matron – Major Agnes McGeary of Chindit fame – who rolled up her sleeves and taught me how to make tea in a bucket! This time it was literally by the bucketful, because with such huge numbers to cater for, plus a dearth of large teapots, it was the only sensible way to make and distribute it.

My office soon became a running buffet and after a night or two it was christened Jill's Grill! During these nightly disturbances there was often something of a party atmosphere amongst the patients, especially those lying on stretchers in the dark cramped corridors, as they cracked jokes about the Gooks and their second-hand bombs. These patients were a wonderful bunch of lads and my only problem was having to waken them when there was an alert, discovering they were usually able to sleep through any amount of noise! My nursing staff was superb, looking after the sick lads so well, and, with the Sergeant-Major, also treated me as though I were a piece of Dresden china.

Later during that week, after handing over the night report to Matron, she asked me if I would like to have the chance to go out of the compound that afternoon with Irene and herself, as she had to buy some flowers. As this was the first opportunity I had had to escape for over ten days, I accepted with alacrity. Sleeping soundly for several hours before meeting them at 1600hrs, we drove into Seoul by jeep to a tiny florist's shop Matron had found not far from the main railway station (another impressive building though damaged in part by shellfire.) We all squeezed into the shop – which was little more than a cubby hole – leaving the jeep in the capable hands of our driver.

Sadly, the few blooms on display were almost past their prime and very expensive but eventually Matron found a small bunch that would do. Returning to the jeep we saw that it was surrounded by a band of jostling, clamorous, tattered little boys who, when they saw us, instantly demanded money. There must have been about ten of them, shouting vociferously, causing something of an upheaval as we clambered into the vehicle. While Matron was getting into the front seat I saw one of the little wretches shove his thin, grubby hand into the pocket of her skirt, trying to grab the Parker pen protruding slightly from it and shouted a warning to her in the nick of time.

Soon after leaving the area, we were held up for some time by a large demonstration of schoolgirls, all of whom were neatly dressed in white blouses and navy skirts. Several carried placards and banners and all were chanting the now familiar slogan, 'Unification or Death', as they marched along. At the time I thought it was sickening that these young schoolchildren had been manipulated into participating in these political demonstrations, feeling instead they should be allowed to live as normal a life as possible in this sad city. Now, with the hindsight of age, I can understand how strongly not only the citizens of Seoul, but also most of the population of South Korea, distrusted the very real threat of partition which menaced them. Tragically, half a century later, the situation remains little changed with the nations of North and South Korea still pretty much divided.

Back in the Mess again, I found that my hair and khaki drill uniform were plastered with the inevitable powdery white dust. Dust was everywhere in this benighted place, embedding one's fingernails, even penetrating one's most private areas, so that we all had the same problem of trying to keep clean and tidy within the limitations of water rationing. Writing my (almost) daily air letter home to reassure my parents that any reports in the Press about the current air raids in Seoul were exaggerated, I included an urgent request for a soft nail-brush! Recently, at night we had been plagued by dozens of horrible fat black flies, which buzzed shamelessly around us, whilst we swatted in vain!

The peace negotiations struggled on and it was rumoured that Dr Syngman Rhee, the President of South Korea, was being difficult about the treaty. Recently, for some obscure reason, he had unexpectedly released an enormous number of North Korean Prisoners of War from Pusan and also from somewhere outside Seoul. None of us could really understand the full implications of his actions – apart from being a slap in the face for the United Nations – and at the time could only surmise that he was crazy to allow these unfortunates to roam around at will.

During my penultimate night on duty there was an unexpected respite from Bedcheck Charlie when things were unusually quiet and our boys had an undisturbed night. My two French Canadian nursing orderlies were a great team and it was fun to listen to their attractive French drawl, as well as the many other accents when I did my rounds. Since working at the hospital, I had met – to my surprise – quite a number of British boys actually serving with the Australian Army, including several Scots, a few Irish and an aggregate of English lads, all of whom wore their distinctive Digger hats with pride.

Bedcheck Charlie revisited us in the early hours of Monday (22 June and my last night) when we were plunged into darkness for over an hour and a half; later we heard that there had been five Red planes circling the city. Some time before the siren blasted off we had a bit of kerfuffle in the hospital when one of the guards saw an intruder attempting to break in, and for about half an hour or so my office was seething with people, whilst one of the French Canadian guards chased after him. Minutes later I heard a couple of shots being fired. Shortly after that the guard returned and reported that all was well, confirming that whoever had entered illegally had just escaped by jumping the wall of the compound. Then, after checking his rifle, handed me the brass cartridge case of one of the bullets he had fired – which I still have to this day.

After finishing night duty, I was given forty-eight hours' leave and spent the first twenty-four sleeping to shake off my weariness. The following morning Anne invited me to visit the lads at the American hospital. The sun was high in the sky and it was baking hot inside the jeep; outside the road looked like a dust bowl and our journey was only enlivened by the presence of our ever-smiling Canadian guard who, when briefly posing for a quick snap, impressively brandished his rifle. Two hours later we were glad indeed to return to the comfort of the Mess for lunch.

At table our kind CO was talking to Gay – a Royal Australian Air Force nursing sister temporarily attached to the unit. To our surprise he was speaking sternly, saying, 'No! I am sorry but it must go – and go very quickly too.' Wondering idly as I enjoyed the roast turkey and cranberry sauce what IT was, I suddenly remembered that I had heard the unit had been given a little Korean goat as a mascot. Where it had come from or who had bequeathed it to us I had no idea. The CO continued firmly, 'You see, Sister, it's much too unhygienic to keep a goat, albeit a small kid, in a hospital.'

'Yes Sir, I understand and I'll do my best to get rid of it today,' replied a downcast Gay.

'But how can you? Unless you give it to one of the Koreans who work in the hospital. Come to think of it, that's a good idea, as I'm sure they would be grateful.'

'Especially to have some nicely stewed young kid for their supper!' chipped one of the young Medical Officers.

'Oh please don't say that – I couldn't bear it – it's such a sweet little thing,' Gay exclaimed. 'But,' she continued 'my boyfriend in the Air Force is serving with a squadron which I just happen to know is without a mascot. And what's more, I'm pretty sure that they would love to have Minnie, as she's been christened by everyone here.'

'But that squadron is some distance away, so how do you propose to get her there, Sister?'

'Quite easily, Sir, that is if you could please lend me a jeep?' Gay said, fixing her large brown eyes appealingly on the CO's stern countenance.

'Okay, once you have contacted your friend and made the appropriate arrangements, I'll fix something up for you. But you will need some help, is there anyone who could go with you?'

'What about you Jilly, you are off duty today – wouldn't you like to come, even if it's only for the ride?'

'Oh yes, I'd love to and I can look after Minnie, whilst you negotiate with the Royal Australian Air Force.'

'That's great. I'll ring Bob now – hopefully he won't be out on a mission – if so perhaps one of his friends will bale me out.'

Luckily for Gay and Minnie, Bob was there and he was given the go-ahead to accept the kid as a mascot, so she was no longer destined as the main ingredient for a Korean Hot-Pot!

Fortunately the CO managed to include the three of us in a jeep, already detailed to transport some stores over to the Air Force Base within the hour, so it was not long before Gay and I climbed into the back of the canvas-topped but open-sided vehicle, carrying a rather forlorn-looking Minnie with a bright red ribbon bow tied askew round her fluffy white neck. Bleating continuously throughout the journey, she stopped only when suckling my fingers. Some distance from Seoul, when driving across a deserted plain, we heard a couple of shots ring out. 'Snipers,' muttered our driver as he accelerated along the near straight and dusty road; speeding onwards, we heard no more.

Bob was waiting at the Air Force base, where he introduced us and little Minnie to several of the crew members. All were delighted with their new mascot and minutes later she skipped off happily to her fresh abode.

As we waited for the jeep to unload before returning to Seoul, Bob suggested that we might like to watch some of the Sabre Jets just about to take off on a mission. This was a thrilling opportunity, as we had heard much concerning these highly sophisticated planes, and walked quickly with Bob from the hutted area of the base to the small airstrip some distance beyond.

On ground level they appeared small and flimsy but only until take off, as the high-pitched whine of the powerful jets rapidly increased to a loud crescendo, before hurtling up into the sky. This was enthralling as we were standing not far from the planes, and as one of them took off, I glimpsed the pilot, waved spontaneously, and to my delight he returned the signal. The tremendous power and speed of these small planes impressed us, because one moment they were sitting quietly on the ground and the next roaring up into the clouds and the battle zone beyond, leaving behind them a trace of black smoke and an empty silence. This brought the reality of war considerably closer and, simultaneously, a lump to my throat.

The returning jeep was full, with two extra passengers, the driver and ourselves as we hastened back to base before the 1800hrs curfew – imposed since the recent unrest in Seoul. All went smoothly until we had been travelling for about half an hour, by which time we were driving at speed along a straight narrow dusty track of loose sand and gravel, steeply banked above some paddy fields. So far so good, I thought peering through the haze, when in the distance I suddenly spotted a huge cloud of dust surging ahead and through this the faint outline of an oncoming jeep, racing closer and closer towards us.

Realising in a flash there was insufficient room for both vehicles to pass in safety, and simultaneously experiencing an unusual sense of calm, I was convinced (at twenty-five) that this was the end. Fate, however, had other ideas. Shaken by a deafening sound of screeching brakes and skidding tyres, our jeep gave a terrifying shudder as it swerved to avoid the oncoming collision, before somersaulting over the bank and landing upside down in a paddy field, several feet below!

For a moment it was eerily quiet. Then came the realisation we had landed safely, if overturned, onto a soft field of rice. Checking each other for possible injuries, we were remarkably composed, remaining in a recumbent position with our feet touching the canvas roof until, slowly one by one, we crawled out of the wreckage. Our good sergeant driver, who had remained cool and calm throughout, unbelievably only sustained a few scratches to his face and hands; miraculously no one else was injured.

The US Military – the occupants of the other jeep – gave us a lift back to the Royal Australian Air Force Base, where we were immediately taken to the First Aid Post to be checked by the Medical Officer on duty. There our sergeant had his cuts and bruises treated and the rest of us were given a small tot of brandy to combat shock. After politely thanking him, because neither of us thought that we should return to the Unit smelling of strong drink, Gay and I discreetly disposed of ours behind the nearest convenient bush!

The subsequent return journey to Seoul occurred without further mishap and it was only as we were approaching the outskirts of the city that one of the passengers, a rather quiet, fair, young RAF pilot officer, mentioned with something of a chuckle that this had been his second misfortune in less than twenty-four hours, modestly explaining that his plane was shot down during the night and that he had had to bale out. What a courageous lad and just one of many…

After giving Matron the briefest of explanations when we apologised about being delayed for the curfew, it was much too late to have a shower. Thankfully I was able to grab a jug of hot water and with it managed to scrub off the thick coating of dust I had amassed, using the remaining few inches to shampoo my gritty hair.

Thursday 25 June was the third anniversary of the outbreak of war with the invasion of South Korea by the North Korean Forces. We understood there were

tremendous demonstrations in the city and consequently everyone was confined to barracks for another twenty-four hours. At least Bedcheck Charlie had ignored us for the last few nights and things were unusually quiet. We had all hoped for definite progress concerning the ceasefire negotiations, but from the news filtering through these were still at something of a stalemate.

Two evenings later, after dinner, Major Black intriguingly invited Irene and me to see the view from the roof of the Mess, adding cautiously that as things appeared to be quiescent, it was safe to go up there. So, we followed him up the narrow staircase until we climbed through one of the dormer windows onto the ledge of a small balcony. By that time it was dark and at first we could only see the sporadic lights of the sprawling city, flickering down below. Pointing to the far distance, he asked, 'Can you see the twin beams of those searchlights in the distance over there, girls?' Sure enough in the darkness, obviously some miles away, we could make out the crossed beams shining upwards. 'Just there?' pointed Irene.

Nodding he said, 'Ladies, that is where, at this very moment, history is being made, because those powerful searchlights are deliberately beamed over a little village called Panmunjom, which is where the ceasefire negotiations are being thrashed out between the Chinese and North Koreans and the United Nations and South Koreans.'

'Presumably the searchlights are to prevent either side in the conflict from bombing them?' I asked.

'Yes, that is correct.'

'What a memorable sight. Do you think there will be an agreement soon?' enquired Irene.

'I hope so, although from what I've gathered, as always, there is a certain amount of stalling taking place,' the Major concluded.

The following twenty-four hours brought a dramatic change in the weather, commencing with a violent thunderstorm – far more deafening than any air raid and the pre-cursor of torrential rain – which partially dampened down the ever-present dust, but with the temperature rising steadily and already up to 87°F, everyone was beginning to feel the humidity. Luckily Irene and I had just discovered the site of the old Olympic swimming pools, located only a short distance behind the Mess, and with freedom of access to them when we were off duty, it soon became a cool and refreshingly relaxing pastime.

Unsurprisingly, neither the deep 18ft diving pool nor the large swimming pool were in their former glory; both suffering from decaying edges with cracked concrete slabs and much overgrown with weeds. However, because the water was heavily chlorinated the pools were safe for swimming and we understood that troops based in Seoul had permission to swim there, though we had met very few, until the one evening when I happened to be the only occupant in the pool, a couple of US servicemen turned up, jumped in, and swam straight across to inspect me (or my swimsuit) a fraction too closely. Baling out smartly, I left them gazing into an empty pool!

CHAPTER FOURTEEN

ORPHANAGE, PEGLEGS AND CHOCOLATE MUD

The UN Command and Communists agreed to negotiate an armistice without South Korean participation. 13 July, Chinese Forces launched another attack on South Korean positions.

For me personally, the last week in June and the first in July were the most significant since my arrival in Seoul, with three totally unexpected diversions; at breakfast on Monday 29 June, when Major Black casually enquired whether or not I was off duty that afternoon. Affirming this, he asked, 'In that case, would you like to come with me to visit the orphanage, as I have to take a delivery of stores up to them?'

After a busy morning on the wards, I dashed back for a quick lunch, changed into khaki drill and grabbed any spare cash I had in my room. Then, rushing over to our small NAAFI I bought a dozen bars of chocolate, three small toys and a few bars of candy, which the kind lad on duty packed into a small, square, cardboard box. Outside the hospital, Major Black and his driver were packing large boxes into the jeep. As soon as they had finished, he looked up with a brusque, 'Ready?' I nodded. 'Right then, jump in because we have a long drive and I don't want to be too late.'

He was quite right, as we drove out some way from the city before continuing through open countryside, where we slowly climbed up a long, steep and lightly wooded hillside. According to the Major, the orphanage was called Myung Jin and it had been established for a considerable time. However, since the outbreak of hostilities things had become extremely difficult, with the partial destruction of the buildings and most of the equipment. During the war the children and staff had been evacuated to the island of Jeju by special arrangement of Chaplain Bressdell of 5th Air Force, until it was safe to return to Seoul. On Jeju Island another detachment continued to support the sister orphanage which remained there. At our BC Z MU we tried to help Myung Jin in Seoul as much as was possible.

On arrival, we were greeted by one of the teachers who was genuinely delighted to see us. Shortly afterwards I was taken off by another for a tour of the orphanage and to meet some of the 179 children living there, whilst Major B and the driver unloaded the stores. Fortunately my guide could speak a little English, just sufficient to show me around the living quarters of the small and dilapidated old building.

The house itself had suffered extensive war damage and passing from one small room to another I noticed that practically all the ceilings were badly cracked, some with large chunks of plaster hanging down in places, whilst a number of the thin interior walls had gaping holes. These, I noticed, were often stuffed with pieces of torn blankets and sheets of old newspapers, presumably trying to insulate them during the freezing winter months. The sheer poverty of it was heartbreaking and although everything I saw within the building was spotlessly clean and tidy, at the same time it was pitifully poor and threadbare.

The children were sweet and very friendly, and on the whole seemed happy enough; each one I observed to be well occupied with some useful task or other. In one tiny, cramped upper room, I met a handful of young girls, sitting cross-legged on some matting, busily sewing and I asked if I might see their work and when they showed me the beautiful designs that each was intricately embroidering I was not only astonished by the excellence of their work but even more by their age, as the eldest looked no more than about eleven. What truly grieved me was to see them stitching away in poor light and on such wretchedly cheap cloth, which would surely disintegrate long before the carefully worked embroidery silks. The girls were justifiably proud of their work and when I enquired as to what happened to the finished items, they told me that they were sold to raise funds for the orphanage. Embarrassed, I turned out my empty pockets – remembering too late that I had invested my all in the few chocolate bars which were in the jeep.

The nice teacher gave me a roneoed leaflet, written in rather quaint English, containing a potted history of the orphanage and a concise account of the children's weekly routine, by Mr Huh Chon Man the Director of Myung Jin

Orphanage, # Shin-Dang Dong, Song O'Dong Ku, Seoul. The following was tabulated under the heading of Daily Life:

A. Three meals a day for each child (Soup, Rice, Kimchi) Quantity ... 414 G per day.

Interval foods are given for small children.

B. Two pairs of clothing for each child.

C. Three sheets of blankets per child.

D. Sanitation Situation.

a) Bath ... once a week.

b) Medical Examination ... once a week.

c) Change of clothing ... once a week.

E. Recreation.

a) Movies ... once a week.

b) Music Concert ... once a week.

F. Church.

Beginning from May 1947, church has been arranged in the orphanage. The church accommodates not only members of the orphanage but also neighbours and friends as well as a meeting place for people to have sacred hours.

ROUTEEN OF DAILY LIFE.

0600hrs	0630–0730hrs	0730–0840hrs
Getting Up	Sweeping	Praying
0900–1200hrs	1200–1240hrs	1300–1600hrs
Lesson and Exercise	Lunch	Lesson
1600-1700hrs	1700–1800hrs	1800–1840hrs
Recreation Playing	Bathing	Supper
1900–2000hrs	2000–2040hrs	2100hrs
Lesson Preparation	Class Meeting	Taking Bed

Some of the bigger boys had their own band and before we left they put on an impromptu concert for us in the yard outside the house. They played well and several of the little girls clapped their hands in time to the music, excitedly watching the boys perform. Then, one of the real babies of the group, a tiny girl who could not have been more than three or four years old, stepped forward smiling prettily at me, bowed and then danced such a lovely little dance; luckily I had my camera, for which she sweetly posed.

When it was time to take our leave, I remembered with shame the small box of goodies in the jeep. By then I was both overwhelmed by the number of orphaned children and acutely embarrassed by the diminutiveness of my gift – feeling at a loss amongst so many, as what on earth to do with it.

Plucking up courage as the band finished playing, I crept forward and placed the box in the circle of children. With a great whoop of joy, they swept up the miserable prize – whereas I left Myung Jin feeling dreadfully inadequate and more than a little humbled.

The following afternoon after lunch, Matron with the other RAANC sister and I drove across the city to the Severance Hospital. We were there to attend the Dedication Service of the newly constructed fifth floor of the remaining wing of this extremely busy and well-established civilian hospital in Seoul. Partially run by Missionaries, it had an extensive history of service and devotion.

As long ago as 1884, a Dr Allen became the first practitioner of Western medicine in Korea, at a time when people were frightened that he might dig out their eyes or livers to make drugs. It was not until the doctor saved the life of a royal prince (the victim of an assassin and bleeding to death) that he won the confidence of the Emperor, and his services were at last accepted. The Emperor built a hospital for Dr Allen, which subsequently developed into the present day Severance Hospital, named after a wealthy benefactor. This became an international interdenominational institution, predominantly supported by the Mission Boards of the Presbyterian Churches of the United States and Australia, the Methodist Church of the US and the United Church of Canada. The medical college commenced in about 1900, seeing 35 per cent of Korean doctors graduate from there, and at the same time the Nurses Training School was begun by a Miss Shields.

During the Korean War practically two thirds of the site was reduced to ruins, including the out-patients building, private patients' wing, maternity wing, three nurses residences, main college building and twenty Korean houses. The remaining buildings were damaged and most of the equipment lost. What was saved was used on Koje Island in a hospital for refugees, where the work of this branch is continued. After much interruption from the war, the hospital in Seoul reopened in April 1952 with cots and bassinets salvaged from the wreckage, plus a forty-bedded unit donated by UNCACK. The college resumed in June 1952 with 125 students of whom, for the first time, some were women. The Nurses Training School has, over the years, graduated 462 trained nurses, with forty-two student nurses under training in 1953.

Driving up to the battered building, I saw piles of rubble close by and many badly damaged buildings in the distance. At the entrance we were warmly welcomed by two of the Missionary nursing sisters, who took us up to the fifth floor where the ceremony was to be held. Already a number of people had gathered in the large, cream-painted foyer of the wing, including a handful of white-coated doctors and several sisters. Opposite us across the room a small group of young Korean student nurses, wearing freshly laundered uniforms and starched caps, talked quietly amongst themselves.

The dedication was conducted in Korean by a Christian Korean priest, who was also assisted by several of the hospital staff during the half-hour service. At the conclusion we had an opportunity to meet more of the Missionary sisters and I was amazed to hear that some of the older ones had been working at the Severance Hospital for thirty years. By nationality the nurses, as these courageous women were called (whereas at home in the UK they would have the title of sister), seemed to be a happy mixture of mainly Americans and Canadians, and several Australians.

Then we were invited to take a tour of the hospital wing and, of course, the brand new floor of which they were justly proud. It was a lovely hospital with such a happy atmosphere and where everything was running in good order, despite the devastation, continuing air raids and general shortages caused by war. For me, all was well until we came to the last ward of the visit: stopping for a moment outside the shabby old swing doors, the Senior Nurse remarked quietly, 'This is the children's ward and it's possible that you may find it rather distressing,' pausing briefly she added, 'You see these particular children are all amputees…'

Then she pushed open the doors and we followed her into a huge, high-ceilinged, drab and dismal ward, crammed full of little children, all chattering away until we appeared when, with a momentary hush, the many pairs of small brown eyes looked with interest at the strangers by the door. Seconds later, pointing to us and smiling broadly, they began to talk excitedly amongst themselves.

Never before had I seen such a pitiful sight and my immediate thought was that even the lost orphans of Myung Jin seemed far better off, because at least they were physically fit. At a glance, I saw that all the thirty or forty vulnerable little children there had lost either an arm or leg and, as I was to discover later, occasionally two limbs. Walking slowly around the closely packed cots I noticed that the only artificial legs that seemed to be available were wooden. However, wooden legs or not, the courage, skill and humour of these very small children was so utterly amazing that I was swiftly shaken out of despair. Hearing a happy chuckling sound beside me, I turned around to see the mischievously impish face of a tiny, thin scrap of a boy grinning at me before he literally threw himself onto a diminutive pair of wooden crutches, hurtling forwards and running at full pelt to meet up with his young buddy waiting for him at the far end of the long ward. Unbelievable, with only one small leg and a small pair of crutches.

Noticing my incredulity, the Nurse said, 'We try our utmost to rehabilitate each one of them and on the whole they do cope wonderfully well and seem to be reasonably happy here.' As we left, she added, 'There is one older lad whom I should like to introduce you to, because after meeting Choi I think you will better understand what above all else we are trying to achieve at the Severance Hospital. Please come with me,' and we followed her along the corridors to return to the foyer. There she enquired of a colleague if Choi was nearby. 'Actually, he's in the Rehabilitation Department: I'll go get him now – hang on,' and off she scurried. While we waited, we were told his story.

During a heavy bombardment in 1952 when Choi was a lad of about twelve, his home was destroyed, killing his parents, grandparents and brothers and sisters and he was seriously injured, resulting in the tragic amputation of both forearms.

'But just wait until you meet him, then you will really understand why things are not as grim as they often appear,' said the Nurse with a broad smile, which illuminated her tired but kindly face.

A few minutes later in walked Choi, a tall, lanky, nice-looking boy, who smiled a quiet 'Hello'. I noticed below his shirt sleeves, replacing his lost hands, two pairs of stainless steel hooks attached to the artificial arms hanging limply at his sides. After introducing him, the senior nurse handed him the telephone and said, 'Choi, please show these ladies how well you can dial a telephone number.' He did, too – quite expertly dialling it with the thinner of the two hooks on his right hand. 'Isn't he great? You see, he can manage practically everything with his artificial hands that is necessary in everyday life, even cutting up his food. So Choi will have a bright future, because he's mastered all this through his own faith, courage and will power. We have only been instrumental in guiding him along the way.'

By then the kind Nurse was bursting with pride over Choi's achievements. Proud she might well be, I thought, because not only was he in good physical shape – after such an horrendous experience – but more importantly, I realised that his confident smile radiated both happiness and trust.

As we left I smiled at Choi who, to my surprise, took hold of my hot sticky hands in his cold steel hooks and then for that brief moment I felt that someone blessedly good was holding them.

Exactly fifty years later, I read of the tragically similar case of twelve-year-old Ali Abbas, who during the Iraq War also suffered a horrendous loss of family, appalling amputations and dreadful burns for one so young. Hopefully he too is recovering from the excellent treatment received. But why, oh why, do the children always have to suffer at the hands of those in power? Despite the incredible advances mankind has made during the five decades since the Korean War, little seems to have changed.

'Yes, I can spare you both, providing you are ready to leave directly after lunch. The jeep will pick you up at 1300hrs and will get you back here again for lunch tomorrow, in time to go on duty at 1300hrs. Is that okay?' Matron asked, adding kindly, 'It's time that you two had a little break.' Leaving her office to return to the wards, Irene and I looked at each other with amazement.

'Heavens! I can hardly believe it, can you?' exclaimed Irene.

'And it's a real twenty-four-hour leave pass we've been granted. What's more, I've heard on the grapevine there are actually baths at the leave centre in Inchon. Think how blissful it would be to have a jolly good soak'.

'I can throw some bits into a grip at lunchtime; can you do the same, Jilly?'

'Of course, I just hope that it will stop raining by the time we leave.'

During the past two days there had been an excessively heavy rainfall, when the Han River had become dangerously swollen. One blessing from the continuous downpour was that whilst the visibility was poor we were no longer bothered by nuisance raids.

Luckily, later that morning there was a break in the weather, when the rain suddenly stopped and the sun came out, so the drive to Inchon was not too bad. It was exactly thirty-one miles from the Unit to the leave centre and the farthest either of us had been since arriving at BC Z MU. Soon after leaving the outskirts of the city, we were engulfed by a sense of freedom and felt quite skittish as we drove on through some of the prettiest countryside that either of us had seen since being in Korea. Somewhat similar to that of rural Devon, with fields of emerald green, banks of rich red soil, occasional clumps of trees, their thick foliage shimmering in the bright sunshine, and ahead a line of fertile hills, several capped by craggy peaks.

The greater the distance we travelled, the worse the condition of the roads, with our good driver constantly having to circumnavigate enormous potholes. He was obviously familiar with, and utterly stoical about, the poor state of the road. Eventually, even this petered out into what appeared to be a cart track, along which we lurched for the last few miles, until finally arriving at the camp.

'Right then, see you tomorrow ladies, I'll be here at 1100hrs; have a good leave,' and saluting smartly, the driver climbed into the jeep to tackle the journey back to Seoul.

The Officers' Leave Centre at Inchon, we discovered, consisted of a quaint little Korean house unexpectedly situated in the middle of an immense military rest camp which was surrounded by open fields. After signing in, we were shown to a small room, sparsely furnished with two mosquito-netted cots and a chest of drawers, and as Irene aptly remarked, 'It's not exactly the Hotel Splendide, but just look here Jilly…' as she poked her head into a small recess to one side of the room, 'we've actually got our very own thunderbox!' Reacting as though it was the end of term, we threw our khaki caps onto our respective cots, dumped our few possessions, before setting off to walk as far as we possibly could in the couple of hours free before dinner.

The grounds of the camp were huge and it was a fantastic feeling to tramp along and to stretch our legs for the first time for six long weeks. We followed a narrow grassy track through several fields, where to the left of us we stumbled across a superb view of the pretty coastline hugging the Yellow Sea, famous for the landing of the UN Forces at Inchon in September 1950 when recapturing Seoul. After the confines of the dusty city and although a disappointing grey, the sea, with its refreshing breeze, was an immediate boost to our morale.

Once or twice during our long walk we passed small enclaves of modest Korean houses where we occasionally met a handful of children, some of whom would trot happily along beside us for a little while. These were happy, rosy-cheeked, real country children and much unlike the thin, waif-like city kids haunting the streets of Seoul. On our way back we met a smiling young peasant girl whose lovely baby was asleep on her back, swaddled safely within a deep sash of black material, which was tied tightly around her waist with the loose ends hanging down over her dress. This appeared to be the traditional method used by the Korean women to transport their young, whilst at the same time leaving their hands free for other tasks – such as working in the rice paddies.

Passing through a different entrance on our return to the camp, we noticed a tiny hillock nearby which had a white painted signpost on top of it. On closer inspection, we saw it had six arms, each of which indicated the name and distance of a capital city: London, we discovered, was 10,000 miles away. Returning to our quaint accommodation, the little Korean girl assigned to us enquired if we should like to bath before dinner and this we accepted with alacrity. The bath was a Korean original and turned out to be nothing more than a large, circular, stone bowl, which the girl had filled with blazing hot water. When it was my turn, all I could do, once I had managed to get into it, was to sit with my knees tucked under my chin, just like the proverbial missionary in a pot!

Emerging a little flushed from the ordeal, I found that a note had been delivered from the Commanding Officer of the camp, inviting us both to join him for dinner at his house. This proved to be a pleasant meal, with six at table – including two of the medical officers from Kure whom we both knew slightly. Afterwards, we all walked over to the Garrison theatre to watch the camp concert. This was pretty ghastly and, unfortunately, was followed by an even worse film. So, after thanking the CO, we dashed back to our little house where we slept blissfully for the next nine hours; but as we slept and slept the rains came down and down!

The rain was still torrential when our jeep arrived promptly at 1100hrs, resulting in a grim first half to the return trip to Seoul. The cart tracks and roads around Inchon took on the appearance and substance of thick chocolate ice cream, as we slithered, lurched and skidded our way through slurries of deep mud. This stuck to the tyres like glue, impeding our progress until our resourceful driver could free them. Indeed, the thirty-one miles seemed to stretch to 131, until we eventually hit the city roads and returned to the quarters just after 1300hrs. However, the long walk, abundance of fresh air and relaxing sleep had worked wonders and we were both surprised to realise how so short a leave could produce such beneficial results.

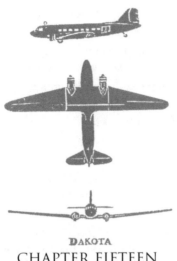

DAKOTA

CHAPTER FIFTEEN

ARMISTICE AT LAST

19 July, Armistice talks at Panmunjom concluded. 27 July 1953, Armistice signed at Panmunjom.

By the middle of July I had completed my seventh week in the Unit. Since being in Seoul, the changes in the climate had been quite dramatic; with the temperature and humidity increasing daily everyone was complaining about the general stickiness. It was the sense of airlessness which affected me worst of all and I noticed others were similarly affected, so by the end of the day when we had finished our duties, we were in a state of lethargy, feeling limp and weary. The hospital was full, but as always, with a large majority of the patients constantly in transit, the actual nursing care remained rather limited and a considerable amount of our time was still spent in documentation.

That week we had a visit from an Army Padre, who amongst his other duties held a service of Holy Communion early one morning in one of the smaller wooden huts in the compound. There, a handful of personnel made up the congregation; the altar was a bare trestle table and the service was simple and quiet.

Sadly the war machine ground on, with further attacks from the Chinese, whilst both the ceasefire negotiations and the people's demonstrations against partition continued. At times the contrast between the abject poverty of a large percentage of the citizens of Seoul and the relative comfort of our own lives in this war-torn city was hard to comprehend – more especially one evening, when Irene and I were invited to a dance at the big American base.

The dance – which neither of us enjoyed and from which we would have gladly escaped had it been possible – was held in a luxuriously appointed Mess with jukeboxes, coloured lights and wall hangings of silk parachutes. Coinciding with our arrival at the door, a large US military bus drew up which to our astonishment was full of Korean ladies who, at a glance, were much made up and dressed to kill in sophisticated Western style.

Later, when chatting idly to our host, we noticed that several of the ladies were dancing with some of the higher ranking US officers. Irene enquired if they were from the Embassy, because – as she explained – it was unusual to see any who were not in national costume. Laughing loudly, before replying brashly he said, 'Oh them – yeah – they're just the home comforts that are bussed in...' This bald remark finished what was left of the evening and we were much relieved when the transport arrived to take us back to our simple surroundings.

One evening just prior to this inauspicious dance, I had had rather an embarrassing encounter with a visiting US medic. When a few of us were sitting on the stone steps outside the Mess admiring the sunset as well as endeavouring to cool off after another busy day, he plonked himself down beside us. Although he appeared to be quite well known to Jess and Irene, I had not met him but perceived for some reason or other that the other two were ignoring him. I misguidedly thought that he was probably a bit homesick and just wanted to talk to someone, so when he suggested that we took a short walk I agreed.

Johnny appeared to know the locality and as the curfew had been lifted I imagined that it was alright to go a little further afield. From the Mess he guided me across an open grassy area and through a gateway into a deserted field, which I briefly noticed was partially secured by an inadequate barbed wire fence. Halfway along the narrow track, he stopped suddenly and made a lunging pass at me. Dodging sideways, I swiftly suggested that we had walked far enough and it was high time we returned to the Mess. 'Gee, just spare me one little kiss, that's all I want,' he pleaded, throwing his arms around my waist. Giving him an almighty push, I managed to free myself and strode rapidly away towards the fence, as he yelled after me, 'Hey! Wait for me – you'd just better be careful – as this field is mined. That's what the notice says over there... Come on, we could have such fun...' Mines or not, my immediate decision was that it was preferable to be blown sky high than to be seduced by a drunken soldier in a Korean minefield!

Retreating hurriedly to the safe perimeters of the Mess, I puffed my way up the steps, to find Jess was still there. Noting my somewhat dishevelled appearance and solitary return, she smilingly enquired, 'Back so soon? Well he is a bit of a lecher and I really should have warned you. He's already tried it on with the rest of us!'

'What minefield and all?'

'Yep, only the minefield was cleared long ago – so you would have been quite safe, Jilly…'

'Safe!' I snorted. 'As it was, I've just had one hell of a job to save my virtue…' and burst into giggles.

Another week passed, although unfortunately it could have been a better one, because for about four days I was under the weather and felt utterly washed up. Matron insisted that I should rest in bed and initially I was thankful to crawl off but after a short rest began to feel guilty about letting the others down, since with so few of us in the Unit, none of us could afford the luxury of being off sick. During the next two days I made two attempts to return on duty – failing miserably each time. However, after a further twenty-four hours thankfully things improved and I managed full-time duty.

Matron was also able to give us some extra time off, which we found particularly helpful as by this time the humidity had intensified to 100 per cent, with a daily temperature fluctuating between 90 and 100°F. It was quite commonplace to wake in the morning to find oneself literally stuck to the sheets, and when writing to my parents I apologised as yet another fat blob of perspiration plopped onto the page!

Daytime was the most uncomfortable, as we coped with wringing wet collars and rivulets of sweat trickling all the way down to the back of our knees. Since the advent of the wet season, everywhere was depressingly damp; a general odour of mouldiness pervaded. During these few enervating weeks – when also suffering the pangs of homesickness – I had a craving for a glass of cool fresh milk and some thinly sliced brown bread and butter.

On Tuesday 21 July, Jess and I were invited to dinner with the nurses of the Severance Hospital and luckily the evening was fine and dry as we were driven over to their living quarters. This was actually a small house, situated in the hospital grounds, surrounded by a mass of rubble and several bomb-damaged buildings. Miraculously their little home – for that was what it truly was – had escaped the onslaught, although once inside we noticed that the plaster was badly damaged in several of the rooms.

After a warm welcome we were shown into a small but comfortable, somewhat shabby, dining room, where we were invited to sit down at the table. To our surprise this was covered with a sparkling white tablecloth and beside each place setting was a starched linen napkin. For us it had been many months since we had eaten in such splendour, albeit the napery was both well worn and exquisitely darned. We had a deliciously home-cooked meal of roast chicken with the luxury of fresh corn on the cob, lots of other lovely fresh vegetables and a wonderful home-made gooey sort of pudding. However, most enjoyable of all for us was being able to relax in such a homely atmosphere, whilst exchanging our different experiences from various parts of the world.

There were about seven or eight of us at table and I was sitting next to a young American girl, whom I discovered had the responsible post of nurse in charge of the operating theatre. She was really friendly and after the meal brought in her two gorgeous dogs to meet us. Pansy the little puppy was especially sweet, and snuggled up and fell asleep on my feet. The Australian nurse tutor talked mainly to Jess regarding the training of the Korean student nurses – another challenging task. At the other end of the table were three of the physiotherapists working at the hospital and with the vast amount of rehabilitation required, they must have been in much demand. When it was time for us leave, I felt sad because for the first time for months – if only momentarily – I had been welcomed into a genuinely happy home and generously made to feel very much a part of it.

The following day was a particularly cheering one for the Unit when we was entertained by a visiting ENSA group from the United States, who kindly took their show to each ward so that all the patients were able to enjoy it. When they visited my ward I was very amused to see the full-skirted lady soprano – of rather mature years and endeavouring to emulate Doris Day – march across the ward and sit on the bed of our youngest patient. There, through heavily mascara-ed eyelids she gazed amorously at him, before bursting into song. Amidst repeated catcalls from his mates, the poor lad – puce with embarrassment – looked around despairingly for somewhere to escape. Thankfully, though, at the beginning of the fourth verse she hopped off his bed, turning her attentions to another.

Matron told me on Saturday morning that she was pretty certain that I should be returning to Kure on Thursday 30 July. So this was my last weekend in the Land of the Morning Calm, the national name of this war-torn country of Korea. In many ways I was pleased to be returning to Japan and the Land of the Rising Sun because, once there, I should only have a limited time to serve in Kure prior to sailing home to the UK.

Initially the lack of urgent nursing care, combined with the swift turnover and continuous chore of documentation at the Unit, had been frustrating. At the same time I had immensely appreciated the invaluable experience I had had during my two months in Seoul. Through meeting and seeing with admiration the manner in which the civilian population had coped with the devastating casualties of war in this benighted land, I hoped that I had gained a better understanding of the realities of life and, hopefully, an increased maturity. In addition – on the lighter side –

during long evenings spent in the small dark ante-room in the Mess, I had finally accomplished the art of playing darts whilst drinking half a pint of beer. And when we were – as frequently happened – confined to barracks, I even finished embroidering my tablecloth. Consequently, I was sincerely sorry to leave this small, happy Commonwealth unit, with its united comradeship and international loyalty.

That Sunday evening it was announced on the radio that the Armistice would be signed in Panmunjom at 1000hrs the following morning, on Monday 27 July 1953. At the British Commonwealth Zone Medical Unit, we were all genuinely delighted and much relieved that – hopefully – hostilities had ended, although most of the people whom we met during the day had taken the news very quietly, almost as though no one could quite believe that it was true.

That night Jess and I went to an impromptu celebration at the Officers' Club in Seoul, where a number of people had gathered. Everyone there was extremely pleased about the Armistice but, again, many were hoping that it would not be breached. On the whole it was a rather subdued evening, which I presumed was because almost everyone was intensely weary of what had seemed to be such a cruel and lengthy war. Albeit, we did have champagne to drink and several of the younger and more high-spirited members of the Club, flourishing their glasses of bubbly, jumped fully clothed into the small swimming pool!

My return journey to Japan, on Thursday 30 July, was far swifter than my outward one to Korea. Leaving the Mess after breakfast, I travelled by jeep to Kimpo Airport in time to catch the 1045hrs plane. It was a pleasant flight and wonderfully cool at 9,000ft, but probably due to turbulence the old Dakota did wobble around a bit during the final lap. We landed safely at Iwakuni at about 1320hrs and, by a stroke of luck, I managed to get a seat on a fast VIP launch to Kure. This was a super trip with a fresh breeze blowing, speeding across a sparkling blue sea and arriving in Kure in just one and a half hours.

Walking into the Quarters once again, things appeared slightly unfamiliar. However, whilst standing in the dark passageway, peering around for the number of my new room, the floor started shaking and the windows rattled noisily, culminating in the strongest tremor yet: I knew exactly where I was!

After dumping my luggage and hastily tidying myself, I went over to the hospital to report back to Matron's office and whilst walking along the dusty old track, I carefully rehearsed my spiel... ('Please Ma'am, as I am still due for at least five days R&R leave and because I'm feeling really tired after my stint in Seoul, may I apply for some leave as soon as possible?') But the moment I entered Matron's office, I realised that my application was a dead duck.

Glancing up from her paper-strewn desk, the new Matron, Lieutenant Colonel Mackaness QARANC, enquired, 'Yes?' whilst the Major-Ma'am, who was sitting at her own desk in the other corner of the spacious room, said, 'Ma'am, this is Hall, who has just returned from our Unit in Seoul; I don't think that you have met.'

'No, that is correct. Well, I am glad that you are back here again in Kure.' Quickly checking the large duty roster, she added brusquely, 'Report to Ward Ten at 0730hrs tomorrow morning and, oh yes, you are going on night duty on Sunday, so this is only a relief duty. That's all.' And nodding at me rather vaguely, I was dismissed. Only I decided that I was not going to go as meekly as that!

'But Ma'am, I have literally just flown in from Korea, so all my gear is in store and I've only the bare necessities of uniform with me and most of that is dirty.' And before she could interrupt me, continued bravely, 'In any case, I was given to understand from Captain Smith in Seoul that, following my service there, I should be due for at least two days leave…' Muttering limply, 'As I'm feeling rather tired too.'

'Well, I suppose if you haven't any clean uniform, we shall have to spare you for one day whilst your house-girl gets on with your laundry. So take tomorrow for your day off and report to Ward Ten on Saturday morning. Right, Hall, that is all.' Off I went knowing that further argument was useless.

Walking slowly back to the Mess, with anger seething in my breast, I could not but help thinking about the cool reception I had received. At the very least I thought, they could have enquired how I had enjoyed the experience of serving in Korea or even – at a push – asked if I had had a reasonably good journey. Things certainly had changed in my absence.

For the next twenty-four hours, I took comfort by wallowing in no less than four steaming hot baths and shampooed my hair twice, gradually ridding myself of the sweaty dust of Seoul. There was more encouraging news, too, because on the recent Postings List, I was due to sail from Kure on 5 September. So, with just over five weeks remaining at the BCGH, I began to suffer from quite a strong dose of 'Funnel Fever'!

DAKOTA

CHAPTER SIXTEEN

'BIG SWITCH', YOKOHAMA CONVOY AND FAREWELL

5 August–6 September 1953, Operation Big Switch, exchange of Prisoners of War, took place.

My ultimate night duty at the Britcom General began on 2 August when I was again destined to take charge of the same three wards: isolation, skin and, of course, detention. Despite the added responsibility of the latter, it was rewarding to have some real nursing to accomplish. Soon after I took over, we admitted two lads to isolation with suspected poliomyelitis, both of whom were immediately placed on the Seriously Ill List. My nights were very busy caring for these sick boys, as well as keeping a good eye on all the others.

During August the temperature in Japan was hotter than that which I had recently experienced in Korea, but at least we had electric fans on the wards and plenty of ice available to help cool the patients. Luckily, being on night duty I was also allocated a fan. This I had on full blast all day, sleeping only under a sheet, but with the suffocating heat it was still difficult to get much sleep.

The UK mail was again delayed but very much appreciated when letters and packages of newspapers finally arrived. Once again I had to send an urgent but final request to my poor mother, for some new pants and a fluffy powder puff to replace those recently disintegrated on active service.

By 6 August, with my embarkation date just over four weeks away, I dashed down to Kure one morning for a shopping spree, and bought as many presents as I could to take home to family and friends. The only item I purchased for myself was a strong second-hand 'tin' trunk, made of heavy oxidised aluminium. The old Poppa-*san* tried hard to rook me for 4,500 Yen, which because it was so grubby it certainly wasn't worth. Eventually, after a lot of haggling, I managed to knock him down to the more reasonable equivalent of £3 10s.

From the grapevine we heard the wonderful news that the repatriation of all Prisoners of War, code-named Big Switch, had just commenced. Meeting Pat and Georgina shortly afterwards, we all began to realise that the release of these large numbers of POWs could well affect our own departure date. 'Although,' Pat added hopefully, 'I'm sure they will need some of us to nurse any that are really sick, on the troopship!' It was fun to meet up with two of my original travelling companions again and they passed on the good news that the Major-Ma'am was extending her overseas tour for another eighteen months in the Middle East, therefore hoping she would only accompany us as far as Port Said.

Tiredness and fatigue seemed to dog me during my second week on duty, and at night I was extremely busy and still anxious about one of my patients with polio who was not making good progress. This poor boy was only twenty-six and a regular soldier, with his future and Army career now uncertain. Fortunately, the other sick lad with polio was making a good recovery. It was on about 10 August that we admitted our first ex-POW. This unlucky lad had been captured in December 1951 and it was almost three years since he had sailed from the UK. Luckily he seemed to be reasonably well, so he would soon be fit for Med-Evac home.

'Jilly! Whatever is the matter with you? You look dreadful,' exclaimed Georgina a couple of mornings later, as we passed each other going on and off duty.

'Oh, I've got the most awful toothache and on top of this I've just had one hell of a night on duty – which is probably why I look so bushed.'

'What on earth happened? Which wards are you looking after? Tell me about it if it will help,' she suggested kindly.

'The three medicals, including detention.'

'Oh that last one's difficult, I know; did you have some trouble there?'

'Yes, but not with the patients, they were all okay. It was one of the Canadian Guards – of all people – who gave me a hard time. For some obscure reason he was troublesome and insolent each time I did my ward round. This came to a head during my final one, when he was so rude and belligerent that he almost struck me, and then of course I had no option but to 'Charge' him. Oh Gina, I really am upset about it all, especially as I can't understand what caused it…'

'Rest assured that it wasn't you, Jilly, because I too have had problems on there with some of those tough guys. Personally, I think that just a few of them resent us because as QAs we're not only commissioned officers but women as well! How did Matron take it?'

'Oh okay, in fact she was surprisingly understanding and so annoyed that she is having the Canadian Guards removed and replaced by others tonight.'

'That's great, but what about your tooth?'

'Yes that too, and she has made an appointment for me to see the dentist this morning.'

'Sorry Jilly, but I'll have to dash on duty now. Good luck with the dentist and you know where I am if you need anything. Take care.'

After X-raying the offending tooth, the dentist diagnosed (as I had suspected) a large dental abscess situated below it, explaining kindly that although the tooth was in perfect condition he had no alternative but to remove it. So after administering a local anaesthetic, he swiftly extracted the molar. Matron – who unknown to me had been keeping a eye on things – suddenly appeared, much concerned for my well-being, insisting that if I did not feel well enough to go on duty that evening, I was to tell her and she would find a relief for me. Gratefully I thanked her but also reassured her that I should feel fine once I had had some sleep. Having sadly misjudged Matron from our initial meeting, this time I truly appreciated her kindness because just when I most needed it, she seemed to fuss over me like a mother… Sleeping soundly for the first time for several days, on waking I was relieved to find the nagging ache had disappeared and felt a lot better, and when reporting on duty that night I heard the good news that the poorly polio lad had at last begun to recover.

Night duty leave on Miyajima was therapeutic, and although the temperature soared, with nothing more strenuous to occupy me than swim, sunbathe and sleep, I was soon rejuvenated. As the only female amongst the few others who were staying there, I pottered about on my own, appreciating the solitude.

My favourite island seemed more beautiful than ever, with the first hints of autumn shading the delicate maple trees.

During my last day, I noticed that there was a definite increase in the activity on the sacred island, with large numbers of Japanese arriving from the mainland ferry, some of whom were setting up small booths amongst the trees above the shore. Later on I discovered the Japanese festival of *Kangensi* would be celebrated that evening. This did not really get going until after sunset, when it became a spectacular event, with the lighting of the ancient stone lanterns hugging the shoreline. These lovely old lanterns illuminated the waterfront by candlelight, which danced back and forth on the gentle wavelets.

It was remarkable, too, to see this normally quiet little island bustling with people, with sounds of happy laughter, aromas of hot noodles, together with the haunting strains of the *shamisen*. A number of Noh plays – one of Japan's oldest theatrical arts – were also performed during that evening and I caught a glimpse of one of them as it took place before a packed audience on the Itsukushima floating shrine.

As the launch slipped away at 0715hrs on that Friday morning, I felt immensely sad as I watched every tree, sandy cove, Mount Missen and all the familiar landmarks of this beautiful island recede into the misty horizon. This was the third time I had been fortunate enough to spend my leave there and on each occasion I arrived pretty much exhausted. However, when it was time for me to leave the island I felt both physically and mentally refreshed, so it was with a somewhat heavy heart that I bade my silent farewell to the magic of Miyajima that morning, wondering if I should ever be lucky enough to return…

Checking the Mess notice board later on that day, I read with glee that the three of us, the Major-Ma'am – not too much glee there, although she was only travelling as far as Port Said – Pat and I were to embark on HMT *Dunera*, on 6 September, whilst Helen and Georgina would sail three days later on the *Orwell*. After some quick mental arithmetic I calculated there were only another sixteen days for us to serve in Kure and, although I had sometimes moaned about it, I realised, too, just how much I should miss living in Japan.

I thought of the familiar scenery surrounding us from the sparkling sea to the wooded hills beyond, where in summertime enormous butterflies sunned themselves; Momma-*san* of the heavenly flower cart with her beaming smile and kindly manner, the long pot-holey road down to Kure where the shopkeepers bowed ingratiatingly when giving their presentos; the school nearby with its plethora of happy laughing children; the smell of *sukiyaki*, noodles and dried octopus.

Above all I should miss the urgent bustle of the huge BCG hospital, and especially the bravery and camaraderie of all the young lads from all over the Commonwealth whom we had nursed.

Returning to day duty as a relief sister was a break and in my off duty I completed the long list of presents to take home, including the purchase of a pretty Japanese doll traditionally dressed in a red silk kimono, with a wig of lovely long black hair, which my little god-daughter Susan would love to brush. The rest of my free time was spent in packing my two tin trunks, as these had to be sent to the QM's stores for crating, otherwise something nasty might happen to them during the six-week voyage home. Three days later we were informed that our embarkation date had been brought forward to 3 September, the apparent change understandably due to the repatriation of the large numbers of POWs ongoing during Big Switch. However, by then with only twelve days to go, Pat and I were both suffering from severe 'Funnel Fever'.

Politely coming to a halt in front of Matron's desk, I said quietly, 'You wanted to see me, Ma'am?' Looking up from the inevitable mass of papers she smiled, 'That's right, Hall, we have a special job for you, though I'm afraid it is rather short notice so let me explain. We have just been notified by the Danish authorities that their hospital ship *Jutlandia* will be sailing from Yokohama on Friday 28 August, on what could only be described as a United Nations' cruise, by proposing to fill the ship with sick and wounded, and transporting them by sea to their home countries. They have offered to take ten of our British patients who are well enough to stand the long voyage.'

This was intensely interesting news but, being so junior, I could not understand how it could affect me. As though reading my thoughts, Matron swiftly added, 'And this is where you come into the picture, Miss Hall. This afternoon, a medical team will select the ten patients who are fit enough to travel from here to Yokohama and transfer to the ship. Because of your previous experience on the ambulance train, we have decided that you will take them up to Tokyo by the night train leaving Kure Station at midday on Thursday.' Pausing momentarily, she continued, 'Let me see, today is Tuesday, which will give you sufficient time to prepare the ambulance coach tomorrow. Incidentally, you do realise that the rail journey will take a good eighteen hours and that you alone will be responsible for these patients from when they leave this hospital until you hand them over to the staff of the hospital ship in Yokohama. However, I have already detailed two reliable RAMC orderlies to travel with you. You will need two, as I imagine that the majority of the patients will be stretcher cases.'

Matron then explained the journey in more detail – regarding the train times and where we should be met and by whom. She also told me that the two orderlies had been given orders to return to Kure via the night train on Friday and then, completely taking the wind out of my sails, added, 'But you, Miss Hall, are to take three days' R&R leave whilst you are in Tokyo, since I've recently discovered that you certainly have not had your full entitlement. So, as I would like you to take this, I have already arranged for you to stay at the Ebisu Leave Centre from p.m. on the 28th until a.m. on 31 August, when you will return to Kure by the night train.' Adding to my growing excitement and near unbelief, she said, 'As you are now due to embark on the *Dunera* on 4 September, this will give you two free days when you return to pack up your belongings, so you see, taking the ambulance train to up Tokyo will be your final duty in Japan.'

Still in a state of shock, I stammered my thanks assuring Matron that I would carry out my duties faithfully. She interrupted me, 'Oh yes Hall, I hope that you have a smart uniform to wear because you will be representing the British contingent and will be bound to meet many others there from the United Nations.'

'I have Ma'am, but I will make certain that it is well pressed and that my shoes are well polished.'

'Come to my office tomorrow at 1700hrs, when I shall have all the necessary papers ready for you – in the meantime here are the keys of the train – you know how to arrange your transport, don't you?' And dismissed at last, my head reeled with excitement.

Twenty-four hours later, the ambulance coach was sparkling and well prepared for its long journey the following day, when it would be hitched up to the Forces' leave train, which set off daily at noon from Kure. For myself, I had also packed a small bag in readiness for my unexpected leave. Collecting my last orders plus the papers from Matron, she was pleasantly helpful, wishing us all a safe and comfortable journey. I had the impression that she was somewhat agitated over the fate of the ambulance train once it had completed its task by arriving at Tokyo Station. Several times she impressed upon me that under no circumstances was I to lose it… In the end I came close to giggling because by then it was quite beyond me that, having arrived in Tokyo with ten patients to look after, how I could either really lose it, or continue to have it in my safe keeping! (As it happened, once there, I was so occupied in transferring my patients to the waiting ambulances that it vanished from my mind. Guiltily, I never discovered from that day to this if it was returned to Kure – perhaps on the orders of some obliging RTO.)

There was an air of great excitement amongst the sick lads, as we transferred them to the waiting train just after 1100hrs on Thursday morning, thus giving us plenty of time to settle them comfortably in their bunks and to stow away their luggage. With only ten patients, the coach seemed quite spacious. Promptly at midday the guard blew his whistle and the long, leisurely leave train, with its unique addition, steamed slowly out of the smoke-filled gloom of Kure Station and into bright sunshine. A cheer resounded, as the boys realised that, at last, they were on their way home.

Our first task was to make lots of tea in the big, brown enamel teapot. While Corporal Smith did this and expertly filled the hungry lads' mugs with the hot sugary brew, Private Walters and I cut a huge pile of mixed sandwiches. We had all been up with the lark and I had guessed that being so excited, they had eaten little breakfast and by that time would be starving; they were! The rest of the afternoon passed pleasantly, with some patients taking the opportunity to snooze, others chattered happily, whilst several smoked the odd fag or two, contentedly reading what ancient newspapers I had managed to salvage. As always, there was a small group of them who played cards throughout most of the day.

Once I had studied their medicine list, dished out the necessary doses and checked to see that the few dressings and plasters were all comfortable, I was able to take stock of the situation and began to enjoy my change of duty. Luckily I had my tiny office to which I could retreat. My two orderlies had a spare bunk at each end of the ward, so that they, too, had somewhere to rest during our eight-een-plus-hour shift and I worked out a sensible rota for us to cover our patients during the journey. The old wind-up gramophone was a tremendous asset and whiled away the long afternoon, with Pte Walters acting as disc jockey to the many requests.

Sometime during the early evening a hot meal was brought to our coach for which we were grateful, as by then we were all feeling hungry. It must have been an hour or so later, when I was in my office writing up the patients' notes, that I heard a tap on the outer door. Looking up I saw a tall and rather bashful American GI standing outside carrying a large, waxed carton. Smiling sheepishly, he thrust this into my hands, saying, 'Say Ma'am, I hear you got some wounded soldiers on board this coach. And I know you Limeys don't get no fresh milk with your rations, so I figured out as to how you just might like to give them this.'

Overwhelmed by the thoughtfulness of the kind lad, I thanked him profusely at the same time trying to persuade him to pop in and see the boys, but sadly he was too shy, just giving them a hasty wave before dashing off down the long corridor. The milk was a type of specially reconstituted dried milk and looked delicious as I poured it into a jug, and when handed round was much enjoyed by the patients, as a welcome change from the usual evaporated stuff.

As the sky and the passing scenery darkened, the lights came on in the coach and I spent my time re-dressing the wounds that needed attention and checked that the lads with heavy plaster casts were comfortable. Before settling them down for the night, we made sure that they all had some sort of a wash. Despite the con-stant running of the central fan, the atmosphere in the coach was always rather hot and grimy from the penetrating smuts. After administering any injections or medicines due at 2200hrs, I tucked them all up for the night and then switched off the main light, leaving only night lights glowing, and they had a good-natured grumble about being sent to bed early! However, to my surprise, lulled by the constant movement of the train, without exception they all slept well.

By 0600hrs, our patients were awake again and well attended to in readiness for our arrival. Exactly forty minutes later, the tired old train steamed slowly to a halt at Tokyo Station. There we were met by ladies from the Canadian Red Cross who welcomed us with mugs of hot coffee, before we were transferred to the waiting ambulances.

From the station, we were driven to the huge American Military Hospital situ-ated somewhere in Tokyo. On arrival we were informed that we should then be given breakfast, prior to forming up into a very large convoy for the final stage of the journey to the docks in Yokohama.

My patients, accompanied by my two stalwart orderlies, were taken by US Medics to a special messing area of the hospital, whilst I was instructed to go with another. After a long hike down endless corridors I was hived off into an enormous cafeteria and told to queue up behind a column of exceedingly tall

GIs. When, eventually, my turn came to grab a plate, the server flummoxed me by shouting, 'Up and over or sunny side up?' At first I hadn't a clue and embarrassingly held up the queue, until suddenly it dawned on me he was referring to the fried eggs that he was about to slap onto my plate, plus a mountain of unidentifiable goodies! After staggering through some of it, I navigated my way back to the meeting point, where I was reunited with my patients and staff – all of whom had thoroughly enjoyed the change of menu.

Half an hour later our small British contingent was transferred to a colossal American ambulance bus, in which we waited for three long hours whilst the enormous convoy of sick and wounded troops from the United Nations' Forces was assembled. This was an impressive gathering, with representatives of almost every one of the different nations serving with the UN during the Korean War. There were tall, handsome, Turkish soldiers leaning nonchalantly on walking sticks, Australians wearing their familiar Digger hats, American GIs chewing gum, Canadians with their famous Maple Leaves, smiling Kiwis, Irish soldiers proudly wearing their emblem of the harp, and so on... This was indeed an historic sight, and in my own quiet way I felt more than privileged to be there, representing the QAs as part of the British contingent and to be (as frequently happened) one of only a handful of women participating in the immense operation.

The boys were very patient about the delay and when the convoy of many ambulances was mustered at last, responded as usual with a loud cheer. Headed by a high-powered escort from the US Military Police, with a dashing detachment of out-rider motorbikes in front, and a bevy of smart jeeps following, the order to move was given. Immediately accompanied by a shrieking of sirens, the long procession gradually lumbered off through the hitherto quiet suburbs of Tokyo.

Almost three quarters of an hour later, to our bewilderment and surprise, it appeared that we were driving along the same route that we had recently taken – in fact several of the larger buildings looked strangely familiar. So it was with some amusement that we in our ambulance bus realised that despite, the high pitched razzamatazz, the convoy had inadvertently lost its way to the docks!

Cautiously coming to a halt, a huge manoeuvre then took place to turn the whole thing around, before setting off in the right direction. However, this time we really were on track and it was not too long until we arrived safely in the busy dock area of Yokohama. Once there, we soon caught sight of the hospital ship *Jutlandia*, her immaculate white hull gleaming in the watery sunshine with large red crosses painted on her superstructure conspicuous for all to see.

The final part of our journey was by far the swiftest, as it only took a short time to hand over my ten Specials to the welcoming Danish nursing sisters who would care for them during their voyage home. And after meeting them and seeing the two small but compact and comfortable wards to which they were admitted, I knew they would be very well looked after. My fleeting impression of this splendid ship was that it resembled a floating palace, with its air of spaciousness, restful colour scheme of pale green, polished chromium and gleaming floors. More importantly, there seemed to be a relaxed and informal atmosphere on board. As soon as I had settled my patients, making sure that each was happy in his new surroundings, I wished them all Bon Voyage, waving goodbye as I left the wards to find Sister and thank her once again.

As I dashed through the narrow doorway, I almost bumped into the ship's captain. He recognised my QA uniform and kindly enquired after the British patients, whom I assured him were in the process of settling down very happily. Then, to my surprise, he asked if I had been on board *Jutlandia* previously and, if not, would I like to see some of the other wards? As I had not, he then gave me a quick tour of his impressive ship.

With what I hoped was one of my smarter salutes, I thanked the captain and then found Sister to thank her, before slipping quietly down the gangway to find my two good RAMC orderlies, without whom the long journey from Kure to Yokohama would have been more than difficult. Their transport had just arrived and would take them into Tokyo, where they could enjoy a few hours before catching the night train. Thanking them again and wishing them a good trip back to Kure, we parted and I then found the jeep which was waiting to take me to Ebisu. As I clambered in, I was instantly enveloped by a feeling of immense relief with the realisation that all had gone smoothly and my mission was accomplished.

It was good to arrive at the Leave Hotel and even better to manage to get there just before lunch had finished. This gave me an excellent start for the afternoon, which I had planned to spend shopping at the huge American PX store in the city. Several of my friends had mentioned that it was the number one place to shop in Tokyo for Western-style clothes and, as I was in desperate need of some new undies (something completely unobtainable in Kure), I was much looking forward to visiting the store. Having been forewarned that sterling was unacceptable there, to avoid any money problems I had wisely saved what US Dollars I had left over from my time in Seoul.

With the prospect of buying something very feminine and pretty, I set off (in uniform) in a taxi-cab for the big store. This was a large, modern building situated in the middle of the city, with several different floors, stacked high with every conceivable luxury. Discovering that lingerie was on the third floor, I made my way there by escalator. With initial dismay at the price tags on the garments, after careful deliberation, I selected one – just affordable – lovely, lacy, white nylon underslip.

Smiling pleasantly at the little Japanese girl behind the counter, I handed the pretty garment to her with the correct amount of cash, waiting for her to wrap up my purchase and dreamily wishing I could have afforded to buy some more of the exquisite undies on display. To my bewilderment she shook her head and indicated that for some reason or other I was not allowed to buy it. I tried again but again she refused and I could not ascertain why. By this time I was becoming rather annoyed, particularly in the knowledge that several of my friends had previously made purchases there.

As a last resort I demanded to see the manager. He appeared within seconds, a tall, broad-shouldered, smoothly spoken American guy who, when the polite Japanese girl had explained her predicament to him, turned to me saying firmly, 'No Ma'am. She's correct, you cannot buy this garment; in fact you cannot purchase anything at all in this store.' By then I was inwardly seething, clearly remembering how the GIs bought up bottles of Scotch in the NAAFI in Seoul and simultaneously feeling desperately weary after the long and responsible journey up from Kure. So, without further thought of damaging international relations, I lost my temper and with an unusual outburst, blasted him, 'You mean that you will not sell me one miserable underslip when I have the required US Dollars?'

'Yes Ma'am, that is correct.'

'Well, as a member of the United Nations' Forces I am absolutely disgusted that you have refused to sell me this garment, because not only have I recently been working alongside the US Forces in Korea, but only this morning took part in the UN Convoy transporting the British contingent of sick and wounded on board the hospital ship *Jutlandia*, during which time we spent several long hours waiting in your military hospital right here in Tokyo… So you can keep your rotten slip!' And turning on my heel I left the shop floor with as much dignity as I could muster.

To my astonishment, he ran after me, calling, 'Ma'am, please wait – don't go – the store is all yours – you can buy whatever you want!' and then he insisted on showing me all the various departments of the fabulous store. However, I only purchased the one gorgeous, frilly white underslip which – at the time – was all that I could afford.

At dinner in Ebisu that evening, I shared a table with the two Australian nursing sisters who looked after the Medical Centre at the Leave Camp. It was great fun to talk and also to share different experiences, particularly as I was travelling solo, and for the next few days we three became good friends. Annie and Kate were very hospitable and invited me to go out with one or other, whenever they were off duty.

The following morning the temperature had plummeted from over 90°F to below 60°F which was quite a shock to one's system, and but for their kindness, I should have been frozen in my summer kit. Instead, I was comfortably wrapped in borrowed woollies and well protected from the sudden cold. On my last evening there, they kindly invited me to a special party which had been arranged for some Commonwealth POWs, and where I had the privilege of meeting several British lads who thankfully would be returning to the UK soon.

Checking with the Information Office on the morning of my departure that my rail reservation was in order, I was delighted to discover there were no available berths on the night train and that my new orders were to return by air to Iwakuni on the early morning flight. What luck to have the chance of another dinner and night of comfort in the hotel and then only a four-and-a-half-hour flight to follow.

In fact, all went swimmingly well until I reported back to Matron's Office mid-afternoon the next day, expecting only to be wished Bon Voyage.

There to my deep disappointment, I was informed that due to the exigencies of the service, my name had been removed from the troopship *Dunera*'s passenger list. Matron told me that, as far as she knew, it would be added to the *Orwell*'s list, but as yet her sailing date was uncertain. She was sorry too that because of this I should have to return to duty as a relief sister and to report to Ward Nine at 0730hrs, 2 September, the next day.

Sensing my bitter disappointment, Matron spoke very kindly, explaining in strict confidence that the reason for my sudden removal from the *Dunera*, was because 'someone' had blotted their copy-book and consequently was being dispatched to Singapore. Wishing that I could strangle the miscreant, I dejectedly walked back to the Quarters to dig some uniform out of a suitcase, which I also knew was bound to need a good pressing.

Less than forty-eight hours later, when I was dishing out the medicines on Ward Nine, the telephone rang. It was Matron – the orderly said – who wanted to speak to me urgently. Putting down my empty medicine tray on the office desk I picked up the receiver, 'Miss Hall speaking, Ma'am.'

'Oh good, I've found you, Hall, because I've just been informed by the shipping authorities that there has been a change in the berthing plans and that, after all, you are to embark on the *Dunera*, at 1100hrs tomorrow – 4 September – sailing from Kure sometime during the afternoon.' Before I could utter a word, she continued authoritatively, 'It is now 1405hrs, which should give you just about twenty hours to complete your packing, providing you go off duty now. Tell Sister on Ward Ten that I have instructed you to leave immediately and give her your drug cupboard keys, as she must cover for you until I can find a relief sister within half an hour… Right off you go now, Hall – no, don't waste time in thanking me – you have too much to do and in any case I shall see you on board the ship tomorrow.'

After giving a brief explanation to the senior orderly, I fled, dropping off the keys as instructed to Sister on Ward Ten. Bursting with excitement I ran almost all the way over to the Quarters, at the same time wondering what had happened to the 'naughty one' – who presumably would be sailing on another ship (she did too…)

Driving through the hot dusty streets of Kure for the last time, Pat and I chattered excitedly in the back of the jeep, whilst the Major-Ma'am kept up appearances in the front. It was a brilliant morning and in the distance the sea was a sparkling blue.

'There she is! That's our ship. Do you see her, Jilly, the one with the squat yellow funnel. I just cannot believe this really is the start of our voyage home – can you?'

'No, and certainly not until we are safely on board, and even then, I still have the feeling, even at this late stage, that some mysterious hand could try to snatch us away!'

Five minutes later we arrived at the dockside as Matron's jeep pulled up alongside us. She was accompanied by three other QAs who had come to see us off, and forming a small procession, we wound our way up the gangway to the saloon where coffee was being served. Half an hour later it was with genuine sadness that I said goodbye to Lieutenant Colonel Mackaness, with the realisation that I had completed my eighteen-month tour at the British Commonwealth General Hospital, Kure. I was indeed sorry to be leaving the hospital and the friends there and even more to be leaving Japan, although at the same time tremendously happy at the thought of returning home.

The Purser allocated Pat and me to a comfortable and spacious cabin, where we quickly dumped our caps and hand luggage and shot back on deck to watch the final stages of our departure. On the quayside there was great activity, with vehicles constantly arriving and departing, troops embarking and stores and crates of luggage still being loaded. Dotted below, amongst the neat lines of soldiers, we occasionally spotted a disoriented straggler, usually accompanied by a couple of hefty Military Police. I pointed this out to Pat, and who thought that they must had been on a farewell binge.

However, after the final draft of troops had embarked and the quayside was less busy, this became more noticeable, with increased numbers of stragglers appearing; many of them capless with crumpled uniforms, and singing lustily as they were supported by the Red Caps. It was a pathetic sight, even though there were only a dozen or so in all. I remarked to Pat, 'Poor things, what a dreadful way for them to begin the voyage home.'

Someone unknown and standing right behind us, added in a deep authoritative voice, 'I have a feeling that those poor devils are all ex-POWs and I imagine, too, that some bloody fool gave them all their back pay, so that they blew the lot last night in Kure and were probably fleeced into the bargain.'

We heard later that this indeed had happened, which to us seemed an inappropriate beginning for what should have been a wonderful homecoming.

Our temporary sadness was quickly dispelled by the sounds of stirring music and marching feet, as the Royal Marine band from HMS *Ocean* halted smartly on the quayside below. There they played all the old favourites, including *Take me back to dear old Blighty* and, of course, concluding with *Auld Lang Syne*. Finally, as the ship pulled gently away from her berth, the haunting strains of *Will ye no come back again* floated upwards. Looking quizzically at each other, Pat broke the silence, 'Do you think that either of us ever will, Jilly?'

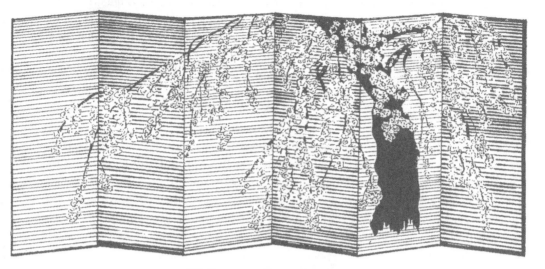

EPILOGUE

October 2006

Twenty-seven years ago, as we were about to leave my parents' home in Sussex, my mother thrust a cardboard box into my hands saying, 'It's high time you took these old letters of yours, as they have cluttered up my bureau for far too long.' Whilst settling our four children in the car and feeling both surprised and a bit miffed – because I had quite genuinely forgotten them – I thanked her briefly and threw the box into the back.

Several years later, having a little more time as our children grew up, I remembered the old box and one cold, wintry afternoon began to re-read the letters that my mother had faithfully kept and that I had started writing almost thirty years before.

These fragile, faded and crumpled sheets of scribbled Forces Air Letters immediately evoked a deep sense of déjà-vu and, once again, I was on the busy wards at the BCGH in Kure and the BC Z MU in Seoul, recalling the innumerable shadows of those sick, wounded, and extraordinarily brave young servicemen of the British Commonwealth and United Nations' Forces. I resolved then that I would endeavour to write an account of life as it was for an Army nurse, in those far off days of 1952–53 during that sadly forgotten war.

Throughout the intervening years, as a member of the British Korean Veterans' Association, I have met many of these ex-servicemen at distinguished gatherings. Likewise, through the QARANC Association after forty years I was very thrilled to catch up again with Jess Fubini (*née* Milton), who was always so helpful whilst we were stationed in both Kure and Seoul. My good friend Cynthia asked me to be her bridesmaid when she married her James and Pat, with whom I sailed back to the UK, actually met Alan, an ex-POW, whilst on board the *Dunera* and some time later they had a lovely London wedding.

During the latter stages of writing this book, I was surprised and delighted to be contacted – through the auspices of the BKVA – by Betty Lawrence (*née* Crocker), my Australian friend of long ago with whom, over the years, I had sadly lost contact. Betty, after recovering from her debilitating illness, continued to serve as a captain with the RAANC, until her marriage to Dr Bill Lawrence in 1955.

Later in life, as I reflected with the hindsight of age, I realised what an enormous debt we owed to the Matrons and Deputy Matrons who ran our hospitals with such distinction. Often they shouldered heavy responsibilities, coping with every exigency and training future generations to respect the qualities of discipline and loyalty. I now appreciate what a handful we four young QAs must have been to Major Priscilla Stewart during our six-week voyage to Japan and will always be grateful to her for keeping an eye on me in Hong Kong!

In 1990, I was privileged to revisit South Korea, as a member of the BKVA, at the invitation of the Korean Veterans' Association (sponsored by the Korean Government). Flying back into Seoul in the brilliance of a September evening was unbelievably impressive, now surrounded by forests of green, neatly terraced paddy-fields, lush meadows dotted with chalk white poly tunnels. Then appeared a vast conglomeration of sky-scrapers and broad tree-lined streets, in stark contrast to the war-torn, barren and mutilated landscape from which I had flown out in 1953.

Driving to the 38th Parallel along the route near the Demilitarised Zone (DMZee) at Panmunjom was fascinating, with an increased military presence and obvious signs of defence, from concrete tank traps to specially constructed port-cullis type bridges. Finally traversing the eerie wilderness of the No Man's Land of the DMZee, with its close proximity to the border and the steep sparse hills of North Korea, a US armed escort was provided before arriving at Panmunjom.

One of the many highlights of this re-visit for me was to stand in the simple blue hutted UN building in Panmunjom, beside the large green baized-covered table where the peace negotiations were still continuing thirty-seven years later and where, in 1953, I saw in the distance from the rooftop of the hospital in Seoul the protective searchlights beaming over Panmunjom.

Later that same afternoon, we tackled an arduous, slippery trek down 75 metres into one of the four infiltration tunnels dug by the North Koreans in 1974, '75, '78 and '90 beneath the DMZee, all capable of massive movements of armaments and troops.

Lastly, we went on to Solmari, encircled by precipitous and formidable mountain sides, the battleground in April 1951 of the Gloucesters and the Royal Artillery on Hill 253. There we remembered the fallen and against the simple memorial stones laid wreaths of yellow chrysanthemums.

In Pusan, following a solemn service of Rememberance in the Memorial Hall and despite the vast and beautifully landscaped grounds, the United Nations Cemetery was tearjerking, with its total of 2,293 graves, 884 of which were British. There we met the families of two brave young men, Corporal J. Mooney, killed in action in April 1953, whose three sisters laid a wreath and took turns in wearing his medals with pride, and also the brother-in-law and three sisters of Lance Corporal L. Williams of the Welch Regiment. They had brought with them a tiny plastic bag of soil from their parents' grave in Wales to place on their late brother's grave, taking home with them a similar amount of Korean soil. Each neat square headstone was enhanced by a fluttering Union flag, an English rose bush and a small box hedge, all well tended by the schoolchildren of Pusan.

The lavish reception in Seoul for the presentation of Peace Medals by General Joon-yeuol So (retired) was the icing on the cake, showing the kindness, warmth and genuine gratitude of the Korean people to those of the UN Forces who had assisted them in their plight.

This was reiterated at every function we attended and endorsed my admiration for the South Korean people, because after over half a century, they still remain divided from their families in the North. Regardless of this, to me, they have shown great resilience and strength in creating a most modern and forward-thinking country.

However, but for the same resilience, strength and sacrifice of those gallant Shadows of the Far Forgotten, the liberation of South Korea could never have been achieved.

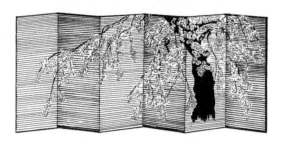

INDEX